Lecture Notes in Computer Science

Commenced Publication in 1973
Founding and Former Series Editors:
Gerhard Goos, Juris Hartmanis, and Jan van Leeuwen

Christian Kop   Günther Fliedl
Heinrich C. Mayr   Elisabeth Métais (Eds.)

Natural Language Processing and Information Systems

11th International Conference on Applications
of Natural Language to Information Systems, NLDB 2006
Klagenfurt, Austria, May 31 – June 2, 2006
Proceedings

 Springer

Volume Editors

Christian Kop
Günther Fliedl
Heinrich C. Mayr
Alpen-Adria Universität Klagenfurt
Institute of Business Informatics and Application Systems
Klagenfurt, Austria
E-mail: {chris, fliedl, mayr}@ifit.uni-klu.ac.at

Elisabeth Métais
CNAM, Chaire d'Informatique d'Entreprise
292 rue Saint-Martin, 75141 Paris, France
E-mail: metais@cnam.fr

Library of Congress Control Number: 2006926265

CR Subject Classification (1998): H.2, H.3, I.2, F.3-4, H.4, C.2

LNCS Sublibrary: SL 3 – Information Systems and Application, incl. Internet/Web and HCI

ISSN	0302-9743
ISBN-10	3-540-34616-3 Springer Berlin Heidelberg New York
ISBN-13	978-3-540-34616-6 Springer Berlin Heidelberg New York

Springer is a part of Springer Science+Business Media

springer.com

© Springer-Verlag Berlin Heidelberg 2006
Printed in Germany

Typesetting: Camera-ready by author, data conversion by Scientific Publishing Services, Chennai, India
Printed on acid-free paper   SPIN: 11765448   06/3142   5 4 3 2 1 0

Preface

Information systems and natural language processing are fundamental fields of research and development in informatics. The combination of both is an exciting and future-oriented field which has been addressed by the NLDB conference series since 1995. There are still many open research questions but also an increasing number of interesting solutions and approaches.

NLDB 2006 with its high-quality contributions tersely reflected the current discussion and research: natural language and/or ontology-based information retrieval, question-answering methods, dialog processing, query processing as well as ontology- and concept creation from natural language. Some papers presented the newest methods for parsing, entity recognition and language identification which are important for many of the topics mentioned before. In particular, 53 papers were submitted by authors from 14 nations. From these contributions, the Program Committee, based on 3 peer reviews for each paper, selected 17 full and 5 short papers, thus coming up with an overall acceptance rate of 32% (41% including short papers).

Many persons contributed to making NLDB 2006 a success. First we thank all authors for their valuable contributions. Secondly, we thank all members of the Program Committee for their detailed reviews and discussion. Furthermore we thank the following people for their substantial organizational collaboration: Kerstin Jörgl, who did a lot of work to compose these proceedings, our Conference Secretary, Christine Seger, Stefan Ellersdorfer for his technical support, and Jürgen Vöhringer and Christian Winkler, who provided additional last-minute reviews.

This year, NLDB was a part of a multi-conference event on Information Systems: UNISCON — United Information Systems Conference. Thus, participants could get into scientific contact with experts from more technical (ISTA 2006) or more business-oriented (BIS 2006) fields. In either case, they profited from UNISCON's organizational environment. We, therefore, express our thanks also to the UNISCON organization team: Markus Adam, Jörg Kerschbaumer and all the students who supported the participants during the NLDB 2006 conference.

March 2006

Christian Kop
Günther Fliedl
Heinrich C. Mayr
Eliabeth Métais

Organization

Conference Co-chairs

Christian Kop   Alpen-Adria Universität Klagenfurt
Günther Fliedl   Alpen-Adria Universität Klagenfurt
Heinrich C. Mayr   Alpen-Adria Universität Klagenfurt
Elisabeth Métais   Cedric Laboratory CNAM, Paris

Organization and Local Arrangements

Markus Adam   Alpen-Adria Universität Klagenfurt
Stefan Ellersdorfer   Alpen-Adria Universität Klagenfurt
Kerstin Jörgl   Alpen-Adria Universität Klagenfurt
Christine Seger   Alpen-Adria Universität Klagenfurt
Christian Winkler   Alpen-Adria Universität Klagenfurt

Program Committee

Kenji Araki   Hokkaido University, Japan
Akhilesh Bajaj   University of Tulsa, USA
Mokrane Bouzeghoub   PRiSM, Université de Versailles, France
Andrew Burton-Jones   University of British Columbia, Canada
Roger Chiang   University of Cincinnati, USA
Gary A. Coen   Boeing, USA
Isabelle Comyn-Wattiau CEDRIC/CNAM, France
Antje Düsterhöft   University of Wismar, Germany
Günther Fliedl   Universität Klagenfurt, Austria
Alexander Gelbukh   Instituto Politecnico Nacional, Mexico
Nicola Guarino   CNR, Italy
Jon Atle Gulla   Norwegian University of Science and
                         Technology, Norway
Karin Harbusch   Universität Koblenz-Landau, Germany
Helmut Horacek   Universität des Saarlandes, Germany
Cecil Chua Eng Huang   Nanyang Technological University, Singapore
Paul Johannesson   Stockholm University, Sweden
Zoubida Kedad   PRiSM, Université de Versailles, France
Christian Kop   University of Klagenfurt, Austria
Leila Kosseim   Concordia University, Canada

Nadira Lammari	CEDRIC/CNAM, France
Winfried Lenders	Universität Bonn, Germany
Jana Lewerenz	sd&m Düsseldorf, Germany
Stephen Liddle	Brigham Young University, USA
Deryle Lonsdale	Brigham Young Uinversity, USA
Robert Luk	Hong Kong Polytechnic University, Hong Kong
Heinrich C. Mayr	University of Klagenfurt, Austria
Elisabeth Métais	CEDRIC/CNAM , France
Farid Meziane	Salford University, UK
Luisa Mich	University of Trento, Italy
Diego Mollá Aliod	Macquarie University, Australia
Andrés Montoyo	Universidad de Alicante, Spain
Ana Maria Moreno	Universidad Politecnica de Madrid, Spain
Rafael Muñoz	Universidad de Alicante, Spain
Günter Neumann	DFKI, Germany
Jian-Yun Nie	Université de Montréal, Canada
Manual Palomar	Universidad de Alicante, Spain
Sandeep Purao	Pennsylvania State University, USA
Odile Piton	Université Paris I Panthéon-Sorbonne, France
Yacine Rezgui	University of Salford, UK
Reind van de Riet	Vrije Universiteit Amsterdam, The Netherlands
Hae-Chang Rim	Korea University, Korea
Veda Storey	Georgia State University, USA
Vijay Sugumaran	Oakland University Rochester, USA
Bernhard Thalheim	Kiel University, Germany
Krishnaprasad Thirunarayan	Wright State University, USA
Juan Carlos Trujillo	Universidad de Alicante, Spain
Luis Alfonso Ureña	Universidad de Jaén, Spain
Sunil Vadera	University of Salford, UK
Panos Vassiliadis	University of Ioannina, Greece
Jürgen Vöhringer	University of Klagenfurt, Austria
Hans Weigand	Tilburg University, The Netherlands
Werner Winiwarter	University of Vienna, Austria
Christian Winkler	University of Klagenfurt, Austria

External Referees

Birger Andersson
Maria Bergholtz
Miguel Ángel García Cumbreras
Theodore Dalamagas
Hiroshi Echizen-ya
Yasutomo Kimura
Nadia Kiyavitskaya
Francisco Javier Ariza López

Borja Navarro
Lluís Padró
Hideyuki Shibuki
Darijus Strasunskas
Stein L. Tomassen
Sonia Vazquez
Chih-Sheng Yang
Nicola Zeni

Organized by:

NLDB was organized by the Institute of Business Informatics and Applications Systems, Alpen-Adria University of Klagenfurt, Austria.

Table of Contents

Concepts Extraction and Ontology

Ontologies and Task Repository Utilization

Query Processing

Information Retrieval and Dialog Processing

NLP Techniques

Short Paper Session I

Short Paper Session II

An Automated Multi-component Approach to Extracting Entity Relationships from Database Requirement Specification Documents

Siqing Du and Douglas P. Metzler

University of Pittsburgh, School of Information Sciences, Pittsburgh,
PA, 15260, USA
sid2@pitt.edu, metzler@mail.sis.pitt.edu

Abstract. This paper describes a natural language system that extracts entity relationship diagram components from natural language database design documents. The system is a fully integrated composite of existing, publicly available
components including a parser, WordNet and Google web corpus search facilities, and a novel rule-based tuple-extraction process. The system differs from
previous approaches in being fully automatic (as opposed to approaches requiring human disambiguation or other interaction) and in providing a higher level
of performance than previously reported results.

1 Introduction

In the database design process, designers first elicit natural language requirements
specifications from users, then transform the requirements into a formal representation
schema. The Entity Relationship Diagram (ERD) model is one of the most popular of
these formal representation schemata [1]. It is a graphic way of displaying entity, relationship, and attribute types, which incorporates some of the important semantic information about the real world situation, and it is considered to be a very natural and
easy-to-understand way of conceptualizing the structure of a database.

The process of translating natural language Database Requirement Specification
(DRS) documents into ERDs is, however, time-consuming, error-prone and costly,
and there have been a series of attempts to automate this process, which is relevant
both to research in sublanguage processing (since the language of database requirement specifications is more limited than general natural language both in structure
and content) and to the general problem of extraction of formal representations from
natural language. Chen [2] first explored the correspondence between English sentence structure and that of entity relationship diagrams and proposed eleven rules for
translation. These rules were neither complete nor fully accurate and a number of
studies have tried to improve on this approach [3-9]. Some of these approaches, e.g.,
[3] emphasized a dialogue tool that helped elicit the natural language description itself, while at the same time avoiding some of the disambiguation difficulties of the
natural language translation process.

Most approaches to this problem have involved extensions of Chen's original approach [2], involving the application of heuristic translation rules to the outputs of a

C. Kop et al. (Eds.): NLDB 2006, LNCS 3999, pp. 1–11, 2006.
© Springer-Verlag Berlin Heidelberg 2006

syntactic parser. Most recently Omar *et al.* [4] used such an approach augmented with a confidence level weighting mechanism to achieve a reported performance of 95% recall and 82% precision in terms of entity recognition. They did not however describe the results in terms of the correctness of attachments of entities and relations.

Automated extraction of entity relationship diagrams from natural language DRS is hard due to the lexical, syntactic and semantic ambiguity of natural language. To avoid the need for human input to resolve such ambiguity, it is necessary to go beyond the simple models incorporating syntactic parsing and simple translation rules, to utilize the semantic information required for such disambiguation. For some natural language applications this can require extensive and explicit knowledge bases that are expensive and time consuming to construct and often do not fully cover the necessary knowledge.

This paper describes an integrated multi-component framework for this problem that brings the necessary semantic knowledge to bear using publicly available, relatively weakly structured, but very large scale resources. It is suggested that this architecture, or ones similar to it, will be applicable to a wide set of similar special purpose natural language to formalism translation problems, and perhaps to a wider set of limited scope natural language problems as well.

2   A Model

Most of the previous research on applying natural language processing to database concept modeling employed a model consisting of the application of heuristic translation rules to the outputs of a syntactic parser. This model proved incapable of adequately dealing with issues such as distinguishing entities from attributes, recognizing conjunctive relations and subtle semantic disambiguation. This section describes an enhanced general model incorporating two knowledge sources capable of providing elements of semantic processing. Each of the components can be realized by different choices according to specific domain and application requirements. The specific components utilized in this system, and the advantages of the approaches taken with some of the components will be described in the following section on implementation.

2.1   A Syntactic Parser

This model follows previous research on ERD extraction, as well as most natural language processing work in general, in having an independent syntactic parser, as opposed to incorporating semantic and syntactic considerations in a single formalism. Some criteria for the choice of syntactic parser are obvious, such as accuracy and lexical coverage. Others are perhaps less so. It is desirable to have an extensible lexicon, so that DRS documents written for particular specialized domains can be covered. The parser should be robust in handling incomplete or incorrect structures, and it should allow for user extensions to cover additional domain specific structures. Finally, the output structures should facilitate the types of processing required by the following components of the system.

2.2   Heuristic Translation Rules

As in previous work, translation rules are employed to extract the ERD components from the outputs of the syntactic parser. In this system, the forms of the translation rules are unusually tightly coupled to the format of the outputs of the syntactic parser. Also, because of the use of semantic filters, the translation rules can be allowed to overgenerate to a certain degree, reducing potential problems of undergeneration. Because of the inherent ambiguity of natural language, it is possible to extract multiple ERDs from a given natural description. What is desired is that interpretations that violate semantic constraints are not retained.

2.3 A Lexical Filter

One form of semantic filtering involves a lexical filter which can help in issues such as distinguishing entities from attributes and relations. Although most modern parsers are lexicalized, it can be useful to employ a separate, post-parsing, lexical filter to deal with semantic disambiguation issues concerned with the semantic interpretations of parsing outputs, as opposed to lexical issues concerned with deriving the correct syntactic interpretations. A post-parsing lexical component can be in the form of a dictionary, lexicon, thesaurus, or general ontology. It can also incorporate domain specific modules. Using a separate post-parsing lexical component allows a system designer to employ a wider and less constrained set of approaches to lexical disambiguation and filtering.

2.4 A Semantic Filter

Some classical ambiguity problems such as prepositional phrase attachment and conjunctive structure interpretation require an analysis of the appropriateness or likeliness of relationships among terms. Some sort of semantic analysis of complex, multi-term structures is necessary to handle these issues. The choices here range from very detailed knowledge-based approaches, which are notoriously difficult to provide for large open-ended domains, to shallow quasi-statistical approaches based on the empirical evidence found in large corpora.

3 An Implementation

In this general approach, one could utilize a number of options for each component. In addition to the specific reasons for the choices made which are discussed below, there were several general considerations that guided the choices. The components utilized (with the exception of the translation rules) are powerful off-the-shelf components that lend themselves to integration in a straightforward environment. We utilized the Link Parser and WordNet, which are open source C language resources that can be readily compiled as dynamic libraries, and Google APIs, which are used to access the Google web corpus via SOAP and WSDL standards. All of them were integrated in the .Net environment.

3.1 Link Parser

The parsing component utilizes Link Parser (LP), which is based on Link Grammar, an original theory of English syntax [10]. The parser has a lexicon of about 60,000 word forms. It covers a wide variety of syntactic constructions, including many rare and idiomatic ones. It also can be easily extended [11]. The parser is robust [12]; it is able to skip over portions of the sentence that it cannot understand, and assign some structure to the rest of the sentence. It is able to handle unknown vocabulary, and make intelligent guesses from context and spelling about the syntactic categories of unknown words. It has knowledge of capitalization, numerical expressions, and a variety of punctuation symbols. Link Grammar and LP have been applied to several sublanguages to extract useful information [13-15]. LP is similar to the Constituent Object Parser [16] and Link Grammar is similar to ideas of [17] upon which [16] was loosely based.

The basic idea of Link Grammar (and these related approaches) is to transfer some of the formal complexity of context-free grammar rules to the data structures representing words. Words are structures with left- and right-pointing connectors. Left- and right-pointing connectors can be joined to form a link, and words have rules that determine how the links can be formed. A sentence is accepted as valid when a complete linkage is formed that includes all the words of the sentence. LP can return more than one complete linkage for a single sentence, reflecting the fact that sentences do have valid alternative syntactic interpretations. LP uses probabilistic information on the creation of links to estimate the likelihood of the correctness of individual interpretations of a given sentence, and its performance in that regard is good. Informally, it appeared that the most likely syntactic interpretation of sentences was almost always among the top three or four interpretations returned. The use of the semantic filters in this architecture made this kind of performance adequate for this application.

3.2 Heuristic Translation Rules

The translation rules extract entity-relation connections which are represented as tuples, e.g. *<has company employees>*. For an *n*-ary relationship, there are total *n+1* objects in a tuple. The first one is the relationship; the following are the entities connected by the relationship. Each of the objects also has some properties. The LP was chosen over similarly powerful parsers because the links correspond relatively directly to the components of entity relation diagrams, as illustrated in Fig. 1. for the sentence " *A company has 3,000 employees*".

In Fig. 1., the "Ss"(subject) and "Op"(object) links in Link Grammar correspond to the two entity-to-relation links in ERD. The "Dsu" and "Dmcn" links provide cardinality information for the relation between the two entities. This basic pattern can be extracted even from a more elaborate and complex version of this sentence, and, in general, such ERD patterns can be extracted from a wide variety of complex sentence forms. The LP employs 107 link types that describe relationships between words, but many of these are not relevant to the style of language used in DRS or are not relevant to the ERD extraction process. The extraction/translation module consists of 50 rules, each of which applies to a single link type. The rules are not strictly declarative, but rather include procedural actions and calls, even to outside modules such as the WordNet component.

The heuristic translation rules we used are link-based, which are more flexible and semantic-richer, compared with syntactic-driven, POS-based approaches in previous research [2, 4, 7]. For each heuristic rule, it is verb-centered. A frame is built for each verb. Then various rules are applied to fill out the values of the slots of the frame,

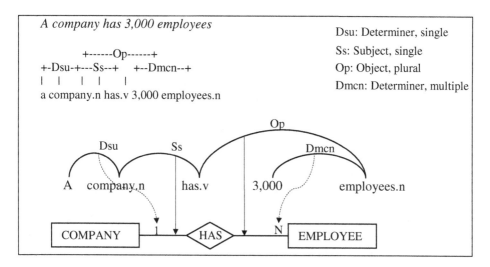

Fig. 1. Links vs. ERD

such as the first entity candidate, possible substitutions for the first entity candidate, the cardinality of the first entity candidate, and so on.

For instance, the following simple rule takes the value found at the "S" (subject) link of a verb, and assigns it to the first entity candidate position of an ERD frame.

if tuple.vword.leftLink.hasLink("S")

    tuple.fentity = tuple.vword.leftLinkWord("S");

The next example illustrates a more complex rule that handles situations that involve identifying the deep subject of sentence structures involving "SF" links to what the Link Grammar refers to as filler subjects, such as "there" or "it" in "there are" or "it is". The first two lines state that if the left link from the verb slot of the tuple frame is an "SF" link, then a call must be made to a procedure that locates the real subject of the sentence. This is usually found as a noun in a prepositional phrase found before or after the surface object, identified by the LP as the right side value of a "J" link. The third line is a call to WordNet to determine whether the subject is plural. WordNet has been compiled as a DLL module so WordNet procedures can be called within rules as can user defined functions (such as *findRealSubject(tuple.vword)*. The last two lines perform a substitution on the verb slot to the plural or singular form of "has" depending on the number of the subject.

if tuple.vword.leftLink.hasLink("SF")

    tuple.fentity = findRealSubject(tuple.vword);

    if WordNetLib.MorphStr(tuple.fentity)

        tuple.vword.substitution = "have";

    else

        tuple.vword.substitution = "has";

Since it is impossible to uniquely determine a correct syntactic interpretation based exclusively on syntactic information, the translation rules are applied to several of the highest ranked interpretations returned by the LP (and its ranking system). The exact number of parses considered is a variable parameter but typically three to four highest ranked interpretations produce good results. Most of the time the first parse is correct, however, by considering more parses, while utilizing filters to eliminate inconsistent ones, we can improve performance by covering cases in which the correct interpretation is not the first returned and cases in which more than one interpretation can be considered correct. This is a unique feature of this system, since other systems work with only the single most preferred parse returned. But processing multiple parsers leads to issues concerning tracking which entity relation tuples came from which parses. In particular, when tuples come from distinct parses, they can not later be incorporated in a single ERD and there is reason to bring semantic information to bear to disambiguate between the two tuples and the parses they came from. To detect the inconsistent tuples extracted from different parses, we record the conflict pairs which will be further processed with WordNet and the Google web corpus. For example, for the following sentence, The LP provided 11 parses. Only the third one is correct, while the first one is syntactically more preferable but semantically wrong.

The company has 50 plants located in 40 states and approximately 100,000 employees. (1)

The extraction module gave the following tuples.

1. <has.v-, company.n, plants.n>

2. <located.v-in, plants.n, states.n>

3. <located.v-in, plants.n, employees.n>

4. <has.v-, company.n, employees.n>

A central ambiguity in this sentence is the conjunctive ambiguity concerning whether the "and" joins "40 states" and "approximately 100,000 employees" as locations of the "50 plants" (semantically impossible), or whether the "and" joins "plants located in 40 states" and "approximately 100,000 employees" as the two things the company has. The former interpretation produces the third (incorrect) tuple while the later leads to the fourth tuple. These two incompatible tuples are noted as a conflict pair which is passed to the filters for disambiguation. The first two tuples are found in all interpretations.

3.3 The Lexical Filter: WordNet

WordNet [18] is a somewhat unusual lexical database with broad coverage and a publicly accessible reference system. It has been developed and maintained at Princeton University since 1985. The current version (2.1) contains about 117,597 synsets, which are the basic unit of WordNet. A synset is a set of synonymous word senses. A word that has multiple word senses (as most words do) will have various separately marked word senses that participate in distinct synsets. Synsets are linked by a variety of semantic relationships, such as *IS-A* (hypernym/hyponym), *PART-OF* (meronymy/holonymy), synonymy and antonymy to form a complex semantic network. The *IS-A* relationship is most fundamental, producing a taxonomic hierarchy of synsets.

WordNet serves a number of functions in this system. The last section illustrated that rules can determine the number of a word/concept by a WordNet call. WordNet can also support merging of redundant tuples when words that represent the same underlying concept appear in different surface forms as with the number of nouns or the tense of verbs.

The most fundamental use of WordNet is to correctly identify entities (in the ERD sense). Although entities (as originally noted in [2]) correspond to nouns, the correspondence is not perfect, with nouns being used to refer to many concepts that are not usually considered entities but are rather abstractions that help describe the nature of the situation but do not refer to the sorts of "things" that are represented as entities in ERD. Words such as "number", "set", or "type" are examples of such abstractions, but in fact, it is not easy to distinguish which nouns can identify entities and which can not. Such distinctions can depend heavily on context and human ability to apply general world knowledge. Fortunately, in this application (a sublanguage domain), the role of context and background knowledge is not as critical or complex as in general natural language understanding, and the use of a large structured lexical source such as WordNet, together with the knowledge of the problematic syntactic structures that signal the need to consult it can largely answer the problem of correctly identifying entity concepts.

For instance, "of structures", (noun phrases modified by prepositional phrases containing the preposition "of"), such as those appearing in (2) and (3), are very common in DRS, appearing in 25% of the sentences in our corpus. In (2), "number" is not an entity and should be ignored since it contributes nothing to the ERD (The cardinality of "employees" is already indicated by the number of that word). But in (3) employee and company are both entities.

A number of employees are working on a project. (2)

Each employee of the company has a direct manager. (3)

The WordNet superordinate chains for "number" and "employee" are:

    number => magnitude => property => attribute => abstraction

    employee => worker => person => organism => living thing => object

Words such as "set, list, range, type, kind, unit, ..." will, like "number" link to this hierarchy of *magnitude => property => attribute => abstraction*, while the kinds of more specific nouns that are more usually indicative of entities will link to general synsets such as "object, physical entity, group, event, act". The system can use such information to correctly interpret problematic structures such as these "of structures", while letting even the abstract words go through as entities when the syntactic structures are unambiguous as in (4).

Each department has a number. (4)

3.4 Google Web Corpus

There has been a recent trend to utilize the web as a corpus for various natural language processing applications and problems including ontology extraction and disambiguation [19]. In particular, there has been work utilizing search engines to find the most probable propositional phrase attachments [20-22]. Coordinating conjunctions and prepositional phrase attachment account for a good deal of the ambiguity in our DRS corpus, as they do in English in general. For instance, *and* and *or* account for approximately 3% of the words in the British National Corpus [23] and 3.27% of the words in our DRS corpus. The propositional phrase attachment problem is reflected as an entity attachment problem in entity relationship extraction.

Section 3.2 discussed sentence (1) and two incompatible tuples (repeated here) that are derived from alternative propositional phrase attachment interpretations that depend on alternative conjunctive interpretations. In one of the interpretations, the sentence is parsed as *"The company has 50 plants located in 40 states"* and *"The company has 50 plants located in approximately 100,000 employees"* which leads to tuple 3.

    3. <located.v-in,plants.n, employees.n>

    4. <has.v-,company.n, employees.n>

To eliminate the inappropriate tuple the system generates calls to Google to determine whether phrases utilizing the terms in the tuple (in that literal form) are found in the Google corpus. In order to account for variations in word forms the system generates variant forms of the queries sent to Google. Table 1. illustrates several variants of the tuples considering only the singular and plural forms of the terms found in the two incompatible tuples. It is clear that the corpus contains a large number of expressions indicative of the meaning of tuple 4, and no cases reflecting the content of tuple 3, thus providing evidence that tuple 4 is the correct interpretation of this sentence. It is noteworthy that the size of the Google corpus largely overcomes the potential problems associated with exact pattern matching. That is, even if the terms in a tuple rarely appear in the exact form produced in the queries, in a very large corpus even a rare form will appear in noticeable numbers.

Table 1. Queries to disambiguate the relationships attachment

Tuple 3. queries	hits	Tuple 4. queries	hits
"plant located in employee"	0	"company has employee"	405
"plant located in employees"	0	"company has employees"	954
"plants located in employee"	0	"companies have employee"	485
"plants located in employees"	0	"companies have employees"	706
sum	0	sum	2550

4   Evaluation

A corpus was constructed of 113 sentences taken from 20 database specification documents collected from database textbooks, past exam papers and examples in related research papers. The average sentence length is approximately 11 words. The authors determined that there is a total of 158 entity-relationship tuples in that corpus. The system extracted 163 tuples in total, of which 147 tuples were judged to be correct. Thus the precision is about 90%, and recall is about 93%, which is somewhat better than the best previously reported results of 82% precision and 95% recall reported in [4]. Performance looks somewhat weaker when viewed in terms of the interpretation of each individual sentence as whole, (rather than individual tuples). 94 (83%) of the sentences were interpreted correctly (with all the relationships and entities extracted and attached correctly), while 19 (17%) sentences were only partially correctly interpreted. Of the partially correct sentences, 6 (5.4%) were undergenerated (where some elements were missed either due to parsing errors or filtering errors), 7 (6.2%) were overgenerated in terms of extraction of incorrect relations, and 6 (5.4%) were overgenerated in terms of incorrect attachments.

Many of the problems were due to incorrect parser outputs (as opposed to the translation rules). 93 (82%) of the sentences were correctly parsed with the first interpretation returned by the LP prioritizing system, and 99 (87.6%) of them were correctly parsed within the first three returned interpretations; the remaining 14 (12.4%) of the sentences could not be correctly parsed by the LP at all. The system was able to correctly extract the correct tuples in 6 (5.4%) of the sentences that the LP could not correctly parse (because the parsing errors concerned aspects of the sentences that were not critical for ERD), but the system failed to correctly extract the correct tuples in 7 (6.2%) of the sentences that were correctly parsed (because of either complex parse structures or pronoun reference issues that are not yet handled by the rules). It is relevant to the architecture of this system that in 5 of the 6 cases in which the second or third parse (but not the first) returned the correct interpretation, the system was able to extract the correct tuples, in effect correctly identifying those lower priority interpretations as the preferred ones.

Although the performance of the system was somewhat better than the best previously reported, (despite the fact that this performance, unlike that previous efforts, was achieved without any human intervention or aid on disambiguation), the semantic filters were not sufficiently accurate to filter all of the incorrect or ambiguous outputs of the parser and translation rules. In some cases (which occurred in 6 of the 19 partially correct sentences), although conflict pairs were identified correctly, the evidence from Google was not sufficient to disambiguate the pairs correctly. Currently, the calls to the Google web corpus account for only about 2% of the precision of the results in our evaluation.

5 Conclusions

The preliminary results produced by this prototype system, evaluated over a small corpus are encouraging. The precision is better than the best previously reported results. However there remain many issues to be further addressed including dealing in the translation rules with issues of pronoun reference, n-nary relationship identification, entity attribute disambiguation, and cardinality information extraction. Also, the performance of the Google corpus as a semantic filter did not prove as powerful as expected (although it may improve as the rule outputs are made more precise) and the use of alternative, more explicit semantic resources such as CYC [24] and Concept-Net [25] will be explored.

References

1. Bagui, S., Earp, R.: Database Design Using Entity Relationship Diagrams: Boca Raton, Fla.: Auerbach (2003)
2. Chen, P.: English Sentence Structure and Entity Relationship Diagrams. In: Information Science Vol.1, No. 1, Elsevier (1983) 127-149
3. Buchholz, E., Cyriaks, H.,Düsterhöft, A., Mehlan, H., Thalheim, B.: Applying a Natural Language Dialogue Tool for Designing Databases. In: Proceedings of the First International Workshop on Applications of Natural Language to Databases (NLDB'95) (1995)
4. Omar, N., Hanna, P., Mc Kevitt, P.: Heuristics-Based Entity-Relationship Modelling through Natural Language Processing. In: Proc. of the Fifteenth Irish Conference on Artificial Intelligence and Cognitive Science (AICS-04), Lorraine McGinty and Brian Crean (Eds.) (2004) 302-313
5. Bouzeghoub, M., Gardarin, G., Metais, E.: Database Design Tools: An Expert System Approach. In: Very Large Data Base Conference (1985)
6. Black, W.J.: Acquisition of Conceptual Data Models from Natural Language Descriptions. In: 3rd Conf. of the European chapter of ACM, Danemark (1987)
7. Tjoa, A.M., Berger, L.: Transformations of Requirements Specifications Expressed in Natural Language into an Eer Model. In: Proceeding of the 12th International Conference on Approach, Airlington, Texas, USA (1993) 206-217
8. Buchholz, E., Düsterhöft, A.: Using Natural Language for Database Design. In: Working Notes of the KI'94 Workshop: Reasoning about structured Objects: Knowledge Representation Meets Databases (KRDB-94), Saarbrueken, Germany, 1994. (1994)
9. Gomez, F., Segami, C., Delaune, C.: A System for the Semiautomatic Generation of Er Models from Natural Language Specifications. In: Data and Knowledge Engineering 29 (1) (1999) 57-81
10. Sleator, K.D., Temperley, D.: Parsing English with a Link Grammar. In: Third International Workshop on Parsing Technologies (1991)
11. Szolovits, P.: Adding a Medical Lexicon to an English Parser. In: Proc. AMIA 2003 Annual Symposium (2003)
12. Grinberg, D., John Lafferty, Daniel Sleator: A Robust Parsing Algorithm for Link Grammars. In: Proceedings of the Fourth International Workshop on Parsing Technologies, Prague (1995)
13. Ding, J., Berleant, D., Xu, J., Fulmer, W.A.: Extracting Biochemical Interactions from Medline Using a Link Grammar Parser. In: 15th IEEE International Conference on Tools with Artificial Intelligence (ICTAI'03) (2003)
14. Madhyastha, H.V., N. Balakrishnan, K. R. Ramakrishnan: Event Information Extraction Using Link Grammar. In: 13th International WorkShop on Research Issues in Data Engineering: Multi-lingual Information Management (RIDE'03) (2003)
15. Rinaldi, F., Dowdall, J., Hess, M., Mollá, D., Schwitter, R.: Towards Answer Extraction: An Application to Technical Domains. In: Proceedings of the 15th European Conference on Artificial Intelligence, IOS Press, Amsterdam (2002)
16. Metzler, P.D., Haas, W.S., Cosic, L.C., Wheeler, H.L.: Constituent Object Parsing for Information Retrieval and Similar Text Processing Problems. In: Journal of the America Society for Information Science 40 (6) (1989) 398-423
17. Moulton, J., Robinson, M.G.: The Organization of Language: Cambridge University Press. (1981) 400
18. Christiane, F.: Wordnet: An Electronic Lexical Database: MIT Press xxii (1998) 423

19. Keller, F., Mirella Lapatay: Using the Web to Obtain Frequencies for Unseen Bigrams. In: Computational Linguistics 2003, 29(3) (2003) 459-484
20. Volk, M.: Scaling Up. Using the WWW to Resolve PP Attachment Ambiguities. In: Proc.of Konvens-2000. Sprachkommunikation, Ilmenau, VDE Verlag (2000) 151-156
21. Volk, M.: Exploiting the WWW as a Corpus to Resolve PP Attachment Ambiguities. In: Proc. of Corpus Linguistics 2001. Lancaster. (2001)
22. Calvo, H., Gelbukh, A.: Improving Prepositional Phrase Attachment Disambiguation Using the Web as Corpus. In: Progress in Pattern Recognition, Speech and Image Analysis. CIARP (2003)
23. Chantree, F., Kilgarriff, A., De Roeck, A., Willis, D.: Using a Distributional Thesaurus to Resolve Coordination Ambiguities. In: Technical Report, Department of Computing Faculty of Mathematics and Computing,The Open University, Walton Hall, Milton Keynes, MK7 6AA, United Kingdom (2005)
24. Lenat, B.D., Guha, R.V.: Building Large Knowledge-Based Systems: Representation and Inference in the Cyc Project.: Addison-Wesley Publishing Company, Inc. (1990)
25. Liu, H., Singh, P.: Conceptnet: A Practical Commonsense Reasoning Toolkit. In: BT Technology Journal. In Submission (2004)

Function Point Extraction Method from Goal and Scenario Based Requirements Text[*]

Soonhwang Choi[1], Sooyong Park[1,**], and Vijayan Sugumaran[2]

[1] Department of Computer Science, Sogang University
{soonhwang, sypark}@sogang.ac.kr
[2] Department of Decision and Information Science
Oakland University, Rochester, MI 48309, USA
sugumara@oakland.edu

Abstract. Efficient processing of software requirements expressed in natural language is still and active area of research in systems development. Function Point is widely used as a basis to estimate software development cost and schedule. This paper discusses a method for extracting function point from requirements text gathered using the goal and scenario based requirements elicitation technique. The proposed method aims to establish and maintain traceability between function point and requirements text. Text based function point extraction guidance rules have been developed. The proposed methodology has been applied to Order Processing System development.

1 Introduction

In the early stages of software development, natural language text is generally used to express customer's requirements [1]. Based on the stated requirements, cost and schedule needs to be estimated for software project management purposes. Function point technique has been widely used as a basis for estimating software cost and schedule [2], [3], [4], [5]. The core purpose of this approach is to count Function Point that is categorized as follows [6]:

- ILF (Internal Logical File): data or control information *maintained* through one or more elementary process of the target application
- EIF (External Interface File): data or control information *referenced* through one or more elementary processes
- EI (External Input): an elementary process to maintain an ILF or alter the behavior of the application
- EO (External Output): a process that presents information to user through processing logic
- EQ (External inQuiry): an elementary process for presenting information to the user through retrieval of data or control information from an ILF or EIF

---

[*] This research was supported by University IT Research Center (ITRC) project, South Korea.
[**] Corresponding author.

C. Kop et al. (Eds.): NLDB 2006, LNCS 3999, pp. 12–24, 2006.

Currently, there is no systematic method for counting function points based on the five categories listed above from the requirements text, and it is dependent on the human engineer's experience. With this situation, there is a problem in that it is very difficult to manage the estimation process throughout the software development life cycle when requirements change is inevitable. This leads to cost or schedule change [7], [8], [9]. There is a tight linkage between requirements analysis and function point analysis. In that sense, a systematic approach for managing traceability between the natural language requirements text and the function point count is very critical. However, existing function point analysis methods do not deal with requirements elicitation in any great detail. So, we need an overall method for extracting function point that is integrated with an existing requirements analysis method.

The goal and scenario approach has been widely used for requirements analysis [10], [11], [12], [13]. This paper proposes a method for extracting function point from goal and scenario based requirements text. The proposed method links function point with natural language based requirements and provides a basis for managing both requirements and cost throughout the life cycle, as depicted in Figure 1.

The remainder of the paper is organized as follows. In section 2 we describe the goal and scenario modeling for requirements elicitation, as well as the order processing system example that is used to explain our approach. In section 3 we present our approach for extracting function point from goal and scenario. In section 4, we provide the extraction results and discussion for the order processing system example. Finally, section 5 concludes the paper.

Text based Requirements   Authoring using Goal and Scenario approach   Function Point extraction Using our approach   Estimate cost Using FP

Fig. 1. Overall concept of our approach

2 Requirements Modeling Using Goal and Scenario

This paper adopts the goal and scenario based approach for requirements engineering described by Kim et al. in [13]. Below, we briefly discuss the key concepts and some additional authoring rules. For a complete description of the approach, refer to [13].

In this paper, we utilize the four level abstraction hierarchy of goal and scenario presented in [13]. The goals are organized in business, service, interaction and internal level. Goal modeling is accompanied by scenarios corresponding to each of the abstraction level.

A Goal is authored using the *<Verb + Target + Direction + Way>* format. Each goal is expressed as a simple sentence with 'Verb' and 'Target' components as mandatory. However, 'direction' and 'way' can be omitted. 'Direction' is the source or destination for objects to communicate with. 'Way' refers to the *means* or the *manner* in which a goal is achieved. The *means* component includes entities which are used as instruments for performing a goal. The *manner* component defines the way in which the goal is to be achieved. Consider the following example:

'*(add)_{verb} (order)_{target} (to order management application)_{direction}*'. In this example, order is the object to be communicated. Order processing system is the destination for adding the transaction. A scenario is authored using the *<Subject + Verb + Target + Direction + Way>* format. In a scenario, the subject is added for detailed description. A scenario describes expected behavior or the activity for achieving a goal. Again, the 'Direction' and 'way' are optional in a scenario. For example, in the scenario '*(Order management application)_{sub} (receives)_{verb} (invoice id)_{target} (from accounting system)_{direction}*', invoice id is the object to be communicated. Accounting system is the source for the object to communicate with.

Our proposed approach for extracting function point from goal and scenario based requirements text is explained using the 'Order Processing System' example. The order processing system discussed here is for a fruit store which has a warehouse. The objective is to improve their manual process through a computer system that tracks their order. A fragment of the goal model (result of the goal modeling process from [13]) for the order processing system is shown in Figure 2. There are four abstraction levels, namely, business level, service level, interaction level and internal level. This paper deals with the interaction level because our approach uses interaction level requirements chunk (G, Sc), where G stands for the goal and Sc stands for the scenario that achieves that goal.

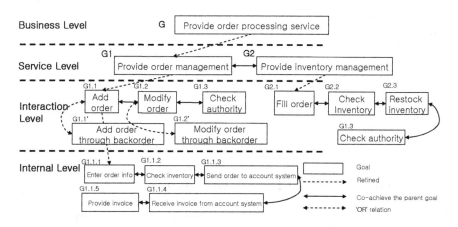

Fig. 2. Partial result of goal modeling for order processing system

3   Extracting Function Point from Goal and Scenario Model

This section describes our methodology for extracting function point from goal and scenario. Specifically, the focus of the proposed method is extracting function point from the interaction level. The main reason for this is that the goal and scenario at the interaction level describes the interaction between user or external application and the target application. It includes data for interaction, which can be used to derive data functions (ILF or EIF), and behavior for data processing that leads to transaction functions (EI, EO or EQ).

Our approach consists of three steps, as shown in Figure 3. In step 1, we extract the context elements from 'subject' and 'direction'. In step 2, we extract data function and its complexity through grouping of 'target'. In step 3, we extract transaction function and its complexity from 'verb' using verb types. The details of each step in our method and the rules are described in the following subsections. After extracting the data and transaction function, we can calculate the unadjusted function point according to the IFPUG standard. It is also described below.

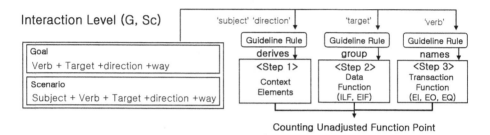

Fig. 3. Approach for extracting FP from goal and scenario

3.1 Step1: Extract Context Elements from Goal and Scenario

The first step of function point analysis is scoping the application boundary. The boundary distinguishes the target application from outside agents such as user or external application. Hence, the users and external applications interacting with the target application should be identified. In the goal and scenario approach, the interaction level requirements chunk (G, Sc) captures the agents that interact with each other and is represented by the 'subject' and 'direction'. It can be a user or an external application interacting with the target application. On the other hand, if the target system's business functions can be decomposed, the system can be decomposed into several applications. In this case, we design each application separately and the other applications are regarded as external applications. We have formalized this into context analysis guiding rules, which are briefly explained below.

Context Analysis guiding rule 1 (CA 1)
Definition: If the target system can be decomposed into several applications, the applications should be decomposed according to business goals. Individual application is refined into service goal.

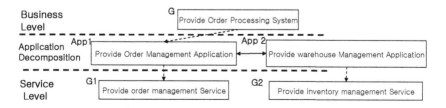

Fig. 4. Application decomposition

Comment: Application decomposition is determined by business functions
Example: Figure 4 shows that 'Order Processing System' is decomposed into two applications because business functions can be decomposed.

Context Analysis guiding rule 2 (CA 2)

Definition: The Agent represented in 'subject' interacts with another agent in 'direction'. If the agent is human, then the agent is a user. The agent that is interacting with the human agent is target application. The agent interacting with the target application can also be an external application.
Example: In example below, accounting manager is the user and order management application (OMA) is the target application. Accounting system is external application

1. (Accounting manager)$_{sub}$ (add)$_{verb}$ (customer name)$_{target}$ (to OMA)$_{direction}$
2. (OMA)$_{sub}$ (receive)$_{verb}$ (**invoice id**)$_{target}$ (from Accounting System)$_{direction}$

Context Analysis guiding rule 3(CA 3)

Definition: If target system is decomposed into several applications, the decomposed applications are designed separately. When each application is designed, the other applications are regarded as external applications.
Example: In figure 4, we should consider 'order management application' and 'warehouse management application' separately. When we design 'order management application', 'warehouse management application' is regarded as external application.

   Using the above rules, we can extract context elements from the goal and scenario model. For the order processing system example, the above rules have been applied to the goal and scenario model and the following agents have been identified – accounting manager, warehouse manager, user management application and accounting system. Order processing system is decomposed into 'order management application' (OMA) and 'warehouse management application' (WMA). Figure 5 shows the context diagram for the order processing system.

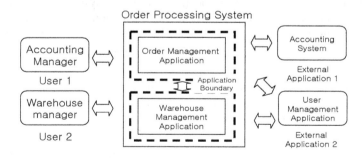

Fig. 5. Context diagram for order processing system

3.2   Step2: Extract Data Functions from Goal and Scenario

After the context analysis, the data functions should be identified. Data functions are characterized by ILF and EIF. In the interaction level requirements chunk, the 'target' expresses data or control information of transmission between target application and the user or external application. This data can be maintained in the target application or the external application. If the data is maintained in the target application, it is ILF. If the data is maintained in the external application, then it is EIF.

After identifying the data functions, the complexity of the data functions should be determined. Complexity of the data function is determined from RET (Record Element Type) and DET (Date Element Type) [6]. DET is a unique user recognizable and unrepeated field in the ILF or EIF. RET is a user recognizable subgroup of data elements within an ILF or EIF. The 'Target' component of a scenario expresses the refined data of the goal. Thus, the refined data in several requirements chunks (G, Sc) can be grouped. We can count the number of refined data elements, represented as DETC (DET Count) and the number of subgroups, represented as RETC (RET Count) [6]. Explanation and examples are given in the following rules.

Data Function Extraction Guiding Rule 1 (DF 1)

Definition: The 'target' of a goal and the group of the 'target' in the scenario which is not related to the 'target' of the goal is ILF or EIF candidate.

Comment: The candidate should be a data element maintained in application and duplication regarded as one. The maintained application can be found in 'subject' or 'direction'.

Example: In the following example, 1 is goal and 2 and 3 are partial scenario refining the goal. 'order' is maintained in Order management application. 'invoice id' and 'invoice contents' are not refined data for 'order' and can be grouped into 'invoice information' maintained in accounting system. So 'order' and 'invoice information' are ILF or EIF.

1. $(Add)_{verb}$ **(Order)**$_{target}$ (to OMA)$_{direction}$
2. $(OMA)_{sub}$ (receive)$_{verb}$ **(invoice id)**$_{target}$ (from Accounting System)$_{direction}$
3. $(OMA)_{sub}$ (receive)$_{verb}$ **(invoice contents)**$_{target}$ (from Accounting System)$_{direction}$

Data Function Extraction Guiding Rule 2 (DF 2)

Definition: Scenario includes refined data of ILF or EIF. If the refined data are maintained in target application, the data function is ILF. If the refined data are maintained in external application, the data function is EIF.

Comment: All goals which include same data function should be considered. The maintained application can be found in 'subject' or 'direction'.

Example: In Figure 6, the refined data for 'inventory' are maintained in WMA. If the WMA is target application, it is ILF and if the WMA is not the target application, it is EIF.

Fig. 6. Example of extracting data function from (G, Sc) 1

Data Function Extraction Guiding Rule 3 (DF 3)

Definition: The identified data function contains refined data. The refined data can be grouped into subgroups. The number of refined data elements is denoted by DETC and number of subgroup is denoted by RETC.

Comment: When the refined data is grouped, all the goals which include the data should be considered. Final complexity is determined by RET/DET complexity matrix for data functions in IFPUG CPM (Counting Practice Manual) [6].

Example: In Figure 7, 'order' is the data function and it is common data for G1.1, G1.2 and G2.1. It includes ten different data elements such as customer name, etc. They can be grouped into two parts, which are 'customer information' and 'order item information'. We can count the number of unique data elements as well as the subgroups. The former represents the DETC and the latter is RETC. Finally we can determine the complexity according to RET/DET complexity matrix.

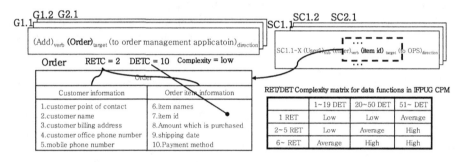

Fig. 7. Example of counting complexity of data function from (G, Sc)

3.3 Step 3: Extract Transaction Function from Goal and Scenario

After identifying the data functions, the transaction functions should be extracted. Transaction functions represent the functionality provided to the user for the processing of data by the target system. They are EI (External Input), EO (External Output), and EQ (External inQuiry). They exhibit the behavior for processing data. In the goal and scenario based approach, the interaction level contains 'verbs' which can represent the behavior for processing data.

In our approach, we identify transaction functions from 'verb' and classify transaction functions using 'verb type' and authoring format. We name the transaction function using the 'verb + target + (direction)' fragment in the goal. This paper restricts the 'verb' in a goal and scenario to active voice. The 'verb type' is defined as the 'data sending type verb' and the 'data receiving type verb'. The main intent of the 'data sending type verb' is sending data, and 'data receiving type verb' is receiving data. Examples of commonly used verbs in requirements statements are in Table 1. The authoring format of the goal used for classification is described in the rules.

Table 1. Two types verb for classifying transaction function

Data sending type verbs	Data receiving type verbs
Send, display, add, dispatch, forward, direct, convey, remit , input, request, modify, fill, output, enter, list	Receive, get, accept, be given, pick up, collect, obtain, acquire, take, validate, check

Complexity of transaction function is calculated from FTR (File Type Reference) and DET (Data Element Type) [6]. FTRC (File Type Reference Count) is the number of ILF or EIF which are referred to by the transaction function. DETC for the transaction function is the number of data elements which are referred to by the transaction + (error, confirm, or complete message) + starting method, etc. We can determine the value of DETC from the 'target' in a given scenario. We can also count the FTR from checking the related ILF or EIF and determine the value of FTRC. Detailed explanation and some examples are given in the following rules.

Transaction Function Extraction Guiding Rule 1 (TF 1)
Definition: 'verb + target + (direction)' components of a goal lead to EI, EO, EQ candidates. 'Direction' can be omitted in the name of a transaction. If several goals are connected with an 'or' relation and only the 'way' component is different, then one transaction is identified by several goals.
Example: In the two goals given below, 'add order' and 'add order through backorder' are transaction candidates. But only the 'way' component is different. So, these two goals derive one transaction.
$(Add)_{verb}\ (order)_{target}\ (to\ OMA)_{direction}$
$(Add)_{verb}\ (order)_{target}\ (to\ OMA)_{direction}\ (through\ backorder)_{way}$

Transaction Function Extraction Guiding Rule 2 (TF 2)
Definition: Goal doesn't have a subject but the subject is regarded as a subject in the scenario that derives the goal. In a goal from which a transaction is derived through TF 1, if the authoring format is $<(User\ or\ External\ application)_{sub} + (Data\ sending\ type\ verb)_{verb} + (Target\ data)_{Target} + (target\ application)_{direction}>$ or $<(target\ application)_{sub} + (Data\ receiving\ type\ verb)_{verb} + (Target\ data)_{Target} + (User\ or\ External\ application)_{direction}>$, then the transaction target is EI.
Example: In the requirement below, the 'subject is' user and the 'direction' is target application. The 'Verb type' is 'data sending type verb' and the main intent is sending order data to the target application. So, 'Add order' is EI for the application.
$(Accounting\ manager)_{sub}\ (add)_{verb}\ (order)_{target}\ (to\ OMA)_{direction}$

Transaction Function Extraction Guiding Rule 3 (TF 3)
Definition: In goal which leads to a transaction through TF 1, if the authoring format is $<(User\ or\ External\ application)_{sub} + (Data\ receiving\ type\ verb)_{verb} + (Target\ data)_{Target} + (target\ application)_{direction}>$ or $<(target\ application)_{sub} + (Data\ sending\ type\ verb)_{verb} + (Target\ data)_{Target} + (User\ or\ External\ application)_{direction}>$, then the transaction which the goal relates to has EO or EQ, which is the behavior for output or inquiry.

Example: In the requirement given below, the 'subject' is user and the 'direction' is target application. 'Verb type' is 'data receiving type verb' whose main intent is receiving inventory data and checking. So, 'check inventory' is EO or EQ.

(Warehouse manager)$_{sub}$ (**check**)$_{verb}$ (**inventory**)$_{target}$ (from WMA)$_{direction}$

Transaction Function Extraction Guiding Rule 4 (TF 4)

Definition: EO or EQ from TF 3 can be classified using this rule. If it includes mathematical calculation, measurement, derived data, changes system behavior or maintaining data function, it is EO. Otherwise, it is EQ.

Example: In the following requirement, 'check inventory' is EO or EQ according to TF 3. However, 'check inventory information' doest not include mathematical calculation, measurement, derived data, change system behavior, or maintain data function. So 'check inventory' is EQ.

(Warehouse manager)$_{sub}$ (**check**)$_{verb}$ (**inventory**)$_{target}$ (from WMA)$_{direction}$

Transaction Function Extraction Guiding Rule 5 (TF 5)

Definition: DETC for transaction functions is the sum of the following:
(The number of unrepeated data in 'verb + target' of the scenario to achieve the transaction ('verb + target'))+ 1 (if there is error, confirm, or complete message) + 1 (if there are starting methods for transaction) + 1 (if there are inputs or data to be retrieved for EO or EQ)

Comment: unrepeated data in 'verb + target' of a scenario should be transmitted between target application and outside and also be in ILF or EIF.

Example: In Figure 8, 'add order' is EI. In the scenario, there are 14 related data items (10 for 'order', 2 for 'invoice' and 2 for 'inventory') and confirming message. We assume there is a starting method for 'ok' button. So its DETC is 16 (10+2+2+1+1).

Transaction Function Extraction Guiding Rule 6 (TF 6)

Definition: FTRC of a transaction is the number of ILF or EIF which is referred by the transaction. If the data elements used for determining DETC is one of the elements of a certain ILF or EIF, the transaction function refers to the ILF or EIF.

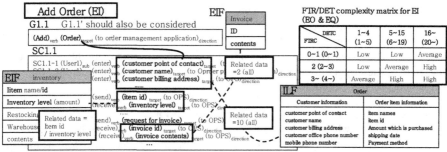

DETC = 14 (10 order + 2 invoice + 2 inventory) +1(confirm/error/complete message) +1(starting method) = 16
FTRC = 3 (related with 1 ILF and 2 EIF)   Complexity = high (3 FTRC/ 16 DETC)

Fig. 8. Complexity of Transaction function ('Add order')

Comment: Final complexity is determined by the FTR/DET complexity matrix for EI, EO and EQ, which is provided by the IFPUG CPM [6].

Example: In Figure 8, 'add order' is EI. The data elements used for determining DETC is included in one ILF named 'Order' and two EIFs named 'invoice' and 'inventory'. Therefore there is one ILF and two EIFs which are referred by 'add order'. So, the FTRC is 3. Final complexity of 'add order' is determined as 'high' by using the FTR/DET matrix.

4   Results from the Order Processing System Example

As a proof-of-concept, we applied our approach and extracted the function point for the order processing system. Parts of this example have been shown in the previous sections. Because of page limit, we provide only an overall summary of the process. Step 1 involves extracting context elements from the goal and scenario model, which is described in section 3.1 and Figure 5 shows the context diagram that resulted from this step. Target system is decomposed into 'Order management application (OMA)' and 'warehouse management application (WMA)'. These two applications should be measured separately. Step 2 deals with extracting data function from goal and scenario. In case of OMA, we extracted 'order' as ILF in addition to extracting 'invoice', 'user' and 'inventory as EIF. In case of WMA, we extract 'inventory' as ILF in addition to extracting 'user' and 'order' as EIF. They were identified by DF 1 and DF 2 (See Figure 6 and related rules). Complexity of the data functions are determined by DF 3 (See Figure 7). Step 3 is concerned with extracting transaction function. In case of OMA, 'add order', 'modify order' is identified as EI and 'check authority' is identified as EQ. In case of WMA, 'fill order' and 'restock inventory', 'check inventory', 'check authority' is identified as EQ. They are identified by TF 1, TF 2, TF 3 and TF 4 (See related rules). Complexity of the transaction functions are determined by TF 5 and TF 6. (See Figure 8 and related rules).

After the three steps, we calculated the UFP (Unadjusted Function Point) from the complexity for each function using IFPUG's conversion matrix [6]. In case of 'add order', it is an EI which has high complexity. We also determined that it has six points using the Functions/Complexity matrix. The sum of UFP for each function is the overall UFP for the target application. We get sixty seven UFP for order processing system. Figure 9 shows the results and the matrices. IFPUG provides an adjustment factor which takes into account the global system characteristics. If UFP is multiplied by that factor, we get the Adjusted Function Point (AFP). This paper deals with only UFP because it is more widely used in cost estimation models.

To show the link between requirements and cost, we estimated the cost of order processing system using a commercial cost estimation model called SEER [14]. Because our estimation is for just showing the link between function point and cost, we used the tool with our UFP result. The estimation result screen is shown in Figure 10. The Estimated Effort Month (man month) is 7.77 for the order processing system.

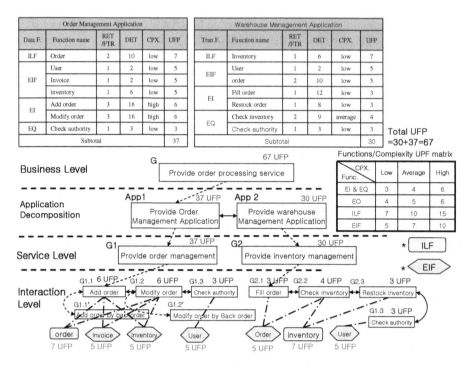

Fig. 9. Extracting the results for the order processing system

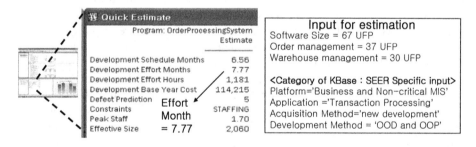

Fig. 10. Cost Estimation using UFP with SEER Model

The proposed method links requirements with function point at multiple abstraction levels and supports traceability activities between requirements and cost through impact analysis, derivation analysis and coverage analysis. However, the IFPUG method does not support it. For example if we remove 'check authority', one EQ named 'check authority' and one EIF named 'user' which is related with 'check authority' are removed from each application. Thus eight UFP is subtracted for each application. Table 2 shows the comparison between our proposed method and the IFPUG method.

Table 2. Comparison between proposed method and IFPUG method

Traceability activity	Proposed method	IFPUG method
Impact analysis	Changed Requirements (G, Sc) are measured again by the rule.	Requirements engineer should be supported by the Function Point Expert (does not facilitate linking with requirements)
Derivation analysis	Following incoming links, in answer to the question. "Why is this here?"	
Coverage analysis	Counting assigned FP values at one level.	

The proposed rules are based on IFPUG's standard and converted for being applied to goal and scenario based requirements text. The rules provide data function and transaction function candidates but final selection should be performed by a human engineer according to the definition. So, Human engineer's mistakes can cause errors.

Function Point approach works well for specific data processing systems but not that well to embedded systems. So, our method may be inefficient for embedded systems because it can generate many invalid candidates. However, it performs extremely well if the system is a data processing specific system. Our rules will be further improved to handle embedded systems as part of our future work.

5 Conclusion and Future Work

Requirements change leads to cost change. Our proposed approach contributes to establishing the link between goal and scenario based requirements and cost. We have described the approach along with the rules and an example. Goal and scenario provide the rationale for requirements, and at an abstract level, requirements and cost can be linked. Thus, our approach supports the integration of traceability management between goal driven requirements and cost. To validate our rules we have also applied the approach to another example, namely, the course registration system. We extracted seventy seven function points in this case and because of space restriction, we have not included it in this paper. As part of our future work, we plan to develop a supporting tool and further refine the methodology. Empirical validation of the approach is also planned.

References

1. V. Ambriola, V. Gervasi, "Processing natural langauge requirements," Proceedings of the 12th international conference on Automated software engineering pp 36, IEEE Computer Society, 1997
2. Albrecht, A. J., "Measuring Application Development Productivity," IBM Applications Development Symposium, Monterey CA, 1979
3. David Garmus, David Herron, Function Point Analysis, Addison Wesley, 2001
4. ISO-IEC, International ISO/IEC Standard 14143-1, Information Technology – Software measurement – Functional size, Part 1: Definition of Concepts, 1998

5. Takuya Uemura, Shinji Kusumoto, Katsuro Inoue,"Function Point Measurement Tool for UML Design Specification," IEEE METRICS 1999: 62-., 1999
6. IFPUG, Function Point Counting Practice Manual Release 4.1.1, International Function Point User Group, 2000
7. Boehm, B., Hoh In, "Software Cost Option Strategy Tool (S-COST)," Proceedings of 20th International Computer Software and Applications Conference (COMPSAC '96) pp15-20, Aug. 1996
8. Karlsson, J., Ryan, K,"A cost-value approach for prioritizing requirements," IEEE Software Volume 14, Issue 5 pp67-74, Sept.-Oct. 1997
9. Boehm, B., Software Engineering Economics, Prentice-Hall, 1981.
10. Hwasil Yang, Minseong Kim, Sooyong Park, Vijayan Sugumaran, "A Process and Tool Support for Managing Activity and Resource Conflicts Based on Requirements Classification," NLDB 2005, LNCS 3513, pp. 114-125, 2005. 6
11. A. Dardenne, A. van Lamsweerde and S. Fickas, "Goal-Directed Requirements Acquisition," Science of Computer Programming, Vol. 20, 1993, pp. 3-50
12. C. Rolland, C. Souveyet, and C. Ben Achour, "Guiding goal modeling using scenarios," IEEE Transactions on Software Engineering, Vol. 24, Dec. 1998, pp.1055-1071
13. Jintae Kim, Sooyong Park, Vijayan Sugumaran, "A Linguistics-Based Approach for Use Case Driven Analysis Using Goal and Scenario Authoring," NLDB 2004, LNCS 3136, Springer-Verlag, , pp. 159-170, 2004. 6
14. http://galorath.com/

Unsupervised Keyphrase Extraction for Search Ontologies

Jon Atle Gulla, Hans Olaf Borch, and Jon Espen Ingvaldsen

Department of Computer and Information Science
Norwegian University of Science and Technology, Trondheim
jag@idi.ntnu.no

Abstract. Ontology learning today ranges from simple frequency counting methods to advanced linguistic analyses of sentence structure and word semantics. For ontologies in information retrieval systems, class concepts and hierarchical relationships at the appropriate level of detail are crucial to the quality of retrieval. In this paper, we present an unsupervised keyphrase extraction system and evaluate its ability to support the construction of ontologies for search applications. In spite of its limitations, such a system is well suited to constantly changing domains and captures some interesting domain features that are important in search ontologies. The approach is evaluated against the project management documentation of a Norwegian petroleum company.

1 Introduction

High-quality ontologies are necessary components in Semantic Web applications. They provide the vocabulary for semantic annotation of data and help applications to interoperate and people to collaborate. The construction and maintenance of ontologies, however, is challenging and has so far been a bottleneck to the realization of the Semantic Web. The ontologies tend to grow huge and complex, and both domain expertise and ontology modeling expertise are needed in ontology engineering. For example, the subsea petroleum ontology proposed as an ISO standard by the Integrated Information Platform project currently contains more than 55.000 classes [10]. As a result, ontologies are expensive and slow to develop, and only few organizations can afford carrying out such a demanding task and set resources aside for subsequent maintenance.

A number of ontology engineering methods have been proposed in recent years (see [4,5]). These are based on traditional modeling approaches and stress the systematic assessment of the domain and gradual elaboration of model descriptions. Several recent projects acknowledge this manual and laborious part of ontology engineering, but would like to speed up the process with automatic tools that can generate candidate concepts and relationships for the new ontology. Most of these semi-automatic approaches use advanced linguistic and statistical methods to analyze a relevant document collection in the domain [7,10,11,13,14,16]. Even though many of the approaches display impressive results, the complexities of ontologies are so fundamental that these generated candidate structures usually just constitute a starting point for the manual modeling task.

C. Kop et al. (Eds.): NLDB 2006, LNCS 3999, pp. 25–36, 2006.

In this paper we present an unsupervised keyphrase extraction system that will be one of several tools made available to ontology engineers. The idea is to use it for constructing and maintaining ontologies to be included in advanced information retrieval systems. The extracted keyphrases will in many cases serve as good concepts (classes) in the ontology and can even give indications for how hierarchical relations should be defined. This is a lightweight extraction system, though cheap and practical to use for domains that evolve and lack available domain experts.

The paper is structured as follows. Section 2 discusses the required qualities of ontologies for search. We then introduce the keyphrase extraction system in Section 3 and briefly presents how it was used to extract keyphrases from the project management domain in Section 4. After evaluating the keyphrases, we investigate how such a system may support the construction of search ontologies in Section 5. Section 6 is devoted to related work, and the conclusions are found in Section 7.

2 Ontologies in Search Applications

Ontology-driven information retrieval incorporates a range of features that are not commonly found in traditional systems. Commercial vector space search engines have started to make use of shallow linguistic technologies, but they do not attempt to expose the real semantics of documents [8]. An ontology-driven information retrieval system operates at three different levels of ambition. At the lowest level, we use concept hierarchies in the ontology to retrieve and present ranked documents to the user. The ontology is either used to reformulate the query in terms of semantic concepts or to construct semantic indices. Slightly more demanding on the ontology side is the browsing of knowledge in the domain. The idea here is to let the user explore relationships and hierarchies in the ontology to help him get an overview of the domain and find related information. At the most ambitious level, we use reasoning to provide answers that are composed of several documents and/or logical proofs in the ontology. A formally defined ontology language like OWL and a complete ontology with constraints and axioms must then be available [1]. Figure 1 illustrates how ontological information is used in these functions.

Function	Focus	Ontology specification needed
Retrieve a document	Concepts	Concepts, hierarchies
Browse knowledge	Ontological structures	+ Properties, relationships
Compose a reply	Reasoning	+ logic, constraints

Fig. 1. Three applications of ontological information in information retrieval

The focus of this paper is on search applications that simply retrieve documents, i.e. we are addressing the lowest level of the ontology-driven retrieval hierarchy. The *ontology value quadrant* in Figure 2 is used to evaluate an ontology's usefulness in a particular application. The ontology's ability to capture the content of the universe of discourse at the appropriate level of granularity and precision and offer the application understandable correct information are important features that are addressed in many ontology/model quality frameworks (e.g. [7,11,14]). But the construction of the ontology also needs to take into account dynamic aspects of the domain as well as the behavior of the application. For search ontologies, this means that we need to consider the following issues about content and dynamics:

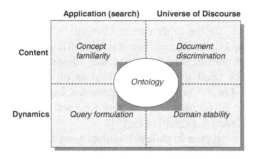

Fig. 2. Ontology value quadrant

- **Concept familiarity.** Terminologies are used to subcategorize phenomena and make semantic distinctions about reality. Ideally the concepts preferred by the user in his queries correspond to the concepts found in the ontology. Analyses of query logs reveal that users tend to use nominal phrases. Whereas we refer to user concepts not found in the ontology as *ignored concepts*, ontology concepts not appealing to users are called *unwanted concepts*.
- **Document discrimination.** The structure of concepts in the ontology decides which groups of documents can theoretically be singled out and returned as result sets. Similarly, the concepts preferred by the user indicate which groups of documents he might be interested in and which distinctions between documents he considers irrelevant. If the granularity of the user's preferred concepts and the ontology concepts are perfectly compatible, combinations of these terms can single out the same result sets from the document collection. Result sets that can be implied by combinations of user-preferred concepts and not by combinations of ontology concepts are called *unfulfilled results*. Result set that can be singled out by combinations of ontology concepts and not by combinations of user-preferred concepts are considered *unwanted results*.
- **Query formulation.** The user queries are usually very short, like 2-3 words, and hierarchical terms tend to be added to refine a query [8]. This economy of expression seems more important to users than being allowed to specify detailed and precise user needs, as very few use advanced features to detail their query.
- **Domain stability.** The search domain may be constantly changing, and parts of the domain may be badly described in documents compared to others. The ontology needs regular and frequent maintenance, making it difficult to depend on the availability of domain experts.

An ontology learning approach for search ontologies, thus, is inexpensive and needs to generate familiar candidate concepts that enable the user economically to retrieve exactly those result sets that he might be interested in.

3 Unsupervised Keyphrase Extraction

Keyphrase extraction is the process of extracting an optimal set of keyphrases to describe a document. Supervised keyphrase extraction employs a collection of documents with pre-assigned keyphrases to train the extraction algorithm. Unsupervised extraction, on the other hand, relies solely on a reference collection of plain unannotated textual data. Despite being more difficult due to the lack of training data, unsupervised keyphrase extraction has the advantage of being more widely applicable. You do not need to know the domain or consult domain experts for extracting keyphrases. On the other hand, supervised keyphrase extraction normally produces more relevant keyphrases and can with repeated training improve the quality of its own keyphrases (see for example [17,19]).

A list of keyphrases gives a high-level summary of the document content. Such summaries can be used on search engine result pages, helping the user to decide which documents are relevant. It is also often used in document clustering or back-of-book index generation. Another important application is in ontology learning. Given a collection of documents describing a domain, keyphrases can be used to identify important concepts and provide a basis for constructing simple ontologies.

Figure 3 presents the architecture for a generic keyphrase extraction system, of which the core components are *data preprocessing*, *candidate phrase generation* and *phrase weighting and selection*.

- **Data pre-processing.** This component includes lexical analysis for tokenizing the data and removing special characters and optionally removing stopwords, normalizing the text and part-of-speech tagging the documents.
- **Candidate phrase generation.** This component applies filters to select the set of words most likely to be keyphrases, called *candidate phrases*.
- **Phrase weighting and selection.** This component *weights* the candidate phrases according to their assumed usefulness to produce a ranked list of keyphrases, and then selects the final list of keyphrases.

Phrases are ranked by their significance within each document and in the reference collection. Selection is done either by outputting a fixed number of keyphrases from each document, or selecting all keyphrases scoring higher than some threshold.

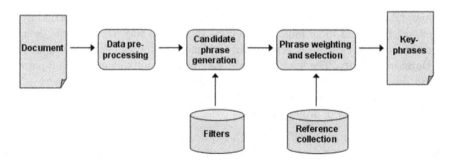

Fig. 3. Keyphrase extraction architecture

4 Extracting Keyphrases in STATOIL

STATOIL ASA, one of the largest companies in Norway, is the leading petroleum company on the Norwegian Continental Shelf and has more than 25,000 employees in 31 countries. Most of their textual documents are structured in NOTES databases, but they are now considering other information management environments and more knowledge-intensive applications. The keyphrase extraction system is developed as part of a cooperation project, KUDOS, between STATOIL and NTNU in Trondheim. The intention of KUDOS is to investigate the benefits of Semantic Web technologies in STATOIL by developing and evaluating ontologies, text mining tools and intelligent search applications.

The domain chosen for the keyphrase extraction system was STATOIL's project management standard, PMI. This standard is enforced throughout STATOIL's organization and is well documented in books and reports. In particular, STATOIL is using a book called PMBOK[1] as a guide to people involved in projects. Every project manager in STATOIL needs to respect the guidelines and advice given in this book, and a project management responsible needs to make sure that the content of PMBOK is known to the right people.

Our unsupervised keyphrase extraction system follows the architecture from figure 3 and incorporates both statistical and linguistic techniques. It takes a collection of plain text documents as input and outputs a ranked list of keyphrases for each document. With our keyphrase extraction system, we extracted keyphrases for all 12 chapters of PMBOK as follows:

Step 1. Data preprocessing
Each chapter in PMBOK is treated as a separate document, and all formatting and document structures are deleted. The resulting input to the extraction system is unannotated plain text, as shown by the PMBOK fragment below:

```
Scope planning is the process of progressively elaborating and
documenting the project work (project scope) that produces the
product of the project.
```

A Brill Part-Of-Speech tagger is then used to tag each word with its respective part of speech (POS):

```
Scope/NNP planning/NN is/VBZ the/DT process/NN of/IN progressively/RB
elaborating/VBG and/CC documenting/VBG the/DT project/NN work/NN (/(
project/NN scope/NN )/) that/WDT produces/VBZ the/DT product/NN of/IN
the/DT project/NN ./.
```

These POS tags come from the Penn Treebank tag set and allows us to filter out words that should not be considered as potential keyphrases. Adverbs (RB), conjunctions (CC) and determiners (DT), for example, will usually not be part of keyphrases, even though you find exceptions like "*Very Large DataBases*" including the adverb "*very*". In fact, since our systems only extracts keyphrases composed of nouns, we concentrate on the words tagged with NN (singular or mass noun), NNP (singular proper noun) and NNS (plural noun). Stopwords are afterwards removed

---

[1] Project Management Institute. A Guide to the Project Management Body of Knowledge (PMBOK), 2000.

from the text, using a list of 571 words that are abundant in the English language and carry little or no discriminating meaning:

```
Scope planning is the process of progressively elaborating and
documenting the project work (project scope) that produces the
product of the project.
```

The words shown in bold are deleted from the text. To get rid of morpho-syntactic variation in the text, we use a lexicon to lemmatize the words. This means that the actual inflections are replaced by their corresponding base forms, giving us plan instead of the progressive planning and produce instead of the third person singular produces. If a word does not occur in the dictionary, Porter's stemming algorithm is applied to the word. This results in the following sequence of words (POS tags hidden):

```
Scope plan process progress elaborate document project work project
scope produce product project
```

Notice that the stemming of progressively to progress makes it appear like a noun, but we keep the tag RB to avoid that progress is analyzed as a noun later.

Step 2: Candidate phrase generation
Different extraction systems tend to adopt different strategies for which structures should be considered potential keyphrases. In our system all consecutive nouns are selected as candidate phrases:

```
{scope planning, process, project work, project scope, product,
project}
```

This list contains all potential keyphrases for the document, but we still do not know which phrases are prominent enough to be suggested as real keyphrases.

Step 3: Phrase weighting and selection
The candidate phrases are weighted using the *tf.idf* measure found in information retrieval. We first calculate the term frequency (*tf*), which gives us an indication of how frequent this phrase is in this chapter compared to other phrases:

$$tf = \frac{n_i}{\sum_k n_k}$$

where n_i is the number of occurrences of the considered phrase in the chapter, and the denominator is the number of occurrences of all terms (phrases) in the chapter. The total tf.idf score is calculated as shown below and takes into account the distribution of this phrase throughout the document collection:

$$tfidf = tf \cdot \log\left(\frac{|D|}{|(d_j \supset t_i)|}\right)$$

where $|D|$ is the total number of chapters in the collection and $|(d_j \supset t_i)|$ is the number of chapters (excluding the current chapter) where the term t_j appears (not equal to 0). The resulting list of weighted phrases are sorted and presented to the user:

```
{(scope planning, 0.0097), (project scope, 0.0047), (product,
0.0043), (project work, 0.0008), (project, 0.0001), (process,
0.0000)}
```

5 Evaluation of Extracted Keyphrases

The experiment was performed with each of the 12 chapters in PMBOK as documents. and for each document the other 11 documents were used as a reference collection. The book contains about 50,600 words, and the average chapter is about 10-11 pages of pure text, or about 4,200 words.

15 phrases were generated from each chapter and rated according to their usefulness as domain concepts using a three-point scale. Score 0 was given to uninteresting phrases, 1 represented a relevant but not ideal keyphrase and 2 was given to phrases that were good descriptions of the chapter. The evaluation itself was performed by Statoil staff that had years of experience with PMI and had been responsible for its application in STATOIL.

Overall Results
The overall results for the top 180 keyphrases (15 for each chapter) gave us 29% relevant phrases (score 2), 18% related phrases (score 1) and 52% irrelevant phrases.

Recall values were impossible to calculate, as it was impossible to know how many relevant concepts that applied to each chapter. Precision is defined as the number of relevant phrases retrieved divided by the total number of phrases retrieved. For the evaluation, we use R-precision curves. R-precision is defined as the precision at the Rth position of a ranked list of results that have R relevant phrases. The curve in Figure 4 tells us that 29% of the first 15 keyphrases of all chapters were considered relevant domain concepts by STATOIL. For the first 5 phrases of each chapter, more than 35% are relevant. We can see that the 5-6 highest ranked phrases tend to be more relevant than the rest, but the difference is not dramatic and ranking seems of little importance after the 10 first phrases.

The results are quite modest and indicate that we cannot uncritically accept the candidate phrases as ontology concepts.   Sometimes you can recognize bad suggestions (like *end* and *build* in Figure 5(b)), but in general you may need domain experts to use these results for domain construction.

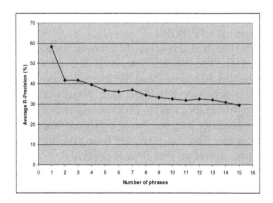

Fig. 4. R-precision curve as an average for all 12 chapters

Detailed Analysis

A more detailed analysis of the keyphrases extracted reveal some interesting features that can help us use unsupervised keyphrase extraction in search ontology learning. Consider the size of the various chapters. The lengths of the chapters span from 1318 words (Chapter 3) to 7811 words (Chapter 11). If we group the chapters together for each interval of 500 words and calculate average R-precision for the top 15 phrases for each group, we get the distribution shown in Figure 5(a).

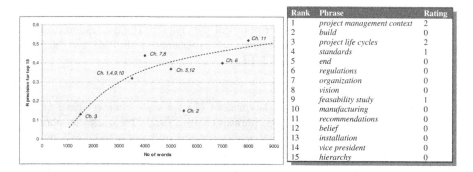

Fig. 5. (a) R-precision and chapter size (b) Keyphrases with domain rates for chapter 2

In general, we observe that the quality of phrases extracted drops fast when the chapters get shorter than 3,000 words. Also, it seems difficult to achieve more than like 50-55% R-precision even if we had much longer documents available.

Chapter 2 (*The Project Management Context*) deserves a closer examination, as it deviates from the general trend. It deals with life cycles, stakeholders, organizational influences, management skills, and social-economic environmental influences, which according to the book is somewhat outside the scope of the rest of the book: "*This chapter describes key aspects of the project management context not covered elsewhere in this document*" (Chapter 2, page 11 of PMBOK). This may explain why the phrases extracted in this chapter were so general and had very little to do with PMI (see Figure 6(b)). It discusses a wider context that was not considered within the domain by the PMI expert at STATOIL.

Secondly we can analyze how the score differences for the top phrases are linked to the rating of the phrases. The score difference is defined as the difference between the average score of the top 10 phrases and the average score of the top 100 phrases. The statistics are not conclusive, but there is a certain correlation for our small experiment. Low score differences tend to produce top phrases of lower quality. This means that we need to consider a larger set of candidate phrases for documents with very low score differences. There is however little statistical support for assuming that high score differences correlate with high R-precision.

Finally, we can see how phrases of different lengths are rated differently by STATOIL. Long phrases are considered more relevant as domain concepts than short ones. In fact, these results are so clear that we should start boosting longer terms in the extraction process. But there is something even more interesting to read from this. Related phrases are phrases that share one or more words, like the phrases *scope changes* and *scope definition*. Of the 38 related phrases suggested in this experiment, as many as 33 were considered relevant (see Figure 6). Almost 90% of related phrases are useful in describing the domain, compared to 60% of two-word phrases and only 4% of one-word phrases.

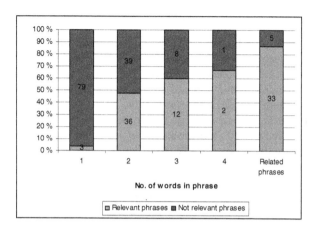

Fig. 6. Relevance of different types of phrases

Keyphrases as Concepts in Search Ontologies

The experiment in STATOIL tells us that we need to consider the results from unsupervised keyphrase extraction with care, though the analysis above can help us make the most out of these systems. The system's results for search ontology engineering can be substantially improved by ignoring very short chapters, include larger candidate sets for documents with low score differences, and boost long and related phrases aggressively.

Concept familiarity is not well supported in general, though we see that the domain experts have a very high rating of long multi-word phrases. The extraction process is set up to focus on nominal phrases consisting of consecutive nouns, which means that we may miss some possibly relevant nominal phrases containing adjectives or adverbs. This is however very easy to modify in the system.

Document discrimination is maybe the most interesting issue for this approach. Since the extraction system copies the standard information retrieval model with tf.idf scores and contrastive reference collections, the generated keyphrases are by nature designed to enable efficient discrimination of documents. This is exactly what ontology concepts need to support in search systems to help the user retrieve the exact set of documents he is interested in.

Query formulation is reasonably well supported, since the discriminatory approach to extracting keyphrases allows you to specify fewer concepts in the query. Moreover, the multi-word phrases help us build hierarchical relations between concepts, enabling the user to generalize or specialize his query. As an example, the phrases *scope changes*, *scope change control* and *scope management plan* from Figure 4 may both suggest more generalized concepts like *scope* and give you ideas about concept relationships.

The lack of *domain stability* in search applications does not pose any problem for this ontology learning system. Unsupervised keyphrase extraction is inexpensive and does not require any training or preparation beforehand.

6   Related Work

In this paper we have investigated to what extent unsupervised keyphrase extraction may be useful in constructing ontologies tailored to an information retrieval context. This idea of taking the intended use of the ontologies into account is not new. Thurmair claims that precision and recall are useless in keyphrase extraction, and the quality of extracted terms must be assessed on the basis of how people can make use of the terms and how fast they can define their own term subsets [14]. Tomokiyo and Hurst propose an unsupervised extraction strategy based on n-grams, and they require that the users themselves characterize what constitutes proper phrases for their particular applications [16].

One of the most well-known workbenches for ontology learning is Text2Onto, which includes a whole battery of statistical and linguistic text mining components [3]. This is a general environments that is meant to support a wide range of analyses and can be expanded with new components when needed. This modular approach to text mining is also adopted in other applications [7,10]. As opposed to these workbenches, our system is more lightweight and tailored to the more restricted need in constructing and maintaining ontologies for search applications.

OntoLT in Protégé includes traditional statistical methods for term extraction, though its main contribution lie in the use of shallow linguistics to extract structured information from individual sentences [2]. It uses a rule-based system for German and English sentence analysis, SCHUG, to propose properties and relationship based on the recognition of heads, modifiers and predicates in the sentences. A similar approach to linguistic sentence analysis is adopted by Sabou et al. to extract concepts and relationships between concepts in a web service context [13]. These methods are able also to suggest relationships between concepts, but it is an open question how this sentence by sentence approach will work for large text collections where individual sentences are statistically insignificant and aggregated data need to be used to produce representative results.

Lastly, there are supervised keyphrase extraction systems that may be used as alternatives to this unsupervised approach. The GenEx system uses a set of training documents to train a steady-state genetic algorithm and optimize the use of 12 parameters for keyphrase extractions [17]. A similar training approach is adopted in KEA [20], which uses many of the techniques included in our extraction system to prepare the documents for keyphrase extraction. Evaluations show that both systems achieve a precision of about 80%, significantly higher than for unsupervised extractors.

7   Conclusions

Unsupervised keyphrase extraction is a flexible and inexpensive method for generating candidate concepts for search ontologies. They do not require any particular preparation or involvement of domain experts and are thus well suited to unstable domains like document collections.

The quality of extracted keyphrases is not at the same level as for supervised extraction. We have to be careful with phrases that are extracted from very short texts or are among a large number of extracted keyphrases with more or less the same scores. However, since multi-word related phrases are the most useful in domain descriptions, these can be boosted to provide better results. Moreover, these multi-word phrases are in many cases useful when defining concept hierarchies. A distinct positive feature of unsupervised keyphrase extraction is also that phrases are chosen on the basis of their discriminating effect.

Unsupervised keyphrase extraction is a promising approach to search ontology engineering, though there are still many aspects of search ontologies that this approach as well as other approaches do not address properly. A good search ontology is specified at a level of granularity that corresponds to the needs expressed in user queries. It should contain concepts that are familiar to the users and allow him to express his information needs in an economic and efficient way. This paper sums up the results of a rather limited experiment at STATOIL and more evaluation is certainly needed. We will also investigate how previously extracted keyphrases (or the resulting ontology concepts) may be consulted to improve the extraction of new keywords. Finally, we intend to compare this keyphrase-enhanced ontology engineering method with a full manual approach to ontology construction in STATOIL.

References

1. Antoniou, G.; Franconi, E.; van Harmelen, F. Introduction to Semantic Web Ontology Languages. In Eisinger, N. and Maluszynski, J. (Ed.), Reasoning Web, First International Summer School 2005, Chap. 1, Malta, July 2005. Springer.
2. Buitelaar, P., Olejnik, D., Sintek, M.: A Protégé Plug-In for Ontology Extraction from Text Based on Linguistic Analysis. In: Proceedings of the 1st European Semantic Web Symposium (ESWS), Heraklion, Greece, May 2004.
3. Cimiano, P., Völker, J.: Text2onto – A Framework for Ontology Learning and Data-Driven Change Discovery. In Proceedings of 10th International Conference on Applications of Natural Language to Information System (NLDB 2005), Alicante, June 15-17, 2005. pp 227-238.
4. Cristiani, M., Cuel, R.: A Survey on Ontology Creation Methodologies. Idea Group Publishing. 2005.
5. Fernandez, M., Goméz-Peréz, A., Juristo, N.: Methontology: from ontological art towards ontological engineering. In Proceedings of the AAAI'97 Spring Symposium Series on Ontological Engineering, pp 33-40, Stanford, 1997.
6. Gene Ontology Consortium. Gene Ontology: tool for the unification of biology. Nature Genet. Vol. 25, pp 25-29. 2000.
7. Goméz-Peréz, A.: Evaluation of ontologies. International Journal of Intelligent Systems, Vol. 16, No. 3, pp 391-409, 2001.
8. Gulla, J. A., Auran, P. G., Risvik, K. M.: Linguistics in Large-Scale Web Search. In Proceedings of the 6th International Conference on Applications of Natural Language to Information Systems (NLDB 2002), Stockholm, June 2002, pp 218-222.

9. Gulla, J. A., Brasethvik, T., Kaada, H. A Flexible Workbench for Document Analysis and Text Mining. In Proceedings of the 9th International Conference on Applications of Natural Language to Information Systems (NLDB'04), pp. 336-347, Manchester, June 2004. Springer.

10. Gulla, J. A., Tomassen, S. L., Strasunskas, D.: Semantic Interoperability in the Norwegian Petroleum Industry. Submitted to the International Conference on Information Systems and Its Applications (ISTA'06), 2006.

11. Lindland, O. I., Sindre, G., Sølvberg, A.: Understanding Quality in Conceptual Modeling. IEEE Software, Vol. 11, No. 2, pp 42-49, March 1994.

12. Maedche, A. Ontology Learning for the Semantic Web. Kluwer Academic Publ. 2002.

13. Navigli, R., Velardi, P.: Learning Domain Ontologies from Document Warehouses and Dedicated Web Sites. Computational Linguistics, Vol. 30, No. 2, pp 151-179. June 2004.

14. Pinto, H. S., Martins, J. P.: Ontologies: How can They be Built? Knowledge and Information Systems, Vol. 6, No. 4, pp 441-464, July 2004.

15. Sabou, M., Wroe, C., Goble, C., Stuckenschmidt, H.: Learning Domain Ontologies for Semantic Web Service Descriptions. Accepted for publication in Journal of Web Semantics.

16. Thurmair, G.: Making Term Extraction Tools Usable. The Joint Conference of the 8th International Workshop of the European Association for Machine Translation and the 4th Controlled Language Applications Workshop (EAMT/CLAW'03). Dublin 2003.

17. Tomassen, S. L.; Gulla, J. A. Ontology Support for Query Interpretation. Submitted to 18th Conference on Advanced Information Systems Engineering (CAiSE'06).

18. Tomokiyo, T.; Hurst, M.: A language model approach to keyphrase extraction. In Proceedings of the ACL 2003 Workshop on Multiword Expressions: Analysis, Acquisitions and Treatment, 2003.

19. Turney, P. D.: Learning algorithms for keyphrase extraction. Information Retrieval, Vol. 2, No. 4, pp 303-336, 2000.

20. Witten, I. H., Paynter, G. W., Frank, E., Gutwin, C., Nevill-Manning, C. G.: KEA: Practical automatic keyphrase extraction. In ACM DL, pp 254-255, 1999.

Studying Evolution of a Branch of Knowledge
by Constructing and Analyzing Its Ontology

Pavel Makagonov,[1] Alejandro Ruiz Figueroa,[1] and Alexander Gelbukh[2]

[1] Mixteca University of Technology, Huajuapan de León, Oaxaca, 69000, México
mpp@mixteco.utm.mx, figueroa@nuyoo.utm.mx
[2] Center for Computing Research, National Polytechnic Institute, 07738, DF, Mexico
www.Gelbukh.com

Abstract. We propose a method for semi-automatic construction of an ontology of a given branch of science for measuring its evolution in time. The method relies on a collection of documents in the given thematic domain. We observe that the words of different levels of abstraction are located within different parts of a document: say, the title or abstract contains more general words than the body of the paper. What is more, the hierarchical structure of the documents allows us to determine the parent-child relation between words: e.g., a word that appears in the title of a paper is a candidate for a parent of the words appearing in the body of this paper; if such a relation is repeated several times, we register such a parent-child pair in our ontology. Using the papers corresponding to different years, we construct such an ontology for each year independently. Comparing such ontologies (using tree edit distance measure) for different years reveals the trends of evolution of the given branch of science.

1 Introduction

Measurement and analysis of evolution of a branch of knowledge is important for various tasks of administration and distribution of resources and human activity. For example, it is possible to predict the trends in the development of science (at least in the periods of stability) for better distribution of capital investment in scientific research [1]. In such periods development of science is based on the previous results (even though in unpredictable direction). It increases in the periods of active development of the scientific infrastructure and decreases some time before the science becomes obsolete and enters the period of stagnation. The latter is an indication of an approaching structural shift—such as a new invention—in the larger system of knowledge embracing the given branch of science, which resolves the difficulties accumulated in this subsystem.

In our previous work we have used the analysis of structured text for portraying the trends in the development of economy. We analyzed the titles of all articles published by the Free Economic Society of Russia for the period of 1983–2000 coinciding with a transitional period of Russian economy [2]. The distribution of the titles in time reveals three clusters of words used in the titles of the articles:

C. Kop et al. (Eds.): NLDB 2006, LNCS 3999, pp. 37–45, 2006.
© Springer-Verlag Berlin Heidelberg 2006

- Words of high level of abstraction (categories of the economy field) that persist during the whole mentioned period, and
- Two different clusters of words, corresponding to the periods 1983–1989 and 1990–2000, belonging to the next, lower level of abstraction (economical processes) that have changed in Russia within the period under consideration.

The two latter clusters reveal the sharp difference between the economical state of the country in the corresponding periods. Indeed, the first period corresponds to the state-controlled economy while the second one to the free market economy.

This suggests that cluster analysis can reveal real underlying processes. In this paper we further develop this idea and apply it to the analysis of the state and development trends of a branch of science. Instead of plain clusters of terms we use a hierarchically organized terminological ontology. We illustrate the methodology on constructing an ontology on a specific thematic domain: *parallel, concurrent, distributed, and simultaneous computing*.

With this research, we introduce a novel view on ontology: not as a static collection of facts about the language and the world but as a snapshot of the state of the language and the world in a specific moment of time, which evolves as the world evolves. This leads to a novel use of (such) ontologies as a tool for describing and studying the evolution of the domain in question: we argue for that the question *what changed in the world (domain)?* is to be more precisely formulated as *what changed in its ontology?* In its turn, this thus gives a tool for qualitative and quantitative studying of the changes in a specific area of interest—which we apply in our case to scientometrics [6].

Since such "time snapshot" ontologies are nearly impossible to construct manually (indeed, their authors would inevitably reflect their own time's view, not the past moment's one), we have developed a novel method of automatic constructing such an ontology, which can be used independently whenever an ontology is to be constructed for a domain for which hierarchically-structured documents are available [7].

Our method for describing the changes in the domain through the changes in its ontology has its limitation. Indeed, changes in the domain, e.g., in science, can be reflected in three different processes:

- Appearance or disappearance of terms;
- Appearance or disappearance of relationships between terms;
- Re-conceptualizing the meaning of terms.

In this paper we mainly discuss the first effect, as the simplest and easier detectable with our methods. The second effect can also be studied by considering structural (qualitative instead of quantitative) changes in the ontology. We do not directly deal with the third effect. However, future research will show whether re-conceptualization is directly reflected in sharp changes of relationships between terms (cf. *trap a mouse* vs. *click with the mouse*) and thus is accounted for in our method.

The paper is organized as follows. Section 2 introduces the basic concepts about the type of ontology we use for our research and its interpretation for our goals. Section 3 briefly presents the algorithm for constructing this type of ontology. Section 4 outlines the experimental results and gives an example of the constructed ontology. Section 5 provides the discussion about the use of our ontology for evaluating the changes in the science. Finally, Section 6 concludes the paper.

2   The Structure of an Ontology of Scientific Texts

By *ontology* we mean a hierarchical structure of concepts and words, which can be represented by a graph. Its root node (zero level of abstraction) identifies the thematic domain under consideration, in our case *parallel, concurrent, distributed, and simultaneous computing*. Each next level contains concepts of lower level of abstraction. The leaves of the hierarchy are the most specific terms. Note that in all algorithms we assume that the texts are stemmed [5]; in what follows for simplicity by words we actually refer to the stems.

To detect concepts and words of a given domain, we use a frequency list of common English words and a corpus of texts with the same list of words of upper level of the hierarchy: the corpus on computer science but not on parallel computing. This allows us to obtain a small but detailed ontology.

We experimented with a corpus of about 2300 articles from IEEE journals and proceedings of various conferences on parallel, distributed, concurrent, and simultaneous computing. The texts in this collection are organized hierarchically: each paper is under title of the corresponding conference or journal, the body of the paper is under its title, etc.; specifically, the hierarchy is as follows:

- Domain description: *parallel, concurrent, distributed, simultaneous computing*
    - Title of the conference or journal
        - Title of the paper
            - Abstract, introduction, conclusions, references
                - Body of the paper

The titles of the sources and of the papers are very short text segments, so we enrich each such segment with the words of the lower levels of abstraction that occur under it. The text segments of each level provide the words of the corresponding levels of abstraction. The bodies of the articles are the source of the lowest level words.

For the present study we considered three levels of abstraction:

- Titles of conferences or journals;
- Titles of papers;
- Abstracts (without titles).

We concatenated the corresponding texts dated by each year (or sometimes several years, when we had too few texts for each year): e.g., all titles of papers for 1997. This gave a relatively small group of larger files T_i (three files per year). For constructing our ontology we used vector space representation of these files with a *tf-idf*-like term weighting.

Namely, we began with constructing weighted wordlists called domain oriented dictionaries (DOD) [3]; such a list includes the domain terms along with their correspondent importance (relevance) weights for the given domain.[1] The DOD includes the words whose frequency in our domain collection is three times higher than that in the general English usage.

---

[1] For constructing the DODs we used the VHCA toolkit (*Visual Heuristic Cluster Analysis for texts*) as well as the *Administrator* and *Reader* toolkits from the IRBIS system [4].

Using the DOD, we obtained a vector space representation (*image*) of each text T_i as a vector of frequencies of the words from the DOD in the text. These images were used to form three matrices: the *texts-by-words* matrix of the frequencies of the words from the DOD in each text; the *words-by-words* matrix of the frequencies of word co-occurrences in a text (the number of texts containing both words); and the *texts-by-texts* matrix of the numbers of DOD words in common in each pair of texts.

Figure 1 shows the text-by-word matrix (histogram) of titles. The horizontal axis corresponds to the words ordered from left to right in the chronological order of their first occurrence in a conference title or (if it does not occur in any conference title) in a paper title. The vertical axis corresponds to the documents—concatenated conference or paper titles for specific years—in the chronological order from top to down, first conference titles and then paper titles. The frequency of each word in each document is represented by the intensity of the color. The new words appearing in a given document (concatenated conference or paper titles for a year) are clearly visible as grey rectangles, and the amount of the new words is characterized by the square of this rectangle. Note that the words appearing in the conference titles have been usually seen in paper titles before: conferences are organized on what people have been discussing for a while in papers.

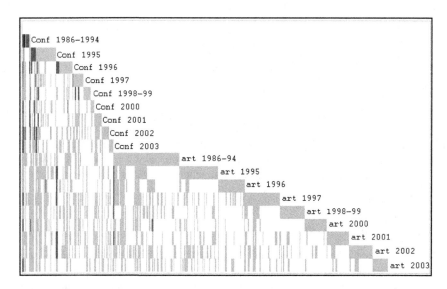

Fig. 1. The portrait of the text-by-words matrix of conference titles and article titles

In Figure 1 one can note two important properties of the word distribution:

– The titles of conferences contain 23% of the DOD; 13% of these words (3% of the total amount of words in the DOD) are represented also in paper titles and 77% belongs to conference titles only. This supports the idea that the 23% of the DOD belonging to conference titles are indeed words of upper level of abstraction.
– The number of new words in conference titles in 1990 to 1997 decreases (the grey rectangles become each time thinner from conferences 1995 and reach their

minimum in 2000), and than a wave of new words occurs in 2001–2002 (the grey rectangles grow wider for the conferences in 2001–2002). A similar effect can be slightly noticed for paper titles. This indicates some change in the interest in main area of research, evidenced by thematic shift in conference topics.

The latter observation allowed us to subdivide the period under investigation into two stages: until 1997 and since 1998. Comparison of these two states allows determining the trends in the development of the science at their boundary. What is more, a similar analysis of a longer period would allow detecting a greater number of stages and thus more detailed development curves.

To compare the two sub-periods, we constructed two texts-by-words matrices (with the same attributes as Figure 1), one for each set of texts corresponding to the periods 1990–1997 and 1998–2003, respectively. Each such set contained the texts of different level of abstraction (conference titles, paper titles, and abstracts bodies). Using the data corresponding to each period, we constructed two corresponding ontologies. Each ontology is based on the three text-by-word matrices (conference titles, paper titles, and abstracts bodies), as described in the next section.

3 Constructing the Ontology

Consider the text-by-words matrix for the period 1998–2003 shown in Figure 2 (this matrix is transposed with respect to Figure 1, i.e., its rows correspond to terms and columns to texts). In this matrix one can distinguish a cluster **A** of words best represented in the conference titles. Obviously these words are also represented in the texts of lower level of abstraction, but with lower and lower intensity.

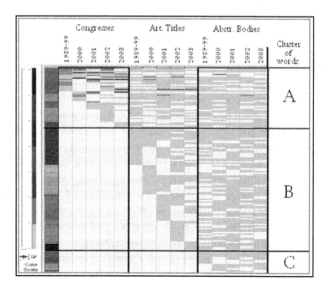

Fig. 2. Distribution of clusters of words by types of documents (conference titles, paper titles, abstracts)

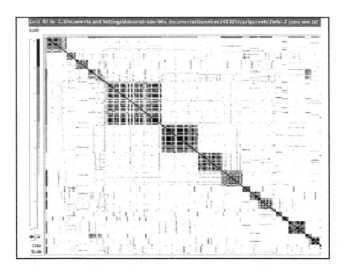

Fig. 3. Clustered word-by-word matrix for the sub-base of word *VLSI* for 1998–2003

These words can belong to two different levels of abstraction:

- The root, most abstract level *LA#1* of our specific ontology, represented by the words *parallel*, *concurrent*, *distributed*, and *simultaneous computing* and their synonyms;
- An even greater level of abstraction: since our ontology is a part of a super-ontology of, say, *computer science*, these clusters contain also the words from this super-system, i.e., general computer science terms.

To exclude the words of the latter type, we constructed the DOD of another branch of computer science (we selected *soft computing* domain) and eliminate from our DOD those words that also belong to the DOD of this another area.

To achieve more reliable statistics, we grouped together highly co-occurring words forming so-called concepts. In our experiments, 25% of all words produced 80% of one-word concepts, the remaining non-trivial "complex clusters" containing 75% of the DOD; the number of concepts was about 20% of that of words.

The subdivision of the concepts (words) into the three clusters: *A, B, C* is the simplest form of our ontology (we call it a pre-ontology). Indeed, it is important to determine the distribution of words of clusters *B* and *C* by vertices of each sub-ontology, i.e., establish the parent-child relationships between these words and the words of *LA#1*. For this, for every vertex (concept) of the given level *LA#1* we select the texts of abstracts under it containing this concept. With this we construct a sub-ontology (create its own DOD, matrices of text-by-word type, and reveal the clusters of words and concepts) for such new sub-domain, as discussed above.

Thus the process of ontology construction is recursive: the lower levels of ontology are constructed by a simple subdivision of a corresponding part of the concepts under an upper level node.

4 Experimental Results

Our initial motivation was to detect trends in computer science development over time. Accordingly, we experimented with two sets of abstracts of conference proceedings corresponding to the periods of 1990–1997 and 1998–2004. Shown below are examples from the two constructed ontologies. The words are represented by stems (not by normal form!), for example, *toleran* corresponds to *tolerance* and *tolerant*. Non-trivial concepts (synset-like ones, consisting of several words) are shown using "{ }", and non-trivial topics (closely related groups of concepts) using "[ ]". Such synset-like groups were obtained by clustering together the words with very similar co-occurrences in the texts [7].

Because of a limited space in the paper, we only show a very small excerpt from the whole ontology: the root, the first level under the root, and the nodes located in the tree under two selected nodes of the first level: the node {*analysi, network, vlsi*} and the node *toleran*. Other nodes have a similar number of sons (not shown here).

Root *parallel, concurrent, distributed, simultaneous* (computing).

1st level, below the root:

- Both periods: *[analysi, network, vlsi], fault, orient, transaction, volum, <u>toleran</u>*;
- 1990–1997: *{graphic, model, securit, communicat, test}, frontier, massive, optic, real, reliabilit, reliabl*;
- 1998–2003: *{autonom, defect, discret, event, foundation, generat, grid, integrat, interact, storag, technologi, tool}, {circuit, date, evolvabl, interconnect, languag, requirement}, knowledg, object*.

2nd level, (example only for one concept) below *toleran*:

- Both periods: *{fault_toleranc}, inject, object, system*;
- 1990–1997: *{allocat, spar}, barri, board, network, critic, efficient, execut, orient, reliabl*;
- 1998–2003: *adapt, adaptat, alternat, amplifi, analog, communicat, control, controller, cost, determin, enhanc, etern, evolut, filter, flexibl, immun, java, motor, path, platform, schedul, test, tool, trigger, upgrad*.

As a gold standard for evaluation of the obtained ontology, we used a deep and elaborated structure of chapters, sections, subsections, and smaller units of good existing textbooks on the corresponding topics (i.e., the textbooks with the title corresponding to a concept from our ontology). We observed that the concepts under the given node in the tree matched well the chapters and sections of the textbooks. This is an independent proof of high quality of the automatically obtained ontology.

Of course, existing of elaborated ontology of textbooks as a gold standard does not make our work useless by providing ready results. Indeed, such a gold standard ontology extracted from a textbook can be constructed only for a period in a rather remote past for which textbook already exist. However, for the currently active research areas the textbooks do not exist yet and will appear only in the future. Actually, our ontology reflects the structure of such a future textbook (and can be used to plan such a new textbook).

The good correspondence between our ontology for a past period and the corresponding textbooks indicates that the ontology constructed with the same method for a recent period should be equally correct. However, more rigorous evaluation is a topic of our future work.

5 Stability of Ontology as a Measure of Its Evolution

For determining stability of our ontology construction procedure we compared three samples of texts: two samples (of similar size) of conferences and papers for the period 1990–1997, and their union.

Accordingly, we obtained three different pre-ontologies. To measure the distance between them, we used cosine metric for distribution of words between different annual aggregated texts. Before measuring this distance, we excluded (as stopwords) some words of other systems and the super-system: numbers, toponyms, and names of events or documents (such as like *workshop*, *conference*, *transaction*).

For the first and the third (joint) samples, we obtained 62 words as vectors of their distribution by years with the mean cosine similarity 0.943 and standard deviation 0.149, and ten words that were not represented in one of the two samples (cosine is zero). However, more important characteristic of stability is the year of the first occurrence. For example, of 89 pairs of words existing in first two samplings, 13 ones have difference in the years of first occurrence. Considering difference of years of first occurrence as the distance between the words in a pair, we obtain the distance of 23 between these samples. This figure can be normalized by the maximum distance (7 years) and by the quantity of words. This approach is similar to the well-known tree edit algorithm for measuring the distance between two trees. This approach can be applied for measuring the distance between different ontology realizations, which can be used for evaluating the evolution of a given branch of science.

The ontology is a hierarchy but not a tree, thus some words can have more than one parent. However, we can measure separately the changes of both parameters (parent changing and level changing) during two given period of time.

In this case we use the criterion of evolution (total discrepancy between the ontologies of the two periods: 1990–1997 and 1998–2003) that consists of three parameters:

- appearing/disappearing of words,
- changes of the levels of words;
- changes of the parents of words.

In a process of detailing of these ontologies these figures are changing.

6 Conclusions

The hierarchical structure of technical documents is useful for automatic learning of a narrow-domain ontology from a relatively small corpus of scientific papers, as the only source of information or an additional source of evidence. The method presented here can be applied to any hierarchically structured texts, for example, HTML web pages.

Experimental results show that the constructed ontology is meaningful. Specifically, it can be used for comparative analysis of the state and development of a branch of science over different time spans. However, the most probable use of the method, as that of many other automatic ontology learning methods, is rapid prototyping of an ontology, with manual post-editing for higher-quality results.

Acknowledgements. This work was done under partial support from Mexican Government: CONACyT, SNI, SIP-IPN, COFAA-IPN. We are grateful to anonymous reviewers for useful comments.

References

1. T. S. Kuhn. *The Structure of Scientific Revolutions.* University of Chicago Press, 2nd edition, 1970.
2. *References Book of Proceedings of Free Economic Society of Russia.* Vol.4. (1983–2000), Moscow, Russia,.2000, pp.756.
3. P. Makagonov P., M. Alexandrov, K. Sboychakov. A toolkit for development of the domain-oriented dictionaries for structuring document flows. In: H. A. Kiers et al. (Eds.), *Data Analysis, Classification, and Related Methods*, Studies in classification, data analysis, and knowledge organization, Springer, 2000, pp. 83–88.
4. IRBIS Automated Library System, Russian National Public Library for Science and Technology; www.gpntb.ru.
5. A.Gelbukh, M. Alexandrov, S.Y.Han. Detecting Inflection Patterns in Natural Language by Minimization of Morphological Model. *Lecture Notes in Computer Science* 3287, Springer-Verlag, 2004, p. 432–438.
6. J.A. Wagner III and R.Z. Gooding, Effects of Societal Trends on Participation Research, *Administrative Science Quarterly*, 32 (1987), pp. 241–262.
7. P. Makagonov, A. Ruiz Figueroa, K. Sboychakov, A. Gelbukh. Learning a Domain Ontology from Hierarchically Structured Texts. *Proc. of Workshop "Learning and Extending Lexical Ontologies by using Machine Learning Methods" at 22nd International Conference on Machine Learning, ICML 2005*, Bonn, Germany.

Document Space Adapted Ontology: Application in Query Enrichment

Stein L. Tomassen, Jon Atle Gulla, and Darijus Strasunskas

Norwegian University of Technology and Science,
Department of Computer and Information Science,
Sem Saelandsvei 7-9, NO-7491 Trondheim, Norway
{stein.l.tomassen, jon.atle.gulla,
darijus.strasunskas}@idi.ntnu.no

Abstract. Retrieval of correct and precise information at the right time is essential in knowledge intensive tasks requiring quick decision-making. In this paper, we propose a method for utilizing ontologies to enhance the quality of information retrieval (IR) by query enrichment. We explain how a retrieval system can be tuned by adapting ontologies to provide both an in-depth understanding of the user's needs as well as an easy integration with standard vector-space retrieval systems. The ontology concepts are adapted to the domain terminology by computing a feature vector for each concept. The feature vector is used to enrich a provided query. The ontology and the whole retrieval system are under development as part of a Semantic Web standardization project for the Norwegian oil and gas industry.

1 Introduction

Lots of business procedures and knowledge are written in natural language and stored in huge information repositories. The procedures are meant to support and guide employees in daily operations. The sizes of these information repositories are constantly increasing and confronting companies with a problem of efficient and effective information retrieval and reuse [7]. Retrieval of precise information at the right time is crucial in knowledge intensive tasks (e.g., monitoring performance of subsea equipment in oil and gas production). However, finding both relevant and good quality information in this sea of information is not a trivial task.

There are different strategies and aspects using IR systems. For a solution to be successful, the right problem should be tackled. In an explorative search, the user does not expect to find the information that he or she seeks at the first attempt and will probably do many searches before satisfied with the result. In these cases, the users are often uncertain about how to phrase the query and therefore will need to do a lot of reading and refining of the query before the goal is reached. Another important aspect is that most users tend to use very few terms (3 or less) in their search queries [9, 11]. Consequently, the search engine cannot *understand* the context of the user based on this little information, which result in lower precision. For instance, the term phrase "christmas tree" can be used in many different contexts, like in Christmas holiday, a component used in the oil and gas industry,

C. Kop et al. (Eds.): NLDB 2006, LNCS 3999, pp. 46–57, 2006.

etc. Furthermore, typically only the top-ranked documents in the result set are considered [9]. However, for enterprise search solutions, the users are more patient and specify their needs in more detail [9]. In particular, [9] reports that there are just about 10% of the users that are using the advanced features of a search engine, which also could have helped to improve the quality of the query. Nevertheless, at the end, the user often finds what he or she seeks but the process can be very time-consuming and frustrating.

For performance monitoring (a scenario is described in section 2), one does not have the same luxury as for explorative search. There is no time available for reading a lot of information to filter out what is relevant or not and refining the query several times. Industry needs a system that can provide correct information at the right time. Preferably, a trusted system that retrieves only highly relevant documents and where the most relevant documents are top-ranked.

An increasing number of recent information retrieval systems make use of ontologies (more details in section 6) to help the users clarify their information needs and come up with semantic representations of documents. A particular concern with these semantic approaches is integration with traditional commercial search technologies. Whereas, in this paper, we discuss how utilizing ontologies in the query process can enhance typical IR systems. In particular, we use text-mining techniques to tailor the ontology concepts to domain terminology, i.e. terms used in documents, but not necessarily aligned to standard terminology. Later, these tailored concepts are used to enrich the query to improve the retrieval quality.

Within the oil and gas industry, many companies usually have their own terminology for all the equipment available. This makes it difficult to exchange information in an efficient manner between business partners. The industry has developed a variety of ad hoc and international standards to meet this problem, though these standards mainly focus on the exchange of data between proprietary applications within a single discipline. The Integrated Information Platform for reservoir and subsea production systems (IIP) project supported by the Norwegian Research Council (NFR)[1] funds this work. The IIP project is creating an ontology for all subsea equipment used by oil and gas industry. Unlike other initiatives, this project endeavors to integrate life-cycle data spanning several standards and disciplines. A goal of this project is to define an unambiguous terminology of the domain and build an ontology that will ease integration of systems between disciplines. A common terminology is assumed to reduce risks and improve the decision making process in the industry. The project will also make this ontology publicly available and standardized by the International Organization for Standardization (ISO)[2].

The paper is organized as follows. In section 2, we present a scenario describing a typical situation where demand for accurate information requires precise query formulation. In section 3, we elucidate the settings and exemplify the ontology created in the IIP project. In section 4 and 5, we present the overall approach where we describe the architecture and techniques used. In section 6, we discuss related work. Finally, section 7 concludes the paper and discusses future work.

---

[1] http://www.forskningsradet.no
[2] http://www.iso.org/

2 Illustrative Scenario

Consider a production engineer monitoring the production efficiency of a well in the area of oil and gas exploration and production. She is located in a control room with several monitors showing the status of the wells. In such a control room, there are constant alarms of some sort with varying degree of importance. One of the most important responsibilities of the production engineer is to look for tendencies among these alarms. One or more of these alarms can indicate an upcoming serious problem that might be handled in advance and hence avoiding a potentially bigger disaster. If she can lower the risk of these potential problems by acting quickly to those relevant alarms, the production can continue smoothly and hence the company would save a lot of money. Therefore, retrieval (or delivery) of the right information at the right time is an essential task here.

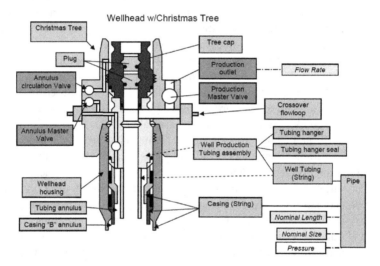

Fig. 1. A drawing of a simplified wellhead with a 'christmas tree'. Shown in the boxes are names of some of the objects and parts of a typical 'christmas tree'. Properties are in italic. [22]

Continuing the scenario, consider the production engineer noticing a tendency of some alarms that might indicate an upcoming problem. Therefore, she has to figure out if anyone has had any similar situations before and a solution to this problem. On one of her many screens she sees that one of the alarms is related to the 'production outlet', which is a part of a 'christmas tree'[3] component found among subsea equipment (see Fig. 1 for a graphical representation of a 'christmas tree'). She selects the 'production outlet' component by pointing at it on the screen. She immediately gets some status information indicating that the temperature and the pressure of the outlet is too high.

---

[3] "An artifact that is an assembly of pipes and piping parts, with valves and associated control equipment that is connected to the top of a wellhead and is intended for control of fluid from a well." [22]

The system did not find an equal situation when searching in the local document base. However, because of the ontology used in this search, describing the relationship of the equipment, information being relevant to this case was found after all. The system found that the 'annulus circulation valve' has a direct influence on the pressure of the 'production outlet', and therefore presents some information describing this relation. With this information presented, she adjusts the 'annulus circulation valve', and in this case prevents the potential upcoming problem.

This case illustrates the importance of information relevance and timing in the oil and gas industry. With costly and complex installations and high production volumes, the industry must make sure that the production systems are up and running at all time. Any problem that shows up needs to be solved quickly and efficiently avoiding decom-missioning or waiting for the symptoms to be escalated. The engineer's task is actually even more complicated since the analysis of a particular problem may involve hundreds of potential causes and require the consultation of a large number of documents.

3   The Ontology of Reservoir and Subsea Equipment

There are many ad-hoc and international standards in the oil and gas industry. One of the main challenges for the IIP project is to integrate these standards in a unified semantic framework [14]. Fig. 2 shows the broad scope of industrial data and technical standards that are proposed for integration.

The ontology created in this project is based on ISO 13628 - 'Design and operation of subsea production systems' and will be modeled in ISO 15926 – 'Integration of

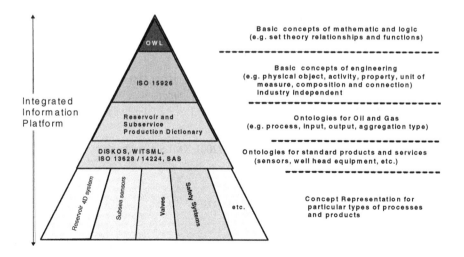

Fig. 2. The different standards being integrated into the IIP ontology [14]

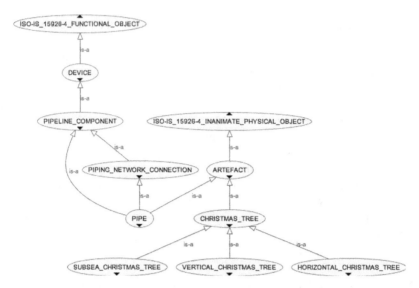

Fig. 3. Showing a fragment of the subsea equipment ontology containing 'christmas-tree'. A graphical representation by Protégé.

life-cycle data for process plants including oil and gas production facilities' Part 4 - Reference Data Library (RDL). In addition, it will include input from Statoil's Tyrihans[4] specifications, which also will serve as the test case for this project.

Fig. 3 illustrates a fragment of the ontology under development, while Fig. 4 illustrates the concept 'christmas tree' represented in OWL[5]. The current state of the ontology mainly includes a hierarchical class structure, as shown in Fig. 3, and contains over 1000 subsea equipment related terms but will be extended with more terms and relations as the project proceeds.

```
<owl:Class rdf:about="#CHRISTMAS_TREE">
    ...
    <dc:description  rdf:datatype="http://www.w3.org/2001/XMLSchema#string">
        An artefact that is an assembly of pipes and piping parts, with valves and associated
        control equipment that is connected to the top of a wellhead and is intended for
        control of fluid from a well.
    </dc:description>
    <dc:title rdf:datatype="http://www.w3.org/2001/XMLSchema#string">
        CHRISTMAS TREE
    </dc:title>
    ...
    <rdfs:subClassOf rdf:resource="#ARTEFACT"/>
</owl:Class>
```

Fig. 4. An example showing some of the information of the 'christmas tree' class being represented in OWL

---

[4] Tyrihans is an oil and gas field in the Norwegian Sea.
[5] Web Ontology Language (OWL), W3C, http://www.w3.org/2004/OWL/

4 Overall Approach

In our approach, we aim for enhanced information retrieval quality by utilizing ontologies to enrich the queries. We use the term *enrichment* in our approach, similarly as in [12], since we aim to enrich the queries to improve retrieval quality.

Fig. 5 illustrates the overall architecture of the ontology-based information retrieval system. First, we describe the individual components of the system and then the system is exemplified in the next section.

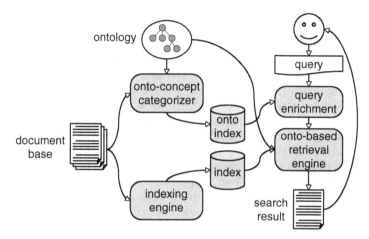

Fig. 5. The overall architecture of the ontology-based information retrieval system. The none-transparent objects illustrate the components of the system.

Onto-concept categorizer: This component extracts the terms from the document collection and associates them with relevant concept(s) from the ontology. An ontology concept is a class defined in the ontology being used. These concepts are extended into *feature vectors* with a set of relevant terms extracted from the document collection using text-mining techniques. We have adopted the k-nearest neighbor (kNN) algorithm [1, 10] to find those terms. The *feature vectors* provide interpretations of concepts with respect to the document collection and needs to be updated as the document collection changes. This allows us to relate the concepts defined in the ontology to the terms actually used in the document collection.

Indexing engine: The main task of this component is to index the document collection. The indexing system is built on top of Lucene[6], which is a freely available and fully featured text search engine from Apache[7]. Lucene is using the traditional vector space approach, counting term frequencies, and using *tf.idf* scores to calculate term weights in the index [3].

Query enrichment: This component handles the query specified by the user. The query can initially consist of concepts and/or ordinary terms (keywords). Each concept

---

[6] http://lucene.apache.org/
[7] http://www.apache.org/

or term can be individually weighted. The concepts are replaced by corresponding feature vectors.

Onto-based retrieval engine: This component performs the search and post-processing of the retrieved results. The ontology is used when post-processing the results before presentation.

5   The Semantic Query Refinement Process

Recall the scenario in section 2. This is a typical example where concept based retrieval could be beneficial for retrieving of documents and ranking them in accordance with user's preferences. This retrieval and ranking process is important, though the result crucially hinges on the user's ability to specify unambiguously his information needs. Query interpretation is the first phase of an information retrieval session and the only part of the session that receives clear inputs from the user. Traditional vector space retrieval systems view the queries from a syntactic perspective and calculate document similarities from counting frequencies of meaningless strings. Whereas we would like the queries' *real intentions* to be exposed and reflected in the way the underlying retrieval machinery deals with them.

This system includes a query enrichment approach that uses contextually enriched ontologies to bring the queries closer to the user's preferences and the characteristics of the document collection. The idea is to associate every concept (classes and instances) of the ontology with a feature vector to tailor these concepts to the specific document collection and terminology used. Synonyms and conjugations would naturally go into such a vector, but we would also include related terms that tend to be used in connection with the concept and to provide a contextual definition of it. The weight for each term indicates to what extent the term is semantically related to the concept. For example, parts of the feature vectors of concepts 'christmas tree' and 'annulus circulation valve' are given as shown in Table 1.

Table 1. An illustration of feature vectors for two ontology concepts

Concept	Term that defines concept	Term's significance to concept
christmas tree	christmas tree	1.0
	x-mas tree	1.0
	annulus circulation valve	0.7
	…	…
annulus circulation valve	annulus circulation valve	1.0
	christmas tree	0.5
	production outlet	0.3
	…	…

As seen from the Table 1, 'x-mas tree' is used synonymously with 'christmas tree' (weight 1.0). 'annulus circulation valve' is also closely related to 'christmas tree', though the weight of 0.7 indicates that they are not semantically as close as 'x-mas tree'. Table 1 does also show that the term 'christmas tree' has less relevance to the concept 'annulus circulation valve' (0.5) than the term 'annulus circulation valve' has to the concept 'christmas tree' (0.7). It is also worth noting that terms identical to concept names may be used to provide contextual definitions of other concepts, like in the case with 'christmas tree' and 'annulus circulation valve'.

When the user posts a query, the query is enriched by substituting the concepts in the query with corresponding feature vectors. In this way, the concepts are adopted to the terminology of the document space. For example, when the user is searching for 'christmas trees' within the oil domain he/she does not expect to get results concerning 'christmas trees' of any other domain. When all substitutions are done and new weights are calculated, the query is sent to a traditional vector space information retrieval system. This enriched query is more complex than the original one, but more precisely reflects the terminological context of concepts in the domain.

Let us now look at the way this is done formally. The query is represented as a vector Q:

$$Q = (q_1, ..., q_n) \tag{1}$$

where $1 \leq i \leq n$ and n is the total number of index terms in the system. Further, q_i is the normalized weight of query term i. Every concept j of the ontology is associated with a feature vector C_j so that

$$C_j = (c_{1,j}, ..., c_{n,j}) \tag{2}$$

where c_{ij} is the normalized weight of term i for concept j. When the query Q is posted the refinement shown in Fig. 6 takes place. Q' is the semantically enriched query in terms of the user's understanding of the domain.

For all $q_i \neq 0$ in Q:
  If $C_i \neq \emptyset$:
        remove q_i from Q
        $Q' = Q + \alpha q_i C_i$

Q *Vector for query*
Q' *Vector of semantically enriched query*
q_i *Weight of term i in query*
C_i *Feature vector for concept i*
α *Concept weight factor (default 0.6)*

Fig. 6. The query enrichment algorithm

Consider now that the query "CHRISTMAS TREE" "production outlet" is posted by the user. This query is turned into the query vector $Q = (1.0_{\text{CHRISTMAS TREE}}, 1.0_{\text{production outlet}})$ before the query refinement. Whereas 'CHRISTMAS TREE' is defined to be a concept since it is capitalized, while 'production outlet' is an ordinary term. In this case, 'production outlet' also happens to be a term of 'annulus circulation valve', but that does not influence on the query refinement. By capitalizing a term, the user may decide if a term should be handled as a concept or as an ordinary term. The user can also set the weight of each concept or term for further control.

Using the ontology in IIP with the user-defined concept feature vectors shown in Table 1, we transform this query into the following enriched query:

$$Q' = (0.67_{christmas\ tree}, 0.67_{x\text{-}mas\ tree}, 0.47_{annulus\ circulation\ valve}, 1.0_{production\ outlet}) \qquad (3)$$

This enriched query contains the original two query terms, where 'christmas tree' was defined to be a concept. The query was expanded by replacing the concept with other terms that are semantically close to the given concept of the domain. 'production outlet' ends up with a higher weight than 'christmas tree' because this is the main term of interest while the terms of the concept 'christmas tree' is given some lower weights. The effect of this is that documents being relevant to the 'christmas tree' concept that also include the term 'production outlet' will be given a higher rank.

The example shown above makes use of very small feature vectors. In practice, these feature vectors may be rather extensive, as they are automatically produced from large sets of documents. For the subsequent retrieval process, though, the contribution of terms with very low weights is negligible. Consequently, we can cut off query terms that fall below a certain threshold.

6 Related Work

Traditional information retrieval techniques (i.e., vector-space model) have an advantage of being fast and give a fair result. However, it is difficult to represent the content of the documents meaningfully using these techniques. That is, after the documents are indexed, they become a "bag of terms" and hence the semantics is partly lost in this process.

In order to increase quality of IR much effort has been put into annotating documents with semantic information [8, 12, 13, 23]. That is a tedious and labor-intensive task. Furthermore, hardly any search engines are using metadata when indexing the documents. AltaVista[8] is one of the last major search engines which dropped its support in 2002 [16]. The main reason for this is that the meta information can be and has been misused by the content providers in the purpose of giving the documents a misleading higher ranking than it should have had [16]. However, there is still a vision that for ontology based IR systems on Semantic Web, "it is necessary to annotate the web's content with terms defined in ontology" [17].

The related work to our approach comes from two main areas. Ontology based IR, in general, and approaches to query expansion, in particular. General approaches to ontology based IR can further be sub-divided into Knowledge Base (KB) and vector space model driven approaches. KB approaches use reasoning mechanism and ontological query languages to retrieve instances. Documents are treated either as instances or are annotated using ontology instances [5, 6, 17, 19]. These approaches focus on retrieving instances rather than documents. Some approaches are often combined with ontological filtering [4, 7, 15].

---

[8] http://www.altavista.com/

There are approaches combining both ontology based IR and vector space model. For instance, some start with semantic querying using ontology query languages and use resulting instances to retrieve relevant documents [19, 20]. [20] use weighted annotation when associating documents with ontology instances. The weights are based on the frequency of occurrence of the instances in each document. [18] combines ontology usage with vector-space model by extending a non-ontological query. There, ontology is used to disambiguate queries. Simple text search is run on the concepts' labels and users are asked to choose the proper term interpretation. A similar approach is described in [25] where documents are associated with concepts in the ontology. The concepts in the query are matched to the concepts of the ontology in order to retrieve terms and then used for calculation of document similarity.

[4] is using ontologies for retrieval and filtering of domain information across multiple domains. There each ontology concept is defined as a domain feature with detailed information relevant to the domain including relationships with other features. The relationships used are hypernyms (super class), hyponyms (sub class), and synonyms. Unfortunately, there are no details in [4] provided on how a domain feature is created.

Most query enrichment approaches are not using ontologies like [2, 24, 26]. Query expansion is typically done by extending provided query terms with synonyms or hyponyms (cf. [21]). Some approaches are focusing on using ontologies in the process of enriching queries [4, 6, 25]. However, ontology in such case typically serves as thesaurus containing synonyms, hypernyms/hyponyms, and do not consider the context of each term, i.e. every term is equally weighted.

[24] is using query expansion based on similarity thesaurus. Weighting of terms is used to reflect the domain knowledge. The query expansion is done by similarity measures. Similarly, [2] describes a conceptual query expansion. There, the query concepts are created from a result set. Both approaches show an improvement compared to simple term based queries.

While an approach presented in [26] is most similar to ours. However, [26] is not using ontologies but is reliant on query concepts. Two techniques are used to create the feature vectors of the query concepts, i.e. based on document set and result set of a user query.

To contrast to above discussed related work we emphasize the main features of our approach as follows. Our approach relies on domain knowledge represented in ontology when constructing feature vectors, then traditional vector-space retrieval model is used for the information retrieval task, where feature vectors are used to enrich provided queries. The main advantage of our approach is that the concepts of an ontology is tailored to the terminology of the document collection, which can vary a lot even within the same domain.

7 Conclusions and Future Work

In this paper, we have proposed a method for utilizing ontologies to improve the retrieval quality. The concepts in the ontology are associated with contextual definitions in terms of weighted feature vectors tailoring the ontology to the content of the document collection. Further, the feature vectors are used to enrich a provided query. Query enrichment by feature vectors provides means to bridge the gap between query terms and terminology used in a document set, and still employing the knowledge encoded in the ontology. We have also proposed that concepts and ordinary terms or keywords of the query should be handled differently since they have different roles.

Main architectural components and techniques constituting the method have been presented in this paper. As research reported here is still in progress, we have not been able to formally evaluate the approach. Though, preliminary results indicate that the quality of the feature vectors is very important for the quality of the search result.

In future work we are planning to inspect and tackle a set of issues as follows. First, there is a need to refine term weight computation. Here we will investigate alternative methods for assigning relevant terms to the ontology concepts, i.e. using association rules, and evaluate the influence on the search results. Second, we will also look into alternative methods for post-processing of the results utilizing the semantic relations in the ontology for better ranking and navigation.

Acknowledgements

This research work is funded by the Integrated Information Platform for reservoir and subsea production systems (IIP) project, which is supported by the Norwegian Research Council (NFR). NFR project number 163457/S30.

References

1. Aas, K., Eikvil, L.: Text categorisation: a survey. Technical report, no. 941. Norwegian Computing Center, Oslo (1999) 37 p.
2. Grootjen, F.A., van der Weide, T.P.: Conceptual query expansion. Data & Knowledge Engineering 56 (2006) 174-193
3. Baeza-Yates, R., Ribeiro-Neto, B.: Modern information retrieval. ACM Press, New York (1999)
4. Braga, R.M.M., Werner, C.M.L., Mattoso, M.: Using Ontologies for Domain Information Retrieval. Proceedings of the 11th International Workshop on Database and Expert Systems Applications. IEEE Computer Society (2000) 836-840
5. Rocha, C., Schwabe, D., de Aragao, M.P.: A hybrid approach for searching in the semantic web. Proceeding of WWW 2004, ACM (2004) 374-383
6. Ciorăscu, C., Ciorăscu, I., Stoffel, K.: knOWLer - Ontological Support for Information Retrieval Systems. In Proceedings of Sigir 2003 Conference, Workshop on Semantic Web, Toronto, Canada (2003)
7. Borghoff, U.M., Pareschi, R.: Information Technology for Knowledge Management. Journal of Universal Computer Science 3 (1997) 835-842
8. Desmontils, E., Jacquin, C.: Indexing a Web Site with a Terminology Oriented Ontology. In I.F. Cruz, S. Decker, J. Euzenat and D.L. McGuinness (eds.) The Emerging Semantic Web. IOS Press, (2002) 181- 198
9. Gulla, J.A., Auran, P.G., Risvik, K.M.: Linguistic Techniques in Large-Scale Search Engines. Fast Search & Transfer (2002) 15 p.
10. Mitchell, T.M.: Machine learning. McGraw-Hill, New York (1997)

11. Spink, A., Wolfram, D., Jansen, M.B.J., Saracevic, T.: Searching the Web: the public and their queries. J. Am. Soc. Inf. Sci. Technol. 52 (2001) 226-234
12. Motta, E., Shum, S.B., Domingue, J.: Case Studies in Ontology-Driven Document Enrichment: Principles, Tools and Applications. International Journal of Human-Computer Studies 6 (2000) 1071-1109
13. Popov, B., Kiryakov, A., Kirilov, A., Manov, D., Ognyanoff, D., Goranov, M.: KIM - Semantic Annotation Platform. In: Fensel, D., Sycara, K.P., Mylopoulos, J. (eds.): The Semantic Web - ISWC 2003, Second International Semantic Web Conference, Sanibel Island, FL, USA, October 20-23, 2003, Proceedings, Vol. 2870. Springer (2003) 834-849
14. Sandsmark, N., Mehta, S.: Integrated Information Platform for Reservoir and Subsea Production Systems. (2004) 9 p.
15. Shah, U., Finin, T., Joshi, A., Cost, R.S., Mayfield, J.: Information Retrieval On The Semantic Web. Proceedings of Conference on Information and Knowledge Management. ACM Press, McLean, Virginia, USA (2002) 461-468
16. Sullivan, D.: Death of a Meta Tag. Search Engine Watch (2002)
17. Song, J-F., Zhang, W-M., Xiao, W., Li, G-H., Xu, Z-N.: Ontology-Based Information Retrieval Model for the Semantic Web. Proceedings of EEE 2005. IEEE Computer Society (2005) 152-155
18. Nagypal, G.: Improving Information Retrieval Effectiveness by Using Domain Knowledge Stored in Ontologies. OTM Workshops 2005, LNCS 3762, Springer-Verlag, (2005) 780-789
19. Kiryakov, A., Popov, B, Terziev, I., Manov, D., and Ognyanoff, D.: Semantic Annotation, Indexing, and Retrieval. Journal of Web Semantics 2(1), Elsevier, (2005)
20. Vallet, D, Fernández, M., Castells, P.: An Ontology-Based Information Retrieval Model. Gómez-Pérez, A., Euzenat, J. (Eds.): Proceedings of ESWC 2005, LNCS 3532, Springer-Verlag. (2005) 455-470.
21. Chenggang, W., Wenpin, J., Qijia, T. et al.: An information retrieval server based on ontology and multiagent. Journal of computer research & development 38(6) (2001) 641-647.
22. DNV: Tyrihans Terminology for Subsea Equipment and Subsea Production Data. DNV (2005) 60 p.
23. Fensel, D., Harmelen, F.v., Klein, M., Akkermans, H., Broekstra, J., Fluit, C., Meer, J.v.d., Schnurr, H.-P., Studer, R., Hughes, J., Krohn, U., Davies, J., Engels, R., Bremdal, B., Ygge, F., Lau, T., Novotny, B., Reimer, U., Horrocks, I.: On-To-Knowledge: Ontology-based Tools for Knowledge Management. In Proceedings of the eBusiness and eWork 2000 (EMMSEC 2000) Conference, Madrid, Spain (2000)
24. Qiu, Y., Frei, H.-P.: Concept based query expansion. Proceedings of the 16th annual international ACM SIGIR conference on Research and development in information retrieval. ACM Press, Pittsburgh, Pennsylvania, USA (1993) 160-169
25. Paralic, J., Kostial, I.: Ontology-based Information Retrieval. Information and Intelligent Systems, Croatia (2003) 23-28
26. Chang, Y., Ounis, I., Kim, M.: Query reformulation using automatically generated query concepts from a document space. Information Processing and Management 42 (2006) 453-468

The Language of Folksonomies: What Tags Reveal About User Classification

Csaba Veres

Norwegian University of Science and Technology
Csaba.Veres@idi.ntnu.no

Abstract. Folksonomies are classification schemes that emerge from the collective actions of users who tag resources with an unrestricted set of key terms. There has been a flurry of activity in this domain recently with a number of high profile web sites and search engines adopting the practice. They have sparked a great deal of excitement and debate in the popular and technical literature, accompanied by a number of analyses of the statistical properties of tagging behavior. However, none has addressed the deep nature of folksonomies. What is the nature of a tag? Where does it come from? How is it related to a resource? In this paper we present a study in which the linguistic properties of folksonomies reveal them to contain, on the one hand, tags that are similar to standard categories in taxonomies. But on the other hand, they contain additional tags to describe class properties. The implications of the findings for the relationship between folksonomy and ontology are discussed.

1 Introduction

The benefits that can be gained from a metadata based annotation infrastructure were discussed at least as early as 2001 [6, 7]. In recent years services offering such an infrastructure have appeared, and gained much popularity. The social bookmarking service "del.icio.us"[1] and the photo sharing service "Flickr"[2] are two, often cited examples of popular annotation based services. Although these differ in aspects of the implementation, the basic idea is similar in that users can annotate resources in a way that organizes them for various retrieval tasks. Importantly, since the annotations are made public, the shared contribution to annotations brings much added value. Let us illustrate with the example of "del.icio.us".

"Del.icio.us" is a web site which requires a user account, and which acts as a central repository for users' bookmarks for web sites. The web sites are indexed by URL and described by a textual description which is typically generated from the title in the web site. As a result, most bookmarks to the same URL will have the same descriptive title, but this is not necessarily the case because users are free to insert their own descriptions. In addition, users are free to annotate each bookmark with any number of single word labels, called *tags*. Users have access to

---

[1] http://del.icio.us/
[2] http://www.flickr.com/

C. Kop et al. (Eds.): NLDB 2006, LNCS 3999, pp. 58–69, 2006.

popular tags for a given URL, and can also see other sites tagged with a particular tag. Because the aggregated "tag use" of all users is available in various forms, users can derive value from each others behavior. For example popular tags for a given URL can influence a user who is also adding that URL to their bookmarks, because they can suggest tags that were, putatively, useful for other users. On the other hand, users can find new web sites by following links that were tagged with the same terms as the current one of interest. As pointed out in [10] the novel feature of services like delicious is not their reliance on keywords in lieu of taxonomies for indexing – that idea has been around for years. Instead, the novelty is the immediacy of the feedback from the community of users.

One important side effect of this process of "social tagging" is the emergence of *folksonomies*, or naive systems of classification that congeal from the mass actions of the users. Folksonomies are a collective classification scheme for resources, which can challenge the role of established taxonomies. At this early stage in thinking about the potential impact of the new paradigm, much of the discussion has taken place through the medium of innumerable web logs, in practitioner magazines and their sites (e.g. InfoWorld) and trade conferences (e.g. O'Reilly Emerging Technologies Conference, 2005). Opinions about its usefulness range according to the philosophical inclinations of the proponents. One vocal advocate of folksonomies, Clay Shirky, appears to despise efforts at systematic categorization and therefore expounds his optimistic views on the promise of folksonomies[3]. In the middle are commentators who suggest that folksonomies could be useful in some way in efforts to develop formal taxonomies or controlled vocabularies [4]. [8] for example consider various techniques for improving the quality of folksonomies, toward this aim. Finally strong advocates of ontology argue that while folksonomies are useful naive indexing schemes, they need to be organized through formal ontologies to facilitate interoperability between folksonomies, for example [4].

A parallel and related debate concerns the relationship between formal categorization and whatever process occurs in the act of tagging. Again there are no solid theoretical arguments concerning this question, as far as we are aware. But there are many opinions, ranging from the claim that they are completely different kinds of phenomena, supported by examples like the tag *toread*: "... these folksonomies are simply the set of terms that a group of users tagged content with, they are not a predetermined set of classification terms or labels" [9], to the apparent admission that they are essentially very similar processes; "... this means that items can be categorized (sic) with any word that defines a relationship between the on line resource and a concept in the user's mind" [8].

There is abundant analysis of "del.icio.us" folksonomies since there are large number of methods and tools already available for viewing tag data from the freely available API and RSS feeds [5]. But these methods tend to be used for

---

[3] http://shirky.com/writings/ontology_overrated.html

[4] also http://www.adaptivepath.com/publications/essays/archives/000361.php

[5] For a list of various applications, see http://pchere.blogspot.com/2005/02/absolutely-delicious-complete-tool.html

uncovering social/cultural factors from historical data. As Clay Shirky points out in his writings (this time about the power law in blogs): "Note that this model is absolutely mute as to why one blog might be preferred over another." Similarly, historical data gives no explanation for why one tag might be preferred over another for a given site, and no explanation of the process of tagging. But surely it seems like some sort of explanation *ought* to be available. After all tags are, presumably, not plucked from thin air but instantiated because they have some cognitive import: they capture some meaning in the web site. It is of course possible that the selection of tags can be influenced by the user interface which can provide hints about how others have tagged the resource. But [3] find remarkable consistency in the relative frequencies of even the less popular tags which are not suggested by the user interface, suggesting that some independent explanation is needed to explain their stable use. In order to find such an explanation we need to know what kind of things these tags are. If we know what tags were, the place for folksonomies in the knowledge management landscape would be more clear, thereby shedding light on many of the debates.

In the remainder of this paper we present a novel approach to analyzing del.icio.us tags, and show some relationships between categorization and tagging. In the following section we briefly present the theoretical framework, which is then followed in section 3 by an experiment. We discuss the results in section 4 and finally conclude.

2   Ad Hoc Categories

Even a cursory look at del.icio.us tags shows that a large number of them could easily be category names in a formal taxonomy: "politics", "science", "research", "travel", etc., suggesting that users are practicing ad hoc categorization. Perhaps the most complete analysis of the nature of ad hoc categories comes from the work of the cognitive psychologist Lawrence Barsalou [1, 2]. He was particularly interested in categories like "things to sell at a garage sale" and "things to take on a camping trip", which are spontaneously generated categories that group entities in goal directed ways. By comparing these to "natural" categories he hoped to discover a more general theory of categorization which subsumes both common and ad hoc categories [2]. Without considering the details of the investigation, we now summarize his proposed model.

The critical role of ad hoc categories is to provide an interface with a person's *world model*, in a way that can help achieve a goal. A world model is " ... a person's knowledge of locations in the environment, together with knowledge of the entities and activities that exist currently in these locations" ([1], p. 53). The world model is not the general knowledge one has about the world, but an instantiation involving "... specific knowledge and beliefs about the current state of the world" ([1], p. 53), which might include culturally shared information and the like. The primary building blocks of the world model are the common taxonomic categories like *bird*, *flower*, *chair*, and so on. Finally, whenever people wish to achieve any goal, they instantiate an *event frame* which describes the necessary components for achieving the goal[6]. The successful realization of the goal described by the frame depends on a satisfactory interface between the event frame and the individual world model. For example if one wishes to *buy* groceries then the relevant frame will include things like *locations* to find groceries, *times* the store is likely to be open, forms of *payment*, and so on. But to achieve this goal we need to know specific locations, times and forms of payment. This is where ad hoc categories provide the mapping, by establishing specific categories like *places to buy groceries*, and so on. Crucially, "mapping different event frames into the same world model defines different partitions on entities in the world model", requiring flexible ad hoc categorization. Taxonomic and goal directed categories are two complementary ways to categorize the world: taxonomies describe the relatively stable kinds of things in the world whereas goal directed categories are ad hoc collections of different taxonomic kinds that are created to map particular event frames to particular world models.

One potential problem in applying this theory to the folksonomy data is that Barsalou's ad hoc, goal derived categories tend to be expressed as multi word phrases whereas the majority of tags are, well, single word tags. Part of the reason for this, on del.icio.us at least, is artefactual since the user interface specifically prevents the use of compound words as tags. [8] report that 10% of tags recovered from delicious showed evidence that people were trying to form compounds by using some sort of punctuation symbol to represent a space. For example there are examples like "Devel/C++", "Devel/perl". But this number does not include the items in which words are simply concatenated, so the prevalence of complex tags may be quite high, opening up the possibility that complex ad hoc categories *are* used in folksonomies. But an equally important point is that goal derived categories may become lexicalized with common usage. Thus *buyer, payment, donor* and *gift* are lexicalized concepts that have an important role in many commonly used event frames [1]. But Barsalou gives no indication of how many lexical items are of this sort, or how to identify them.

This is where the work of linguist Anna Wierzbicka becomes relevant. She comes to some remarkably similar conclusions from an entirely different motivation rooted in linguistic anthropology. She argues a more radical position that in fact most lexical items are in some sense goal derived and very few are truly taxonomic. For these categories "... we no longer ask, What kind of thing is it?; rather, we ask, What is it for? How can you use it? Where does it come from? Why is it there? In other words, we view such things largely in terms of our human interests ..." [14]

For Wierzbicka, *weapon* is not taxonomic: it describes a set of heterogeneous entities (rockets, guns, knives, teeth, claws, sex (according to Pat Benatar)) which are united by a common function. Similarly *furniture* is not taxonomic: it describes a set of heterogeneous entities (chairs, tables, lamps, pillows, televisions (?), refrigerators (??)) united by a common function and the requirement that they are somehow collocated, or at least collocated as part of some goal directed

---

[6] This is similar to the various ideas discussed in the artificial intelligence community since the days of Marvin Minsky.

Table 1. Wierzbicka's non taxonomic categories

Type of category	Characteristics
Functional	(e.g. WEAPON) Artifacts are often made to fulfill specific roles, so it is easy to think of a GUN as a *kind of weapon*. But really it is some specific artifact that can be used as a WEAPON. These categories are fuzzy and to some extent open, such that almost anything *could* be a weapon but nothing definitely is. Is a KNIFE a kind of WEAPON? Is it a WEAPON as much as a GUN is? Is a ROCK a kind of WEAPON? Is a FEATHER PILLOW a kind of WEAPON?
Functional collocation	(e.g. FURNITURE, TABLEWARE, NIGHTWEAR) These are defined by function but in addition, they have to be collected in a place (and/or time). That they differ from purely functional categories is demonstrated by the observation that a table that never made it out of the manufacturer's warehouse is not FURNITURE, but a home made explosive device kept in the basement can still be considered a WEAPON.
Origin collocation	(why is it together?) (e.g. GARBAGE, CONTENTS, DISHES (as in "dirty dishes" after a meal)). These are collections that require a unity of place, but without reference to function. LEFTOVERS form a collection because they came from the same place/source: they have the same immediate origin. The CONTENTS of a bag have all been placed together by someone, for some reason.
Function + origin	(Why is it there? "What for?" and "Where from?") As an example, the term VEGETABLE means, roughly: "a thing of any kind that people cause to grow out of the ground for people to cook for food" [14], (p. 323). Similarly, MEDICINES have a function to cure disease, but must also be manufactured by people. This class classifies heterogeneous entities by their function, origin, and sometimes mode of use. But they are not collocations because the entities are not 'used together'. The terms for these concepts have an interesting syntax in English: they appear to be count nouns but their interpretation is not that of typical count nouns. If I say "I had two vegetables for dinner", I am likely to mean two different sorts of vegetable (e.g. carrot and broccoli) rather than two pieces of the same vegetable (e.g. two carrots). Compare this to "I have two birds in my cage", which could easily refer to two parrots.

state. Electric chairs make for bad furniture because they were never meant to be part of an ensemble to make rooms livable. Refrigerators could *become* furniture with sufficient motivation and creative flair.

An important claim following these observations is that taxonomic relations (of the type often called "is-a", "is-a-kind-of") are often misapplied. In fact, Wierzbicka identified a number of different relationships that are commonly mistaken for taxonomic relations (table 1).

Some implications of Wierzbicka's observations for ontology engineering were investigated in [11,13] who argued that confounding these relationships in ontologies leads to confused semantics. They note that a particularly important feature of Wierzbicka's categories is that they can be characterized by different syntactic distributions, which means their identification can be automated. For example *functional collocations* are all examples of *singularia tantum*, which are words that appear only in the singular. Most people would judge "tablewares", "a lot of furnitures", and "three nightwears" as unacceptable. [12] discusses the usefulness of automatically extracting Wierzbicka categories in generating ontologies from database schemas.

The claim that distributional evidence can differentiate between these semantically significant categories makes them useful in uncovering potential patterns in the goal directed classification behavior of users tagging resources. We therefore decided to analyze the spontaneous classifications observed in folksonomies according to these categories. In addition a comparison between folksonomies and formal, top down category schemas should reveal something about the relationship between the two.

3   The "Language of Thought"

In this section we describe an experiment in which we analyze the kinds of classification observed in user tags. We then compare the patterns to those observed for two well known sources of classification schemes on the Internet: the open directory project (DMOZ) and the Yahoo directory[7]. We first use the syntactic distribution of the terms to classify them semantically. Then we use the semantics to make inferences about the intent of the classification.

3.1   Procedure

The first step in the experiment was to precisely characterize the distributional patterns for the different semantic categories, since [14] only provides cursory definitions. We did this in terms of a set of sentence frames that could uniquely distinguish between the categories, and which could be manually consulted for each tag. We chose this method instead of the fully automatic method described in [12] because that method was not completely reliable. The set of frames is show in table 2. In addition to the Wierzbicka categories, table 2 lists the typical distributional properties of taxonomic concepts like *bird*.

---

[7] http://dmoz.org/ and http://dir.yahoo.com/

Table 2. Sentence frames to distinguish Wierzbicka's categories

Type of category	Sentence frames
Taxonomic	the parrot/flower/tree a parrot/flower/tree parrots/flowers/trees three parrots/flowers/trees many parrots/flowers/trees * a lot of parrot/flower/tree a lot of parrots/flowers/trees * much parrot/flower/tree
Functional	the toy/vehicle/weapon a toy/vehicle/weapon toys/vehicles/weapons three toys/vehicles/weapons many toys/vehicles/weapons * a lot of toy/vehicle/weapon a lot of toys/vehicles/weapons * much toy/vehicle/weapon
Functional collocation	the furniture/cutlery/clothing *a furniture/cutlery/clothing *furnitures/cutlerys/clothings *three furnitures/cutlerys/clothings *many furnitures/cutlerys/clothings a lot of furniture/cutlery/clothing *a lot of furnitures/cutleries/clothings much furniture/cutlery/clothing
Origin collocation	the leftovers/refreshments/groceries *a leftover/refreshment/grocery leftovers/refreshments/groceries ?three leftovers/refreshments/groceries many leftovers/refreshments/groceries *a lot of leftover/refreshment/grocery a lot of leftovers/refreshments/groceries *much leftovers/refreshments/groceries
Function + origin	the vegetable/cereal/medicine/herb a vegetable/cereal/medicine/herb vegetables/cereals/medicines/herbs many vegetables/cereals/medicines/herbs a lot of vegetable?/cereal/medicine/herb a lot of vegetables/cereals/medicines/herbs *much vegetable/cereal/medicine/herb

The alert reader will immediately notice a potential problem: our current analysis cannot distinguish between taxonomic and purely functional categories. This distinction is therefore made by manually deciding if the category contains homogeneous entities or not. As we already saw, purely functional categories include very diverse sorts of entities that have little in common apart from the ability to function in the defined capacity. The category members lack the cohesion displayed by taxonomic classes which allows a large number of inferences to be drawn based on class membership. For example if someone says that a moving truck has only a *chair* remaining in it, this enables a wider set of inferences than if there was only one item of *furniture*. What is the expected size, weight, shape, of each item? How many people are needed to carry it? Clearly many more such inferences are possible in the former case. A prolonged discussion of this is beyond our scope, but the reader is invited to think about the kinds of featural similarities observed for taxonomic categories like *cat*, *dog*, and *apple*, as opposed to functional categories like *weapon*, *tool*, and *pet*. The final decision about the appropriate category type for a tag that could syntactically be either taxonomic or functional was based on a consideration of the heterogeneity of its possible members.

Data was then collected about sites selected randomly from the 50 most popular delicious bookmarks of all time [8]. The sites were: Slashdot (News for Nerds), Flickr (Photo sharing), Pandora (Music site), DIGG (community driven news and link aggregation), IMDb (Internet Movie database), BoingBoing (blogging about what's new in science, technology, industrial design, toys, and art), NewYorkTimes (News Service). The data was collected about the way these sites were represented in the three sources, in the following ways:

del.icio.us Tags: The Firefox Web Browser plugin *Scrumptious*[9] queries the delicious API and returns the most popular tags, together with their frequency of usage. For each site we therefore obtained a list of the most popular tags (between 20 - 30 per site).

DMOZ: each DMOZ search returns a list of sites together with a link to the complete directory branch under which it is filed. Each level of the the branch is taken as a unique term.

YAHOO: a search returns the requested site, together with the category name for the leaf node in the relevant branch. Clicking on this name redirects the browser to a site that includes the compete branch, as with the DMOZ search.

The terms returned for all three sources were entered into a mind map[10], purely as a convenient form of representation. They were then annotated with the appropriate Wierzbicka category by judging the acceptability of each word in the sentence frames. Very soon into the process we realized that additional categories would need to be introduced.

First, many tags in del.icio.us were not nominals. Sometimes people use adjectives to describe a resource, for example *cool*, *social*. In some instances where adjectival and nominal uses of a word are both available, it is not easy to decide how to code it. We often called on WordNet for assistance. For example *social* has just one nominal meaning with the gloss "a party of people assembled to promote sociability and communal activity". On the other hand the adjectival

---

[8] This data can be obtained at http://populicio.us/fulltotal.html. The data in this paper was taken at 11/02/2006.

[9] https://addons.mozilla.org/extensions/moreinfo.php?
application=firefox&category=Bookmarks&numpg=10&id=738

[10] http://freemind.sourceforge.net/wiki/index.php/Main_Page

use has an interpretation as "relating to human society and its members" which seems a more apt description of the URL. But there is an additional possibility that people were using property descriptors (e.g. *cool*) as surrogates for the category made up of entities fitting that description (e.g. *cool things*). In such cases the classification was double checked by making sure that no Wierzbicka category was appropriate (syntactically and semantically).

Some examples of tags were verbs as in *tagging* and *search*. There were slightly fewer ambiguous examples in this category, which were resolved as above. There were also some examples of proper names. Many of these were del.icio.us tags that simply repeated the name of the site, but some included names like *New York*.

The assignment of Wierzbicka categories was usually straightforward, except for the occasional taxonomic/functional ambiguity which was difficult to reconcile. For example *gadget* is somewhat unclear but was finally classified as *taxonomic,* whereas the equally ambiguous *reference* was classified as *functional* because instances of *reference* are much less well delimited than gadget. After each category was assigned, we did a cursory "sensibility check" on the Wierzbicka categories. Overall the semantics of the syntactically assigned categories were sensible. For example; *news = functional collocation* (functionally related items in one place); *technology = function + origin.*

3.2   Results

Figure 1 shows the relative proportion of the assigned category for each label from each source. The relative proportion is more meaningful than average num-

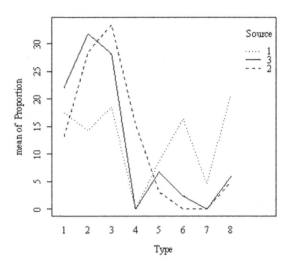

Fig. 1. Mean proportion of categories in three sources (1 = Tags, 2 = DMOZ, 3 = YAHOO) for 8 distinct word type categories (1 = taxonomic, 2 = functional, 3 = functional collocation, 4 = reason collocation, 5 = function + origin, 6 = adjective, 7 = verb, 8 = proper name)

ber because del.iciu.os contained more tags on average (18.86 in our collection) than DMOZ and YAHOO had category labels (4.57 and 4.71 respectively).

There is a clear difference between folksonomy tags on one hand and the two classification schemes on the other. Tags are drawn from most categories while DMOZ and YAHOO were biased toward *functional* categories. Additionally, the nominal sub categories differentiated between the directories and the tags.

The effects were statistically significant with the main effect of category type, $F(1,160) = 27$, $p < 0.01$, and more importantly, a significant interaction of type with source, $F(1,160) = 9.22$, $p > 0.01$.

4 Discussion

The results clearly show that the different classification schemes differ in their use of category types. The established category structures of DMOZ and YAHOO are dominated by categories whose members are heterogeneous collections united primarily by function. That is, categories tend have labels of functional categories like *weapon, pet* and *toy* rather than taxonomic ones like *cat* and *dog*. Taxonomic categories, when they occur, tend to do so near the leaves of branches, as in the DMOZ branch: *shopping ¿ pets ¿ cats* and *dogs*. This provides interesting evidence for the hypothesis that taxonomies have mixed semantics [13, 14], and that directories group sites if they s*erve the same purpose for users*, and only at the leaves do they distinguish them in a taxonomy. The most remarkable point is that the "taxonomies" in the study contain relatively few genuinely taxonomic categories, as predicted by [14], and consistent with their purpose for collecting resources related for particular goals and perspectives. On the other hand "naive taggers" tend to use similar proportions of taxonomic and non-taxonomic categories, almost as if they were "sprinkling ingredients" in a recipe in an intuitive attempt to cover the domain in all possible ways. This also results in the finer granularity displayed in folksonomies, as evidenced by the relatively higher number of tags than directory categories.

But the results show that folksonomies and the studied directories are involved in similar categorizations. What is different between folksonomies and the directories is that the former also includes information which is best expressed by adjectives, verbs and proper names whereas the latter do not. These are the sorts of examples (like "to_read") which are often cited as arguments that taggers are not categorizing. But now we have a different interpretation. In fact, taggers *are* categorizing, but they are *also* supplementing the categories with descriptions. In other words they are creating an ontology of categories and a list of property relations. For example the *New York Times* has adjectival tags *english* and *national* which is clearly a property describing its language and one describing its coverage.

The use of proper names is another feature that appears to distinguish folksonomies from taxonomies. Many of these are simply a repetition of the site name. This is fairly obviously designed as a simple memory cue, which could have some utility for a small number of highly distinctive sites which the user already knows. Clearly these have no utility in large directories.

Finally, we acknowledge that the study is limited in a number of ways including the relatively low number of sites studied. However, the statistically significant findings mitigate this to some extent. Also decisions about how those sites were selected (all of them popular), and the fact that least popular tags were ignored biases the selection somewhat. Finally the manual classification of labels into category types is less than ideal from both an experimental and practical perspective. This study provides a proof of concept which motivates further work on the implementation of an automatic classifier.

5   Conclusion

On a theoretical level this study demonstrates that users engaged in resource tagging are performing classification according to principles not too dissimilar from those imposed by (at least some) formal taxonomies. This contradicts many claims to the contrary in the popular literature. In addition we showed the importance of non taxonomic categories for classification, which is an emerging field of study in the area of ontology engineering [11, 5]. We also showed a novel combination of a psychological [1] and a linguistic [14] theory that together help in uncovering the hidden nature of user tags and explaining why they come to represent web sites.

But the practical implications are even more impressive. In achieving a detailed understanding of the structural properties of tag sets as they relate to web sites, we are part way to automating the process of producing them. While "automatic user classification" would appear to mock the entire enterprise, it would certainly be useful if tags turn out to be as widely adopted as the early enthusiasm suggests. But in addition the way we characterize tag sets facilitates their translation into ontologies which suggests a new methodology for automated ontology extraction, which is a topic of much on going research. The results reported in this paper are encouraging for future development.

Acknowledgments. This work was sponsored by the Norwegian Research Council, WISEMOD project, 160126V30 in the IKT-2010 program.

References

1. Barsalou, L. W. Deriving categories to achieve goals. in Bower, G. (Ed.) The Psychology of Learning and Motivation: Advances in Research and Theory, Academic Press, 1991.
2. Barsalou, . W. Ad hoc categories. Memory & Cognition, 11 (3), 211 - 227, 1983.
3. Golder, S., and Huberman, B. A. The Structure of Collaborative Tagging Systems, http://www.citebase.org/cgi-bin/citations?id=oai:arXiv.org:cs/0508082 (2005)
4. Gruber, T. Ontology of Folksonomy: A Mash-up of Apples and Oranges. http://tomgruber.org/writing/ontology-of-folksonomy.htm#_edn4 (Jan 19, 2006)
5. Hepp, M. Products and Services Ontologies: A Methodology for Deriving OWL Ontologies from Industrial Categorization Standards. International Journal on Semantic Web and Information Systems, Vol. 2, Issue 1, p. 72 - 99, 2006.

6. Koivunen, M-R. and Swick, R., R. Metadata Based Annotation Infrastructure offers Flexibility and Extensibility for Collaborative Applications and Beyond, A position paper for KCAP workshop on Knowledge markup and semantic annotation, 2001. (http://www.w3.org/2001/Annotea/Papers/KCAP01/annotea.html)
7. Koivunen, M-R. Annotea and Semantic Web Supported Collaboration. (http://kmi.open.ac.uk/events/usersweb/papers/01_koivunen_final.pdf)
8. Marieke, G. and Tonkin, E. Folksonomies Tidying up Tags? D-Lib Magazine January 2006 Volume 12 Number 1 (ISSN 1082-9873) http://www.dlib.org/dlib/january06/guy/01guy.html
9. Mathes, A. Folksonomies - Cooperative Classification and Communication Through Shared Metadata. http://www.adammathes.com/academic/computer-mediated-communication/folksonomies.html
10. Udell, J. Collaborative knowledge gardening. InfoWorld. August 20, 2004. http://www.infoworld.com/article/04/08/20/34OPstrategic_1.html
11. Veres, C. Aggregation in Ontologies: practical implementations in OWL. Proceedings of the 5th International Conference on Web Engineering, ICWE2005 (2005).
12. Veres, C. Automatically Generating Aggregations for Ontologies from Database Schema: some alternatives to type hierarchies. In Proceedings of ODBIS2005, VLDB Workshop on Ontologies-based techniques for DataBases and Information Systems, Trodheim (2005)
13. Veres, C. and Sampson, J. Ontology and Taxonomy: Why "is-a" still isn't just "is-a". In Proceedings of The 2005 International Conference on e-Business, Enterprise Information Systems, e-Government, and Outsourcing. Las Vegas, Nevada (2005)
14. Wierzbicka, A Apples are not a 'kind of fruit': the semantics of human categorization. *American Ethnologist* 313–328 (1984)

A Task Repository for Ambient Intelligence

Porfírio Filipe[1,2] and Nuno Mamede[1,3]

[1] L²F INESC-ID, Spoken Languages Systems Laboratory, Lisbon, Portugal
{porfirio.filipe, nuno.mamede}@l2f.inesc-id.pt
http://www.l2f.inesc-id.pt/
[2] ISEL, Instituto Superior de Engenharia de Lisboa, Lisbon, Portugal
[3] IST, Instituto Superior Técnico, Lisbon, Portugal

Abstract. This paper describes a task repository, a device semantic interface to express device capabilities, and an advice algorithm that suggests the best task-device pair to satisfy a request. The purpose of the task repository is the adaptation of a pervasive environment (Ambient Intelligence) to support natural language applications, such as a natural language interface. The task repository has a predefined group of concepts linked to linguistic and semantic resources and is updated, at runtime, with task descriptors associated with a set of heterogeneous devices. We assume that each device, belonging to the pervasive environment, holds its own semantic interface essentially composed of task descriptors. This approach tries to reach the ubiquitous essence of natural language, because the coverage of handmade lexical resources is limited, coverage problems remain for applications involving specific domains or involving multiple languages. Furthermore, we reduce the interface device problem to a database access problem. An environment simulator with the respective set of devices is depicted.

1 Introduction

This paper describes a task repository to support natural language applications, such as natural language interfaces (see Androusopoulos et al. [1] for a survey), within Ambient Intelligence (AmI) [2]. This repository includes an advice algorithm, which suggests the best task-device pair to satisfy a request. We assume that each device, spread in AmI, holds its own semantic interface essentially composed of task descriptors.

AmI is a recent paradigm in information technology. It can be defined as the merger of two important visions and trends: ubiquitous computing and social user interfaces. It is supported by advanced networking technologies, which allow robust, ad-hoc networks to be formed by a broad range of mobile devices and other objects. By adding adaptive user-system interaction methods, digital environments can be created to improve the quality of life of people by acting on their behalf. These context aware systems combine ubiquitous information, communication, and entertainment with enhanced personalization, natural interaction and intelligence.

This kind of environment can be characterized by the following basic elements: ubiquity, awareness, intelligence, and natural interaction. Ubiquity refers to a situation in which we are surrounded by a multitude of interconnected embedded systems, which are invisible and moved into the background of our environment. Awareness

C. Kop et al. (Eds.): NLDB 2006, LNCS 3999, pp. 70–81, 2006.

refers to the ability of the system to locate and recognize objects and people, and their intentions. Intelligence refers to the fact that the digital surrounding is able to analyze the context, adapt itself to the people that live in it, learn from their behavior, and eventually to recognize as well as show emotion. Finally, natural interaction refers to advanced modalities like natural speech and gesture recognition, as well as speech synthesis, which allow a much more human like communication with the digital environment than it is possible today.

Ubiquitous computing [3] or pervasive computing is an emerging discipline that brings together elements from distributed systems, mobile computing, embedded systems, human computer interaction, computer vision and many other fields. Its vision is grounded in the belief that processors are becoming so small and inexpensive that they will eventually be embedded in almost everything. Everyday objects will then be infused with computational power, enabling them as information artifacts and smart devices. By bringing computational power to the objects of the physical world, ubiquitous computing induces a paradigm shift in the way we use computers.

1.1 Pervasive Computing Environments

Pervasive or ubiquitous computing environments are far more dynamic and heterogeneous than enterprise environments. Enterprise network services operate within a network scope protected by firewalls and managed by human expert administrators. The increasing need to simplify the administration of pervasive environments introduces new requirements. A variety of new protocols has been proposed to attempt to satisfy these requirements and to provide spontaneous configuration based on service discovery.

Examples in academia include the Massachusetts Institute of Technology's Intentional Naming System (INS) [4], the University of California at Berkeley's Ninja Service Discovery Service (SDS) [5], and the IBM Research's DEAPspace [6]. Major software vendors ship their service discovery protocols with their current operating platforms, for example, the Sun Microsystems' Jini Network Technology [7], the Microsoft's Universal Plug and Play (UPnP) [8], and the Apple's Rendezvous [9].

Perhaps the most serious challenge to pervasive computing is the integration of computing devices with people. Normally, users are not prepared to deal with frequent reconfiguration problems. Unfortunately, we now spend precious time actively looking for services and manually configuring devices and programs. Sometimes the configuration requires special skills that have nothing to do with the tasks we want to accomplish.

Our research issue is exploring ways to enable non-technical people to use, manage and control their computational environment, focusing the home environment that is particularly hostile. In our standpoint, the use of natural language combined with a service discovery plays an important role in this scenario. To address this need, we propose in Section 2 a task repository that is a semantic service discovery infrastructure (that includes the environment linguistic resources), in Section 3 a device adaptation process, and in Section 4 an advice algorithm, which suggests the best task-device pair to satisfy a request.

2 Task Repository

This section describes the task repository data infrastructure that is represented by a relational data model. The main goal of the task repository is the adaptation of the pervasive environment to support semantic service discovery in order to facilitate the use of natural language applications. The task repository holds, at designed time, concept declarations that employ linguistic and semantic descriptors. The concepts that represent device classes are organized into a hierarchy or taxonomy. When a device is activated or deactivated the task repository is automatically updated using the device semantic interface. We propose a relational database to maintain the task repository. The database tables, of the task repository, are structured in three groups named: (i) DISCOURSE, (ii) WORLD, and (iii) TASK. The design of the relational database model was inspired in the *Unified Problem solving method Modeling Language* (UPML) [10] that refers decoupled knowledge components for building a knowledge-based architecture. The notation used to describe the task repository model is the *Integration DEFinition for Information Modeling* (IDEF1X). The requirements about fault tolerance, load balance, and other requirements forced by the pervasive computing environment should be supported by the adopted database implementation technology.

2.1 DISCOURSE Group

The group of tables named DISCOURSE defines a conceptual support. Fig. 1 shows the relational model of the DISCOURSE group.

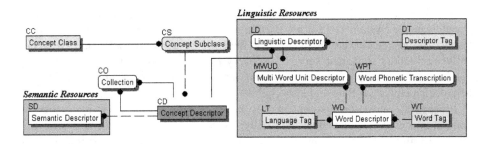

Fig. 1. DISCOURSE Group Model

The DISCOURSE group supports concept declarations used to describe device classes, devices, and the tasks they provide. A concept is an atomic knowledge unit, represented in table *Concept Descriptor* (CD). The CD table refers a unique *IDentifier* (ID), a *Concept Class* (CC), a *Concept Subclass* (CS), a *Semantic Descriptor* (SD), and a *Linguistic Descriptor* (LD). Table *Collection* (CO) links a concept used as a collection name with the respective concepts that are the collection members (*Attribute* concepts).

The concept classes (*Category, Class, Task,* and *Value*) and concept subclasses (*Collection, Unit, Active, Passive, Action, Acquisition, Attribute,* and *Quantity*), described in Table 1, allow the organization of the concept declarations.

The use of classes and subclasses are important to prevent the mismatch of concept references and to prevent task execution conflicts. The most relevant classes of concepts are (device) *Class* and *Task*. For instance, the class *"microwave oven"* is represented by a concept belonging to the *Active* subclass and the class *"thermometer"* is represented by a concept belonging to the *Passive* subclass.

Table 1. Concept Classes and Subclasses

Class	Subclass	Description
Category	Collection	For names of concept collections
	Unit	For physical units (International System of Units)
Class	Active	For subclasses of devices that provide task actions
	Passive	For subclasses of devices that only provide acquisition tasks
Task	Action	For task names that can modify the device state
	Acquisition	For task names that do not modify the device state
Value	Attribute	For property names (members of a collections)
	Quantity	For numeric values or quantities

In order to guarantee the vocabulary used to designate a concept the concept declarations include linguistic resources. This approach tries to reach the ubiquitous essence of natural language. Although, the coverage of handmade resources such as WordNet [11] in general is impressive, coverage problems remain for applications involving specific domains or multiple languages.

Each concept declaration has linguistic resources describing the concept in linguistic terms. The linguistic resources are express by linguistic descriptors in table Linguistic Descriptor (LD). Unlike a terminology-inspired ontology [14], concepts are not included for complex terms (word root or stem) unless absolutely necessary. For example, an item such as *"the kitchen light"* should be treated as an instance of a *"light"*, having the location *"kitchen"* without creating a new concept *"kitchen light"*.

A linguistic descriptor holds a list of terms or more generically a list of Multi-Word Unit (MWU) [12]. A MWU list, see table Multi Word Unit Descriptor (MWUD), contains linguistic variations associated with the concept, such as synonymous or acronyms (classified in table Descriptor Tag (DT)). Each word, in table Word Descriptor (WD), has a part of speech tag, such as a noun, a verb, an adjective or an adverb (classified in table Word Tag (WT)); a language tag, such as *"pt"*, *"br"*, *"uk"* or *"us"* (classified in table Language Tag (LT)); and some phonetic transcriptions in table Word Phonetic Transcription (WPT). For instance, if the language tag of a word is *"pt"* its phonetic transcription is encoded using the Speech Assessment Methods Phonetic Alphabet (SAMPA) for European Portuguese [13]. The content of table WD can be shared with other concept declarations.

The CD table refers optionally semantic resources. Each one of the semantic resources is referred by one semantic descriptor in table Semantic Descriptor (SD). A semantic descriptor has references to other knowledge sources, for instance, an ontology or a lexical database, such as WordNet. The knowledge sources references in the task repository must be unique.

The references to knowledge sources must be encoded using a data format allowing a unique identification of the concept in the knowledge source. The syntax of the knowledge source reference do not need to be universal it is enough to keep the same syntax for a particular knowledge source. We recommend the use of a generic Uniform

Resource Identifier (URI) format to encode the knowledge sources references. In particular, could be used a Uniform Resource Locator (URL) or a Uniform Resource Name (URN). For instance, the declaration of the concept *"device"* can have the reference *"URN:WordNet21:device:noun:1"* meaning: the concept *"device"* is linked to the first sense of the noun *"device"* in WordNet 2.1, where it is described by *"an instrumentality invented for a particular purpose"* (in WordNet 2.1 this noun has five senses).

2.2 WORLD Group

The group of tables named WORLD represents a device class hierarchy and its instances that describe active devices. Fig. 2 shows an example of a device class hierarchy, in a home environment.

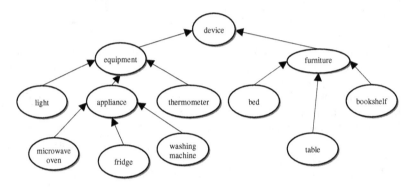

Fig. 2. Device Class Hierarchy

In a home environment, a device class may be either an appliance, or a thermometer, or a window, or a table.

Fig. 3 presents the relational model of the WORLD group. Table *Device Class Descriptor* (DDD) supports the hierarchy of the common device classes linking IDs of concepts that represent device classes. Table *Device Descriptor* (DD) keeps data about the active devices. At design time, DD table is empty. However, when a device is activated, its name (see Table 1) is automatically declare as a concept name and when the device is deactivated, this concept is removed.

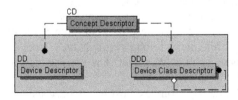

Fig. 3. WORLD Group Model

2.3 TASK Group

The group of tables named TASK represents the set of available tasks provided by the active device(s). When a device is activated, its semantic interface descriptor (see Table 2) is processed and when the device is deactivated, the respective task descriptors are removed. All concept IDs used to fill the slots of the task descriptors must exist in CD table, as we can see observing the relations in Fig. 4.

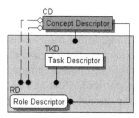

Fig. 4. TASK Group Model

Tables *Task Descriptor* (TKD) and *Role Descriptor* (RD) support the device's task descriptors. Table TKD maintains the task name and assumptions available to check the state of the world. Table RD keeps data about the allow input and output parameters of the tasks. The list of input parameters is described by an input role list. The list of output parameters is described by an output role list. One role describes one task argument.

2.4 Bridges

The task repository model is essentially based on the main descriptors represented in tables TKD, DD, and DDD. Nevertheless, these descriptors should be coupled/decoupled (when a device is activated/deactivated) to indicate the device class and the tasks they provide.

Fig. 5 presents the employ of bridges to couple the main descriptors. Table *Device Class Bridge* (DCB) couples the device descriptors in DD table to the respective device class descriptors in DDD table. Table *Device Task Bridge* (DTB) couples the device descriptors in DD table to the respective task descriptors in TKD table.

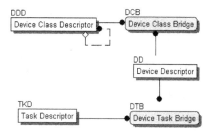

Fig. 5. Coupling of Descriptors Using Bridges

3 Device Adaptation

This section describes the adaptation of a device to work with the task repository. This adaptation is achieved by building a set of three layers, which would potentially cover all the relevant device features:

(i) The first layer is a device driver that provides an elementary abstraction of the device expressing the primitive capabilities. For instance, if the device is a light bulb we must be able, through the device driver, to turn on or to turn off the light and to ask about the associated state (on/off);

(ii) The second layer is an adapter that transforms the first layer into a more convenient interface, considering the device class. For instance, the adapter might transform labels into infrared command codes;

(iii) The third layer includes particular features of the device, bearing in mind, for instance, variations of the device commercial model.

The second and the third layer can be extended with local data about particular features of the devices. For instance, if we have a microwave oven we have to convert the power (100 watts) into a particular cooking process (defrost). In order to allow a semantic description of the device capabilities the third layer must be personalized to the user's needs, defining a device semantic interface descriptor. Table 1 represents a device semantic interface descriptor.

Table 2. Device Semantic Interface Descriptor

Slot	Value
device name	string
device class	ID-Class
task descriptor	
other task descriptors ...	

A semantic interface descriptor starts with the slot *device name* followed by the slot *device class* and ends with a group of one or more *task descriptors* (detailed in Table 3). The value of the slot *device name* is a string. Other slot values, including the values of the task descriptors, refer IDs of concepts declared in the task repository, at design time.

Table 3 depicts a task descriptor where the "*" means mandatory fulfilling.

Table 3. Device Task Descriptor

Slot			Value
name*			ID-Task
input list	input role	name	ID-Attribute
		range*	ID-Category
		restriction	*rule*
		default	ID-Value
	other input roles ...		
	pre-condition		*rule*
output list	output role	name	ID-Attribute
		range*	ID-Category
	other output roles ...		
	pos-condition		*rule*
assumptions	initial condition		*rule*
	final condition		*rule*

A device task descriptor is a semantic representation of a capability or service provided by a device.

A task descriptor has a *name* (concept from the *Task* class) and optionally an *input list*, an *output list*, and *assumptions*.

The *input list*, that describes the task input parameters, has a set of optional input roles. An *input role*, that describes one input parameter, has a *name*, a *range*, a *restriction*, and a *default*. The *name* is a concept from the *Attribute* subclass and is optional. The *range* is a concept from the Category class. The *restriction* is a rule that is materialized as logical formula and is optional. The *range* rule and the *restriction* rules define the set of allowed values in parameters. For instance, if the range is a positive integer and we want to assure that the parameter is greater than 3, then we must indicate the restriction rule: "name > 3". The *default* optional slot of the input role is a concept of the *Value* class. If the default is not provided the input role must be filled.

The *output list*, that describes the output parameters, has a set of optional output roles. An *output role*, which describes one output parameter, is similar to an *input role* without *restriction* rule and *default*.

The rules of the *task descriptor* allow three kinds of validation: *restriction* rule to perform individual parameter validation, *pre-condition* to check input parameters before task execution, and *pos-condition* to check output parameters after task execution. *Restriction* can refer the associated input role, *pre-condition* can refer task input role names and *pos-condition* can refer output role names. *Assumptions* perform state validation: the *initial condition* (to check the initial state of the world before task execution) and the *final condition* (to check the final state of the word after task execution). *Assumptions* can refer role names and results of perception task calls.

The state of the world is composed by all device states. The state of each device is obtained by calling the provided acquisition tasks. For instance, if the request is "*switch on the light*", we have to check if the "*light*" is not already "*switched on*" and after the execution, we have to check if the "*light*" has really been "*switched on*".

4 Advice Algorithm

This section describes an advice algorithm that suggests the best task-device pair to satisfy a request. The goal of this algorithm is to facilitate the exploration of the repository by natural language applications or directly by people (human administrators). The task repository supplies an interface to execute this algorithm. The suggestion of the task-device pair is based on the individual ranking of tasks and devices. The advice algorithm uses as input a list of terms that are compared against the linguist descriptors in order to identify the pivot concepts.

The pivot concepts references to tasks and devices are converted into points that are added to the respective individual rankings. The ranking points are determined considering two heuristic constants values: *nBase* and *nUnit*. The *nBase* value is equal to the maximum number of task roles (arguments) plus 1 (one). The *nUnit* value is equal to 3 (three) that are the number of ways to reference a task role (by *name*, *range*, and *value*).

The device ranking is modified following the heuristic rules:

1. If the pivot concept is used in a device descriptor (device name), the *nBase* value is added to the respective device ranking;
2. If the pivot concept is used in a device class descriptor (class name), the value obtained from the expression *nBase/2* is added to the respective device ranking;
3. If the pivot concept is used in a device super-class descriptor (super-class name), the value obtain from the expression *nBase/2-n*nUnit* is added to the respective device ranking, considering *n* is equal to the number of concept classes (in the hierarchy) between the device class and the device super-class.

The task ranking is modified following the heuristic rules:

4. If the pivot concept is used as a task name, the *nBase* value is added to the respective task ranking;
5. If the pivot concept is used as a task role name or as a task role range, the value obtained from the expression *nUnit/2* is added to the respective task ranking;
6. If the pivot concept is used to fill a task argument (is validate by the task role), the value obtained from the expression *nUnit/3* is added to the respective task ranking.

Finally, the pair task-device is formed by the task with the best ranking and by the device with the best ranking, which provides the task.

5 Experimental Evaluation

Our current work is based on an environment simulator in which we are testing the proposed task repository to represent a set of common home devices that are essentially present in the kitchen. Fig. 6 shows a screenshot of the home environment simulator, developed originally for Portuguese users.

This simulator allows the debug of the task invocation and the simulation of the interaction with a particular appliance. Using the simulator, we can activate and deactivate devices, do requests of tasks, obtain the answers and observe the devices behavior. We can also consult and print several data about the device semantic interfaces. Actually, the environment simulator incorporates nine device simulators:

- An air conditioner simulator with 24 tasks using 63 concepts;
- A freezer simulator with 13 tasks using 96 concepts;
- A fryer simulator with 23 tasks using 92 concepts;
- A light source simulator with 20 tasks using 62 concepts;
- A microwave oven simulator with 26 tasks using 167 concepts;
- A kitchen simulator table with 13 tasks using 48 concepts;
- A water faucet simulator with 24 tasks using 63 concepts;
- A window simulator with 13 tasks using 44 concepts;
- A window blind simulator with 22 tasks using 65 concepts.

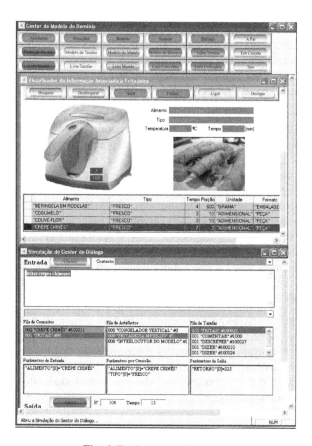

Fig. 6. Environment Simulator

On the top of the screen, is showed the Fryer simulator after the execution of the request: "*frying Chinese spring rolls*". The Fryer simulator screen shows the automatically select temperature (180 ºC) and duration (7 minutes) of the frying process. On the bottom of the screen, we can see data processed by the advice task algorithm. In order to determine the best task-device pair, the advice algorithm selects two pivot concepts associated with "*frying*" and with "*Chinese spring rolls*". The concept "*frying*" is used as a task name (rule 4). The concept "*Chinese spring rolls*" can be used to fill and argument in tasks "*frying*", provide by the "*fryer*" and "*tell*", provided by the "*freezer*" (rule 6). The task "*frying*" is the best choice with $nBase + nUnit/3$ points. Finally, the device "*fryer*" is selected only because it provides the task "*frying*". So, the suggested task-device pair is "*frying*"-"*fryer*". In this case we do not have a ranking of devices because the request does not refer any device.

6   Discussion and Future Work

The growth in pervasive computing will require standards in device communication interoperability. These devices must be able to interact and share resources with other existing devices and any future devices across the network. The current technologies require human interventions to solve environment reconfiguration problems. We believe that these technologies must be improved with more human like ways of interaction that must include natural language support.

In this context, we have already identified two future application scenarios:

(i)   Automatic generation of multilingual device descriptions. The lexical knowledge linked in a concept declaration can be combined with the task descriptors to generate a systematic report (easily understandable) of the available services of one device and even of the entire environment. The generation can be targeted to a preferred language and the part of speech tags can be used for syntactic validation. The phonetic transcription can be used to disambiguate terms (homograph vs. homophone);

(ii) Automatic build of device's graphical user interfaces. The knowledge about the class of concepts (see Table 1) and other appropriated extensions can be used to determine the convenient graphical item to represent them. For instance, when a task input role is represented by a concept of the Collection class the respective argument should be graphically represented by a combo box.

As future work, we also expect to evaluate the task repository and the advice algorithm within an improved context, integrating the progresses already achieved in our lab [15] [16] [17]. Currently, our goal is the development of a Device Integration Process (DIP) that will update automatically the DISCOURSE group. DIP will resolve ambiguities in the vocabulary that should be included into each one of the device semantic interfaces.

7   Concluding Remarks

Our approach reduces the interface device problem to a database access problem and is a definitive contribution to facilitate the use of natural language applications, namely natural language interfaces (with or without dialogue) in a pervasive computing environment. This approach tries to reach the ubiquitous essence of natural language, because the coverage of handmade lexical resources is limited, coverage problems remain for applications involving specific domains or involving multiple languages.

The task repository supports semantic service discovery, which is an important feature to achieve spontaneous configuration of a heterogeneous set of devices. The presented ideas have been applied, with success, in a set of devices that represents a home environment.

References

1. Androutsopoulos, I., Ritchie, G., Thanish, P.: Natural Language Interfaces to Databases – An Introduction, Natural Language Engineering, vol 1, part 1, 29-81, (1995)
2. Ducatel, K., Bogdanowicz, M., Scapolo, F., Leijten, J., Burgelman, J.: Scenarios for Ambient Intelligence in 2010, IPTSSeville, ISTAG (2001)
3. Weiser, M.: The Computer for the Twenty-First Century, Scientific American (1991)

4. Adjie-Winoto, W., Schwartz, E., Balakrishnan, H., Lilley, J.: The Design and Implementation of an Intentional Naming System, Proc. 17th ACM Symp. Operating System Principles (SOSP 99), ACM Press, pp. 186–201 (1999)
5. Hodes, T., Czerwinski, S., Zhao, Ben., Joseph, A., Katz, R.: An Architecture for Secure Wide-Area Service Discovery, ACM Wireless Networks J., vol. 8, nos. 2/3, pp. 213–230 (2002)
6. Nidd, M.: Service Discovery in DEAPspace, IEEE Personal Comm., pp. 39–45, Aug. 2001
7. Jini Technology Core Platform Specification, v. 2.0, Sun Microsystems (2003)
8. UPnP Device Architecture 1.0, UPnP Forum (2003)
9. Cheshire, S., Krochmal, M.: DNS-Based Service Discovery, IETF Internet draft, work in progress, (2005)
10. Fensel, D., Benjamins, V., Motta, E., Wielinga, B.: UPML: A Framework for Knowledge System Reuse, IJCAI (1999)
11. Fellbaum, C. (editor): WordNet: An Electronic Lexical Database, MIT Press (1998)
12. Daille, B., Gaussier, E., Lange, J.: Towards Automatic Extraction of Monolingual and Bilingual Terminology, COLING 94, 515-521 (1994)
13. SAMPA (SAM Phonetic Alphabet), Spoken Language Systems Lab (L^2F), http://www.l2f.inesc-id.pt/resources/sampa/sampa.html
14. Gruber, T.: Toward Principles for the Design of Ontologies Used for Knowledge Sharing, In International Workshop on Formal Ontology, Padova, Italy (1992)
15. Filipe, P., Mamede, N.: Databases and Natural Language Interfaces. V Jornadas de Bases de Datos, Valladolid, Spain (2000)
16. Filipe, P., Mamede, N.: Towards Ubiquitous Task Management. 8th International Conference on Spoken Language Processing, Jeju Island, Korea (2004)
17. Filipe, P., Mamede, N.: Ubiquitous Knowledge Modeling for Dialogue Systems, to appear in 8th International Conference on Enterprise Information Systems, Paphos, Cyprus (2006)

Formulating Queries for Assessing Clinical Trial Eligibility

Deryle Lonsdale, Clint Tustison, Craig Parker, and David W. Embley

Brigham Young University, Provo, UT, USA, 84602
lonz@byu.edu

Abstract. his paper introduces a system that processes clinical trials using a combination of natural language processing and database techniques. We process web-based clinical trial recruitment pages to extract semantic information reflecting eligibility criteria for potential participants. From this information we then formulate a query that can match criteria against medical data in patient records. The resulting system reflects a tight coupling of web-based information extraction, natural language processing, medical informatic approaches to clinical knowledge representation, and large-scale database technologies. We present an evaluation of the system and future directions for further system development.

1 Background and Overview

Researchers design information extraction systems to perform various tasks, and these tasks require various levels of linguistic processing. Some systems are only concerned with parsing out the extracted information and therefore only require the use of a syntactic parser. Others need more in-depth processing and include a semantic component that can give some meaning to the extracted information. Yet other systems are dependent on real-world knowledge and require a pragmatic component to relate the data gathered from the system to outside information. One area receiving recent attention is the medical domain. Much of the natural language processing (NLP) research done with medical literature has involved developing systems that extract different types of relationships from text. For example, NLP techniques have been used on Medline[1] abstracts to extract information on genes, proteins, acronyms, and molecular binding relationships.

For its part, the field of medical informatics has produced large-scale resources, largely in database format, that specify the vast knowledge required for medical research and patient services. Highly specialized tools for representing clinical information and patient data have also been developed. Unfortunately, there has been only a modest amount of crossover between the NLP and medical informatics fields. The topic of information extraction is a salient one for demonstrating how applications can leverage the developments from both fields. This paper[2]

---

[1] See http://www.medlineplus.gov.
[2] This work was partially funded under National Science Foundataion Information and Intelligent Systems grant IIS-0083127. See also www.deg.byu.edu.

C. Kop et al. (Eds.): NLDB 2006, LNCS 3999, pp. 82–93, 2006.

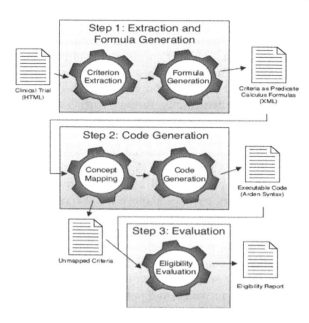

Fig. 1. Stages of processing in the system with data formats (input, intermediate, and output)

describes our approach to identification, extraction, and query formulation of information regarding medical clinical trials. Figure 1 shows an overview of the system. In Step 1, extraction and formula generation, we extract patient criteria from a web-based natural language description of qualifications for clinical trial participants, and create predicate logic expressions (PLE's) that reflect the semantic content of the text. In Step 2, code generation, the system processes parsed criteria and their PLE's. The system then attempts to map the criteria to concepts in an electronic medical record. For the criteria that map successfully, the system outputs appropriate logic for computing patient eligibility.

In Step 3, eligibility assessment, the system evaluates the eligibility of a potential participant by executing the logic generated in Step 2 against that patient's electronic medical record. The system produces a generated report that can help a clinician make an informed decision about whether to further evaluate the patient for enrollment in the clinical trial. In Section 2 we describe Step 1 of the system, which involves the NLP component. Section 3 describes the subsequent medical records database query component. We then discuss the system evaluation in Section 4. Finally, we sketch ways the system could be enhanced in the future to provide better results.

2   Extraction and Formula Generation

The domain that our system addresses is clinical trials, which medical professionals use as a tool to assess diagnostic and therapeutic agents and procedures.

Such trials require voluntary human subjects to undergo the new treatments or receive experimental medications. With the increasing cost of bringing experimental new drugs to the public, there is a crucial need for improving and automating access to the information in clinical trials including the directed recruitment of experimental participants, which is otherwise costly and labor-intensive. In this section we first discuss the web corpus we have targeted. Then we sketch the first stage of the system—how the pertinent text is processed by the NLP components of the system. From 1997 to 1999 the U.S. National Library of Medicine (NLM) and the National Institutes of Health (NIH) developed an online repository of clinical trials [5]. This repository currently contains about 25,000 trials which are sponsored by various governmental and private organizations[3]; the repository receives about 8,000,000 page views per month[4].

Providers develop web pages for the clinical trials website using a simple user interface[5] including a text box for the eligibility criteria. No format restrictions are currently enforced on the text, though some boilerplate material can be entered (e.g. patient ages and gender) via dropdown boxes. Each trial in the online repository comprises a series of sections that contain specific information regarding the trial that is useful to providers and patients. Figure 2 shows a sample web page for an individual clinical trial and the hierarchy of different components it contains. For this paper we extract information from one section of the web page: the Eligibility section. This section contains a listing of the requirements that a person must satisfy in order to participate in the trial. For example, nearly every eligibility section specifies the patient age and also the gender.

Each web page undergoes two levels of preprocessing: (i) locating, retrieving, and converting the Eligibility section to an XML format with each item embedded in <criterion> tags; and (ii) manipulating the natural language text of some criteria to enable further processing. Often eligibility criteria are expressed telegraphically, for example with elided subjects or as standalone noun phrases. Parsing works best on full sentences, but only a small percentage have eligibility criteria structured as complete sentences. For elided subjects, a dummy subject and verb (i.e. *A criterion equals...*) are prepended to the criterion.

In other instances the first word in the criterion needs to be nominalized in order to produce a grammatical sentence. For example, the criterion *able to swallow capsules* is reformulated as *an ability to swallow capsules*, and then the dummy subject and verb are prepended. Figure 2 shows an example clinical trials web page, its corresponding XML version, and the linguistically-annotated rendition of its eligibility criteria. The next step in the process involves using a syntactic parser to process the natural language criteria and produce a corresponding syntactic representation. We use the link grammar (LG) parser [10]. We chose this tool because of its open-source availability, efficiency, robustness in the face of ungrammaticality and out-of-vocabulary words, and flexibility[6].

---

[3] See http://www.clinicaltrials.gov.
[4] See http://www.clinicaltrials.gov/ct/info/about.
[5] See http://prsinfo.clinicaltrials.gov/elig.html.
[6] See http://www.link.cs.cmu.edu/link.

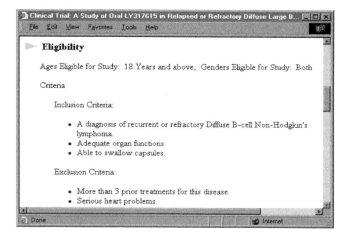

(a) *Clinical trial web page NCT00042666.*

```
<criteria trial="http://www.clinicaltrials.gov/ct/show/NCT00042666">
 <criterion>
  <text>Eligibility</text>
  <text val="1">Ages Eligible for Study: 18 Years and above,</text>
 </criterion>
 <criterion>
  <text>Eligibility</text>
  <text val="2">Genders Eligible for Study: Both</text>
 </criterion>
 ... (ADDITIONAL CRITERIA) ...
 <criterion>
  <text>Eligibility</text>
  <text>Criteria</text>
  <text>Exclusion Criteria:</text>
  <text val="6">More than 3 prior treatments for this disease.</text>
 </criterion>
 <criterion>
  <text>Eligibility</text>
  <text>Criteria</text>
  <text>Exclusion Criteria:</text>
  <text val="7">Serious heart problems.</text>
 </criterion>
</criteria>
```

(b) *Criteria annotated with XML tags.*

> 1. *A criterion equals* an age greater than 18 years.
> 2. *A criterion equals* both genders.
> 3. *A criterion equals* a diagnosis of recurrent or
> refractory Diffuse B-Cell Non-Hodgkin's lymphoma.
> 4. *A criterion equals* adequate organ functions.
> 5. *A criterion equals* an ability to swallow capsules.
> 6. *A criterion equals* more than 3 prior treatments for
> this disease.
> 7. *A criterion equals* serious heart problems.

(c) *Criteria with linguistic elements added.*

Fig. 2. Portion of clinical trial NCT00042666 and preprocessed versions of eligibility criteria

The system reads in a .txt file containing each criterion (as extracted from the XML file described above) on a separate line in the file and parses each sentence individually. Because of structural ambiguities in English, a single input sentence might produce multiple parses; in this project, we only consider the highest-scored parse for subsequent processing. Figure 3 shows how a parse of *A criterion equals serious heart problems.* would be represented syntactically by the LG parser. Different labeled links connect the words in the sentence in a way that expresses their dependencies. These links are the key to the next step, extracting the semantic meaning from the syntactic output.

Once syntactic parsing of a sentence has been completed, the sentence is analyzed by the syntax-to-semantics conversion engine. This is a component (that was previously developed for other applications) specifically designed to take the output from the LG parser and convert its content to PLE's (though other semantic formats are also supported by the system). The engine is built on Soar[7], a rule-based symbolic intelligent agent architecture that uses a goal-directed, operator-based approach to problem solving [6]. Several dozen pertinent rules have been developed to interpret the LG parse links and convert their associated words to logical predicates and their associated arguments. Variables are generated for predicates to specify with appropriate arity which referents the predicates refer to. For example, the parsed sentence *A criterion equals serious heart problems.* would yield the PLE "criterion(N2) & serious(N6) & heart_problems(N6) & equals(N2,N6). Note that the dummy subject and verb, which were added for parsing purposes, are present in the PLE. For this reason, a postprocessing stage removes this extraneous information. Then the resulting PLE is placed in the abovementioned XML file. Figure 3 illustrates the parse, its PLE, and the XML file after the NL processing stages have finished.

3   Query Generation

Once the source web page has undergone the NL processing techniques described above, the resulting extracted information feeds a database query stage to match them with patient medical records. In this section we can only briefly mention the technologies germane to the task at hand; more details are available elsewhere [8].

3.1   The Target

Medical information systems manage patient information for a wide variety of tasks including patient care, administration (e.g. billing), research, and regulatory reporting. Coded medical vocabularies have been developed in order to ensure consistency, computability, and sharability. Often they are conceptually based and have associated lexicons or vocabularies which are sometimes hierarchical in nature. For example, the SNOMED-CT [11] coded vocabulary has a code "254837009" that represents the concept "breast cancer". Representing patient data usually requires more information than simple concepts. A data model

---

[7] Soar is freely available at http://sitemaker.umich.edu/soar.

```
+--------------------------------Xp------------------------------+
|                              +-------------Op------------+      |
+-----Wd-----+                 |        +--------A--------+ |     |
|    +--Ds--+-----Ss----+      |        +----AN---+       | |     |
|    |      |           |      |        |         |       | |     |
LEFT-WALL a criterion.n equals.v serious.a heart.n problems.n  .
```

	LEFT-WALL	Xp	<---Xp---->	Xp	.
(m)	LEFT-WALL	Wd	<---Wd---->	Wd	criterion.n
(m)	a	Ds	<---Ds---->	Ds	criterion.n
(m)	criterion.n	Ss	<---Ss---->	Ss	equals.v
(m)	equals.v	O	<---Op---->	Op	problems.n
(m)	serious.a	A	<---A----->	A	problems.n
(m)	heart.n	AN	<---AN---->	AN	problems.n
	.	RW	<---RW---->	RW	RIGHT-WALL

(a) *Link grammar output for a criterion's sentential form.*

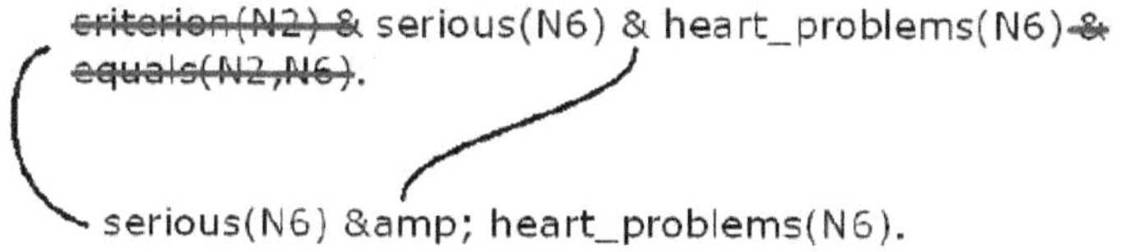

~~criterion(N2) &~~ serious(N6) & heart_problems(N6) ~~&~~
~~equals(N2,N6).~~

serious(N6) & heart_problems(N6).

(b) *Predicate logic expressions before and after postprocessing.*

```
<criteria trial="http://www.clinicaltrials.gov/ct/show/NCT00042666">
 <criterion>
  <text>Eligibility</text>
  <text val="1">Ages Eligible for Study: 18 Years and above,</text>
  <pred val="1">age(N4) &amp; quantification(N5,greater_than)
                &amp; measurement(N4,N5) &amp; units(N5,years)
                &amp; magnitude(N5,18)</pred>
 </criterion>
 <criterion>
  <text>Eligibility</text>
  <text val="2">Genders Eligible for Study: Both</text>
  <pred val="2">both_genders(N4)</pred>
 </criterion>
 ... (ADDITIONAL CRITERIA) ...
 <criterion>
  <text>Eligibility</text>
  <text>Criteria</text>
  <text>Exclusion Criteria:</text>
  <text val="7">Serious heart problems.</text>
  <pred val="7">serious(N6) &amp; heart_problems(N6)</pred>
 </criterion>
</criteria>
```

(c) *XML file with tagged predicate logic expressions added.*

Fig. 3. Final result of natural language processing stages

called a detailed clinical model defines relationships between coded concepts or
(other data values) and information of clinical interest. For example, a detailed
clinical model might define a diagnosis in terms of a type and a subject/person,
so that a statement "The patient has breast cancer." could be encoded with the
diagnosis type from SNOMED-CT as described above, and the subject/person
with the relevant patient ID number. Detailed clinical models thus combine

coded concepts into meaninful expressions of a higher-order nature. We make extensive use of both coded concepts and detailed clinical models in the concept mapping process shown in Step 2 in Figure 1.

The target electronic medical record for this project is Intermountain Health Care's Clinical Data Repository (CDR)[8]. The CDR makes extensive use of coded vocabularies; it also defines detailed clinical models using Abstract Syntax Notation One (ASN.1) [3], an ISO standard for describing electronic messages [1], including binary and XML encodings for many different application areas ranging from telecommunications to genome databases. All coded concepts in the CDR are drawn from IHC's Healthcare Data Dictionary (HDD) [9], a large coded vocabulary (over 800,000 concepts with over 4 million synonyms). The names of all the detailed clinical models used in the CDR and the fields they contain are defined as concepts in the HDD. The CDR comprises a database and its associated services. Besides providing a common access mechanism (for security, auditing, and error handling), the services crucially provide for handling of detailed clinical models as the basis for information access and retrieval. For example, an application can pass an instance of a detailed clinical model to the services, which will then return relevant instances of other detailed clinical models.

One of the outputs of Step 2 in Figure 1 is executable logic in Arden Syntax format [2], an ANSI standard for handling medical data. Arden Syntax is written in units called medical logic modules (MLMs). Each MLM contains the logic necessary for making one medical decision. One category of information in an MLM defines knowledge required for making clinical decisions; this category is what we use in this project. The most significant slots in this category are the data slot and the logic slot. The data slot contains mappings of symbols used in an MLM to data in the target electronic medical record. The logic slot, as its name implies, contains the logic that operates on the data. Finally, since electronic medical records vary widely in content and structure across applications, it has been useful to use an abstraction called the virtual medical record (VMR) [7]. This assures that any number of healthcare organizations can write, maintain, and share clinical decision logic no matter what the structure of their own repositories. For eligibility criteria we use a small subset of VMR attributes called observations.

3.2   Concept Mapping

The process outlined in Step 2 of Figure 1 takes the XML file described above as input. It attempts to map each criterion to concepts and data structures in the target electronic medical record. For each successful mapped criterion we generate executable code for determining if any patients meet the criterion. Since IHC's CDR stores clinical data as instances of clinical models with coded concepts, and since all coded concepts are in the HDD, the mapping task involves

---

[8] See http://www.3m.com/us/healthcare/his/products/records/data_repository.jhtml. Intermountain Health Care (IHC) is a regional, nonprofit, integrated health system based in Salt Lake City, UT. The CDR is the result of a joint development effort between IHC and 3M Health Information Systems.

matching words and phrases from the eligibility criteria to concepts in the HDD that represent either names or values in detailed clinical models. The concept mapping portion of the system thus iterates through each criterion, attempting to map it to coded concepts from the HDD used in the CDR's detailed clinical models. The system uses multiple matching strategies executed sequentially, and once a match is found, subsequent matches are not sought. Seven decision points formulate the matching strategy; we sketch each below.

(1) Execute special case handling. We use string comparisons and regular expression matching for processing predictable boilerplate material (e.g. age and gender). (2) Match the raw text of a criterion to concepts in the database, in case subsequent processing does not succeed. Note that these two steps do not require PLE's and thus are executed for every criterion. The remaining steps, however, are executed only for criteria that successfully convert to PLE's. (3) Match predicate names to the HDD. For example, the criterion "heart disease" yields the formula: heart(x) & disease(x). In this stage the mapper retrieves the best coded concept from the HDD that includes both predicate names. (4) Match the predicate with a measurement. Measurements are extracted as predicates; they include magnitudes, units, and other information. Here the criterion "LDL-C 130-190 mg/dL" is successfully matched to a query that searches LDL-C measurements (a valid HDD concept) in medical records and returns those within the acceptable range.

If the full matches above are not possible, partial matching is then tried.

(5) Match name-value pairs. The predicate names are processed to find possible name-value pair relationships. For example, the criterion "diagnosis of appendicitis" does not map to a single concept in the HDD, but it does map to concepts in the CDR. Furthermore, the HDD recognizes "diagnosis" as a valid name for a clinical observation, and "appendicitis" as a valid value. We thus combine them to form a name-value pair. (6) Match a conjunction/disjunction. Often criteria are conjoined, and in such cases we process all elements. For example, the elements of the criterion "Hyperthyroidism or hypothyroidism" are mapped separately and then related with the relevant operation (conjunction or disjunction). (7) Partial match. The best possible match with all available predicate names is attempted, preferring nouns over other parts of speech. Thus, for example, a criterion "active neoplasms" would not match on the predicate "active" but would on the other one, "neoplasm". This heuristic is generally useful, though not always correct. For example, in the concept "renal disease," the adjective "renal" is more useful than the noun "disease".

3.3 Code Generation

The second stage of Step 2 is code generation, where we generate executable code from the output of the concept mapping process. The code that we generate for this project is an Arden Syntax MLM (Medical Logic Module) that specifies VMR queries for data access[9]. The process has two steps. The first step

---

[9] Generating code in a different language would only require an appropriate reimplementation of the generator interface.

```
Criterion1 := READ {
  <VMRQuery class="Observation">
      <value op="equals">
          <cd code="1450395" displayName="heart disease"/>
      </value>
  </VMRQuery>
```

(a) *A sample Arden Syntax read statement containing a VMR query.*

Eligibility Report	
Header	
Title of Trial	A Study of Oral LY317615 in Relapsed or Refractory Diffuse & Large B-Cell Non-Hodgkin's Lymphoma
Patient Name	J. Doe
Medical Record #	1234567
Eligibility Summary	
Criteria met	6
Mapped Criteria for which eligibility could not be determined	7
Criteria not mapped	5
Total criteria	18
Criterion Detail	
Criterion 1	
...	
Criterion 3	
Criterion	LDL-C 130-190 mg/dL
Mapped	Yes
Status	Patient meets this criterion
...	
Criterion 11	
Criterion	Heart disease
Mapped	Yes
Status	Unable to determine if patient meets this criterion

(b) **Portion of sample eligibility report.**

Fig. 4. Results for query generation and assessment stages

takes place in tandem with the mapping process described above. Each database mapping for a criterion spawns a related VMR query. Abstracting away from the details, this process can be summarized as a rather straightforward conversion from and to nested attribute/value structures. The second and subsequent step in generating code involves creating the Arden Syntax MLM. For our database query we only use a small subset of the possible MLM slots (most of which are meant for human perusal). To generate the query, we iterate through the criteria, generating an Arden Syntax "read" statement when a mapping to the target electronic medical record is possible. Assessing the applicability an encoded criterion involves the straightforward querying of electronic patient records. A report summarizes for the clinician which criteria parsed and matched the stated values. Figure 4 shows an Arden Syntax VMR query and a sample eligibility report.

4   Evaluation Results

We recently carried out an end-to-end system performance evaluation. We randomly chose one hundred unseen clinical trials from www.clinicaltrials.gov and ran them through Steps 1 and 2 in Figure 1. Afterwards we manually inspected each report, comparing them to the generated queries, and characterizing their

Trials evaluated	100
Trials successfully completing Steps 1 & 2	85
Criteria extracted	1545
Criteria parsed into logical forms	473
Criteria parsed but not mapped into queries	49
Queries generated	520
Completely correct queries	140
Other useful queries	113
Technically correct queries	4
Incorrect queries	263

Fig. 5. Results from end-to-end system evaluation

success or failure. A numerical tally of these results appears in Figure 5. The 85 parsable trials varied in size and complexity, having from 3 to 71 criteria per trial. They also varied widely in subject matter, covering conditions from cancer to infertility to gambling. Two main factors contributed to the failure of 15 trials: some had unexpected special characters (e.g. the HTML character "ü" representing the umlat u character), and others had sentences of such complexity that the parser failed.

These 85 trials yielded 1,545 eligibility criteria; logical forms were successfully created for 473 of these criteria. All but 49 of these yielded queries, and another 96 queries could be generated without logical forms, so a total of 520 queries were formulated. Of these, 140 completely and exactly represented their original eligibility criteria. Another 113 of the queries were not entirely correct or complete but still yielded useful information for clinician decision-making. Four queries were technically well-formed based on the logical form though did not reflect the intent of the original criteria. In total, 257 queries were either completely correct, usefully correct, or technically correct. The remaining 263 queries were neither correct nor useful in determining eligibility. Figure 6 summarizes the system's processing stages along with their associated heuristics, assumptions, challenges, and issues.

Processing stage	Heuristic/Assumption	Challenges/Issues
Retrieve criteria	Standard tokenization	Ad-hoc abbreviations
Convert to XML	Scripting (Perl/Python)	—
Make full sentence	Elision predictable	Some ill-formed input
Parse sentence	LG parser + scoring	Some sentences fail to parse
Extract predicates	Soar linguistic agent	Negation, modals, quantifiers
Postprocess predicates	Scripting	—
Map concepts to HDD	String matching	HDD coverage, match cost
Create query structures	Recursive descent	Execution time/complexity
Create query statements	Arden Syntax	Defining relevant subset
Query patient records	Existing software	Patient data completeness
Generate final report	Scripting	End-user usefulness

Fig. 6. Summary of processing stages with relevant assumptions and issues

5   Discussion and Future Work

Our experimental system demonstrates that some degree of automatic evaluation of eligibility criteria is feasible. The system currently generates useful queries for about half of the number of criteria that produce formulas. We are encouraged by these preliminary results, and anticipate that planned improvements like those discussed below will substantially increase system accuracy and performance. One issue has been the consistent authoring of parsable natural language statements by data providers. Tighter editorial controls could help solve this problem. So far we have done little to customize the LG parser for our purposes, and we foresee improving it in at least three ways: (i) extending the range of acceptable grammatical structures; (ii) refining the parse scoring algorithm to return the most plausible parse; and (iii) integrating it with a large-scale medical lexicon as others have done [12]. Currently the semantics engine only handles a limited number of syntactic structures—far less than those provided by the LG parser— and we yet to explore its inherent machine learning capabilities. In several cases the system correctly mapped the name portion of a pair, but incorrectly mapped the value portion, rendering the query incorrect. For example, consider the criterion *blood products or immunoglobulins within 6 months prior to entering the study*. The system found a mapping to an appropriate concept, "blood products used"; it also found a mapping to the valid concept "months". However, the latter is not a permissible value for the former, so processing failed. If appropriate constraint checking could mediate name-value pairings, the system would be able to more gracefully reformulate such instances.

The synonyms supplied by the HDD produced frequent successes, but occasional ambiguity proved problematic. The system mapped the abbreviation "PCP" to the drug "phencyclidine", whereas the trial intended "pneumocystic carinii pneumonia". It also mapped "PG" to "phosphatidyl glycerol" whereas the trial used it in an ad-hoc fashion for "pathological gambling". Often unsuccessful queries reflected an absence of relevant concepts from the HDD. This is not unexpected, given the domain's focus on experimental medications. We could use additional sources of clinical concepts such as the National Library of Medicine's Unified Medical Language System [4] or a database of experimental drugs. New concepts, though, would not be helpful unless patient records contain such concepts, which is unlikely. Several queries provided partial information that was useful, but could not fully assess eligibility. For example, the system mapped the criterion "uterine papillary serous carcinoma", to the concept "papillary carcinoma". Matching "papillary carcinoma" in a patient's record does not necessarily satisfy the criterion, but it could suggest further action by a clinician. With some criteria a match will never be possible. EMR's typically do not store patient information that would reflect such criteria as "plans to become pregnant during the study" or "male partners of women who are pregnant". Criteria we missed could be evaluated based on data in the EMR, by adding further inferencing with external knowledge. For example, "meets psychiatric diagnostic criteria for depression" requires the system to know what these diagnostic criteria are before this criterion can be evaluated. Another possibility for improving the system include mapping criteria to more VMR classes than just the observation class. This would facilitate more accurate queries against information such as procedures, demographics, and medications.

References

1. International Standard ISO/IEC 8824-1. Information technology—Abstract Syntax Notation One (ASN.1): Specification of basic notation. Technical report, International Telecommunications Union, 2002. ITU-T Recommendation X.680.
2. G. Hripcsak, P. D. Clayton, T. A. Pryor, P. Haug, O. B. Wigertz, and J. v. d. Lei. The Arden Syntax for Medical Logic Modules. In R. A. Miller, editor, *Proceedings of the Fourteenth Annual Symposium on Computer Applications in Medical Care*, pages 200–204. IEEE Computer Society Press, Washington D. C., 1990.
3. S. M. Huff, R. A. Rocha, H. R. Solbrig, M. W. Barnes, S. P. Schrank, and M. Smith. Linking a medical vocabulary to a clinical data model using Abstract Syntax Notation 1. *Methods of Information in Medicine*, 37(4-5):440–452, 1998.
4. C. Lindberg. The Unified Medical Language System (UMLS) of the National Library of Medicine. *Journal of the American Medical Reccord Association*, 61(5):40–42, 1990.
5. Alexa T. McCray. Better access to information about clinical trials. *Annals of Internal Medicine*, 133(8):609–614, October 2000.
6. Allen Newell. *Unified Theories of Cognition*. Harvard University Press, 1994.
7. C. G. Parker, R. A. Rocha, J. R. Campbell, S. W. Tu, and S. M. Huff. Detailed clinical models for sharable, executable guidelines. *Medinfo*, 11(Pt 1):145–148, 2004.
8. Craig Parker. Generating medical logic modules for clinical trial eligibility. Master's thesis, Brigham Young University, 2005.
9. R. A. Rocha, S. M. Huff, P. J. Haug, and H. R. Warner. Designing a controlled medical vocabulary server: the VOSER project. *Computers and Biomedical Research*, 27(6):472–507, 1994.
10. Daniel Sleator and Davy Temperley. Parsing English with a link grammar. Technical Report CMU-CS-91-196, Carnegie Mellon University, Oct. 1991.
11. K. A. Spackman and K. E. Campbell. Compositional concept representation using SNOMED: Towards further convergence of clinical terminologies. In *Proceedings of the American Medical Informatics Association Annual Symposium*, pages 740–744, 1998.
12. P. Szolovits. Adding a medical lexicon to an English parser. In *Proceedings of the American Medical Informatics Association Annual Symposium*, pages 639–643, 2003.

Multi-lingual Web Querying: A Parametric Linguistics Based Approach

Epaminondas Kapetanios[1], Vijayan Sugumaran[2], and Diana Tanase[1]

[1] School of Computer Science
University of Westminster, London
E.Kapetanios@westminster.ac.uk, dtanase@shodor.org
[2] Department of Decision and Information Sciences, School of Business Administration
Oakland University, Rochester, MI 48309, USA
sugumara@oakland.edu

Abstract. Developing efficient and meaningful search mechanisms for the Web is an active area of research in Information Management. With information explosion on the Internet, existing search engines encounter difficulty in accurate document positioning and retrieval. This situation is exacerbated by the language barrier for accessing web content provided in different languages. Sophisticated content-based search engines are needed for helping users find useful information quickly from multilingual knowledge sources on the Web. This paper presents a parametric linguistics based approach for flexible and scalable multilingual web querying with low complexity in query translation. The proposed methodology and the system architecture are discussed.

1 Introduction

The World Wide Web has become a valuable knowledge resource and the amount of information written in different languages and the number of non-English speaking users has been increasing tremendously. Although 68% of web content is still in English, this trend is changing and a large number of web pages are being written in almost every popular language. This increasing diversity has created a tremendous wealth of multilingual resources on the Web. However, one of the major difficulties in accessing these knowledge sources is the language barrier. Moreover, these resources are highly unstructured, contain a diverse and dynamic collection of contexts, and are used by individuals who have little knowledge of search techniques.

While some of the existing search engines support limited translation capabilities, the potential to tap into multilingual Web resources has not been materialized. Current search engines are primarily geared towards English and have several limitations. In addition to the language constraint, the search engines use different syntax and rely on keyword based techniques, which do not comply with the actual needs and requirements of users as reported in [1]. In particular, expert users such as the librarians at the Library of Congress need to search a database of documents by making use of meaningful associations. Other expert user communities such as lawyers, researchers, scientists, academics, doctors, etc., have reported similar requirements. Ideally, users should be able to formulate search queries such as "the list of students who took my

C. Kop et al. (Eds.): NLDB 2006, LNCS 3999, pp. 94–105, 2006.

database course last quarter", "the e-mail that John sent me the day I came back from Athens", or "the papers where we acknowledged a particular grant" that make use of concepts, relationships and terms in his/her native natural language.

Multi-Lingual Information Retrieval (MLIR) facilitates searching for documents in more than one language. Typically, two approaches are used in MLIR – translating the query into all target document languages or translating the document information to match the query language. As pointed out in [2], the output quality of these techniques are still not very satisfying because they rely on automated machine translation and do not consider contextual information to correctly perform word sense disambiguation. In addition, these techniques have been developed based on standard TREC collections, which are somewhat homogeneous and structured. However, the Web documents are highly heterogeneous in structure and format. Hence, multilingual querying on the Web is more complicated and requires a systematic approach.

The overall objective of our work is to integrate the salient features of Web search technology, distributed database querying, and information retrieval with respect to multilingual aspects of querying. In particular, the specific objectives of this research are to: *a) develop a flexible and scaleable methodology for concept based multilingual querying on the Web,* and *b) develop an architecture for a system that implements the methodology.* The contributions of this research are threefold. First, unlike the MLIR techniques which are mostly designed for specific pairs of languages, our approach is general enough and flexible that it can be applied to any language. This is possible because our approach is grounded in the parametric theory of linguistic diversity. Second, our approach is not dependent on the structure and format of the target documents. Hence it is scaleable and well suited for searching documents on the Web. Third, the architecture that we have developed incorporates existing resources and tools.

2 Background

Search by important *associations* to some related concepts or user context or profile has been addressed by the emerging *concept or knowledge based* querying approaches [3, 4]. With the emergence of the Semantic Web, information retrieval in terms of *search by associations* within a more domain specific context has been addressed as a way to alleviate the problems in locating the most relevant links and reduce the search space of links and or documents to be examined. There has also been an attempt to focus on generic solutions as suggested by [5], and therefore, improve the effectiveness of search on the Semantic Web.

In general, these approaches make use of domain specific ontologies and semantic annotations in order to augment and improve query semantics either interactively [6] or as performed by the system [3, 4] for different purposes, e.g., search engines and information retrieval [4], and mediation across heterogeneous data sources [3]. However, they mostly rely on intelligent techniques and knowledge-based approaches for mappings across concepts and query expansion. Querying by integrating semantic associations among entities, instances, properties, etc., into a conceptual search or query language has not been addressed, especially when multi-lingual natural language based querying is concerned.

Even within the realm of cross-lingual information retrieval (CLIR) [7, 8], a number of challenges have been reported, especially the *problem of query translation* [8]. To make query translation possible, existing IR systems rely on bilingual dictionaries for cross-lingual retrieval. In these systems, queries submitted in a source language are translated into a target language by means of simple dictionary lookup. If this functionality doesn't exist, query translation is performed by corpus-based techniques [7] in which translation equivalents are extracted from parallel corpuses.

The major difference, however, with our approach is twofold: (a) the underlying query language is still keyword based and does not come closer to the expressiveness of a database (DB) querying paradigm, (b) query translation takes place in a word-by-word or sentence-by-sentence translation and not at a conceptual level. Improving (a) in terms of query expressiveness, i.e., querying by associations, naturally leads to increase in complexity of (b). To this extent, our approach takes a different direction in that we preserve (a) and simplify the task of query translation.

With respect to (a), several DB and IR merging approaches have emerged [9], which either try to tie together the two systems by treating them as a black box or by extending one system with the features of the other, however, with considerable integration drawbacks and difficulties. This kind of querying and search is mostly defined as "*combining search technologies and knowledge about the query and the user context into a single framework to find the most appropriate answer for the user's information need*" [10].

Context based and personalized IR/DB querying paradigms, however, aim at either a contextual proactive content delivery or information filtering according to a model reflecting user behavior and profile [9]. A multi-lingual, natural language based querying by associations, however, is still out of the scope of these approaches.

The only approach for a *concept-based natural language query system*, to our knowledge, has been addressed by [11], in particular, the CQL/NL query language. It relies on the premise that concept-based or conceptual query interfaces reduce the cognitive load in querying DBs by allowing users to directly use constructs from conceptual schemas. Unlike other concept-based query languages, which require users to specify each query-path in its entirety, CQL requires users to specify only the end points, i.e., the starting and terminating entities and relationship roles of query-paths. The CQL system automatically deduces the correct intermediate entities to use on a given query-path. It also performs logical operations such as conjunction or disjunction on the derived paths. A controlled natural language interface like the one we propose in this paper and the methodology is also provided. The CQL/NL system combines natural language interface methods with the CQL querying approach into a single approach that is referred to as the semantic grammar (SG) approach. Despite the similarities, our approach considerably differs from [11] in that we facilitate flexible parsing of multi-lingual queries using *associations*, which is simple and scalable, whereas [11] only deals with imperfect information in concept-based querying.

3   Proposed Approach

Our approach builds on the methodology presented by Burton-Jones et al. [12] for semantic augmentation of web queries. They have developed a heuristic-based methodology for building context aware web queries. Our approach also uses the query language described by Kapetanios et al. in [13]. They present a high level query language (called MDDQL) for databases, which relies on an ontology driven automaton. We provide a brief overview of MDDQL in section 3.1 before describing our multilingual web querying approach in section 3.2.

3.1 MDDQL Parsing

Overview of Language Automata Theory: MDDQL is conceived as a concept based query language to operate with natural language terms. Given that the only potential models of natural or computer languages are defined in terms of four classes of languages, i.e., *recursively enumerable, context-free, context-sensitive,* and *regular,* according to Chomsky's *hierarchy theorem,* a formal specification mode of *MDDQL* is expected to follow these principles.

All these classes of languages can be formally specified by an automaton, which lies within the range of **Finite State Automaton** (FSA) and **Turing Machine** (TM), if *acceptance* of a sequence of words is emphasized. Alternatively, a kind of grammar in terms of

- a finite set N of *non-terminal symbols*
- a finite alphabet Σ of *terminal symbols*, disjoint from N
- a start symbol S, and
- a finite set of some set P of productions of the form $\xi \rightarrow \omega$

is usually specified when the emphasis is put on *generation* rather than *acceptance of sequences of words.* To this extent, a language $L(G)$ can be defined by a grammar $G = \{N, \Sigma, S, P\}$ meaning that all words can be derived by S by repeated applications of the productions P.

These rules, however, adhere to the basic structure of a natural language such as *English* or other natural language, which adhere to the *subject-verb-object* word type order of natural languages. Moreover, *generation* might be turned into an *acceptance* mechanism when *parsing.* Therefore, we might formally define the parser of a language $L(M)$ in terms of an automaton M, which is equivalent to some grammar G, meaning that L consists of all those words in Σ^*, with Σ^* the set of all words, which can be constructed out of elements of Σ and can be accepted by some automaton M. In addition, either the whole set of production rules P or a particular set of words in Σ^* as accepted by M can be represented by a tree, which is called *derivation* or *parse* tree. Normally, the vertices of a derivation tree are labeled with terminal or non-terminal (variable) symbols.

The specification of all kinds of automata, however, underlie the same philosophy having, for example, some finite set S_q of states, some alphabet Σ called the *input alphabet,* a transition function δ as a mapping $S \times \Sigma \rightarrow \Sigma$, some start state s_0 and some set of accepting or final states $F \subseteq S$. In other words, M can be roughly defined as $M=(S_q=\{q_1,...,q_n\}, \Sigma, \delta, s_0, F)$. An underlying assumption is that the specification elements of the language need to be known *a priori* and bound to a particular language. *MDDQL Meta-Parsing:* The formal specification of a *flexible and scalable cross-lingual parser* for a concept based query language such as *MDDQL* needs to be done at a higher level of abstraction and, therefore, be independent of and easily adaptable to any controlled natural language, even those with still unknown grammar. In other words, the formal specification of *MDDQL(M)* or *MDDQL(G)* is driven by universal features holding for all kinds of natural languages, i.e., some atoms of languages as expressed in terms of *parameters* such as *word type order*, *head directionality*, etc.

Formally speaking, a cross-lingual *MDDQL* is defined as $MDDQL(M_L(V \subseteq P_1 \times ... \times P_n, A \subseteq L))$ or $MDDQL(G_L(V \subseteq P_1 \times ... \times P_n, A \subseteq L))$ meaning that the underlying automaton *M* or grammar *G* is a *functional mapping* of an input alphabet (set of words) *A* as a subset of a lexicon *L* for a particular language and a set or subset *V* of the Cartesian product $P_1 \times ... \times P_n$ of values of a set of the applicable parameters $P=\{P_1,...,P_n\}$, which roughly characterize the given natural language *L* in which a concept based query has been constructed, to the specification elements of *M* or *G*.

In other words, given the inherited nature of the *MDDQL* concept based querying paradigm, with the exception of a small set of *non-terminal* or *variable* symbols as common to all natural languages such as *noun phrase, verb phrase, possessed nouns, adjectives, subject, object,* etc., all other specification elements of *M,* e.g., $Sq=\{q_1,...,q_n\}$, Σ, δ, s_0, *F*, or of *G*, e.g., *N*, Σ, *S* and *P* as the set of production rules $\xi \rightarrow \omega$, become subject to the rules, which reflect a deeper understanding of the atoms - other than *words* - and structure of natural languages in terms of *parameters* and *patterns* rather than specific rules for each language. Therefore, the *MDDQL* parser becomes subject to a dynamic specification. To this extent, there is no need for specifying a new automaton or grammar each time a natural language is used, even if it is an unanticipated one. Therefore, besides lowering the overall system *complexity*, *flexibility* and *scalability* become an important issue as well. Let us consider, for example, the parameter P_1 = *word type order* as one parsing dimension, with the following patterns *subject-verb-object, subject-object-verb, no word type order,* which apply to *English, Japanese, Walrpiri,* respectively.

If $M_{L=English}(v=\{P_1 = subject\text{-}verb\text{-}object\} \in V, A \subseteq L)$, then the starting symbol S_0 could be any *English* word from *A* standing for a noun or adjective, whereas the parser is expecting a verb phrase to follow the noun phrase. However, when $M_{L=Japanese}(v=\{P_1 = subject\text{-}object\text{-}verb\} \in V, A \subseteq L)$ holds, the starting symbol S_0 could be any *Japanese* word from *A* standing for a noun or adjective and the parser expecting another noun phrase, this time the *object* of the phrase, to be followed by a verb phrase. In the third case $M_{L=Walrpiri}(v=\{ P_1 = no\text{-}word\text{-}type\text{-}order\} \in V, A \subseteq L)$, where special markers are used in order to distinguish the semantic roles of words within a *Warlpiri* sentence, the parser should be guided according to the indications of those special markers. Further parameters such as the *null subject*[1], *verb attraction*[2], etc., might be considered as *parsing dimensions* which might also have an impact on grammatical patterns to be determined dynamically. It is out of the scope of this paper to explain the impact of all these parameters on parsing of a concept (controlled natural language) based query language. It is, however, important to realize that given a set of all *potential* parameters *S* shaping a multi-dimensional space, the formal specification of *MDDQL* is a functional mapping of a subspace $P \subseteq S$ to all potential specification elements of the

---

[1] Languages like *Spanish, Romanian* and *Italian* do not necessarily need a *subject* within a sentence.

[2] Subjects in languages such as *French* or *Italian* go with an auxiliary verb phrase, however, in languages such as *Welsh* and *Zapotec,* subjects go with a verb phrase.

automaton or the grammar, with P as a multi-dimensional sub-space of potential parameters within which a particular natural language can be characterized.

The mathematical notation of the *MDDQL* automaton for cross-lingual, concept based querying takes the form $M=\{S_q(V), \Sigma(A), \delta(V), s_0(A), F(V)\}$ rather than the conventional $M=(S_q, \Sigma, \delta, s_0, F)$, reflecting the functional dependency of potential states, input alphabet, transition function, start symbol and set of finite acceptable states, respectively, from multi-dimensional space V, as formed by a set of linguistic parameters (universals), and a corresponding lexicon A. In terms of a grammar, it takes the form $G = \{N, \Sigma(A), S(A), P(V)\}$ rather than the conventional form $G = \{N, \Sigma, S, P\}$. Additionally, the *derivation* or *parse* tree, as the outcome of a parsed query, takes the form $G_{MDDQL}=\{V,E\}$, with V representing words together with their semantic roles. Therefore, it is independent of a particular set of production rules P and, therefore, natural language. It reflects compositional semantics of the query. For example, $G_{MDDQL}=\{(<v_1\text{: } car \ (noun, \ class), \ v_2\text{: } wheel \ (noun, \ class)>, \ e\text{: } "part\text{-}of")\}$ is the parse tree of *"car wheels"* or *"wheels of cars"*, in Japanese and English, respectively.

Given that the specified automaton and the computational model of the MDDQL parser can be considered as an *abstract machine*, which consists of more than one *input tape*, each of which has a *finite control* and a *head* to be moved either to the right or the left of the input tape (alphabet) and, therefore, causing a transition from a state q_{i-1} to a state q_i, it is necessary to augment this automaton with *stacks* memorizing not only what are the words, which have been scanned at a state q_i, but also the syntactical/semantic structure at that particular state q_i. The algorithm presented in Table 1 exemplifies the transition function and logic of this abstract machine with respect to a simple case, where the query[3] q: *"big children-SU the neighbors dogs-OB chasing"*, in *Japanese*, and only the parameter P: *word-order-type* as a dimension of the space V, are considered.

3.2 MDDQL-Based Web Querying Approach

Our concept based multilingual web querying adapts the semantic query augmentation method discussed in [12]. It consists of the following five phases: 1) MDDQL Query Parsing, 2) Query Expansion, 3) Query Formulation, 4) Search Knowledge Sources, and 4) Consolidate Results. These phases are briefly described below.

Phase1 - MDDQL Query Parsing: This phase involves parsing the natural language query specified by the user. The query is segmented and the MDDQL parser parses the segments and creates the query graph. The vertices in the conceptual query graph are translated into English (or any other target language) to generate the initial query terms. A detailed description of the parsing algorithm is given in section 3.1.

Phase2 – Query Expansion: The output of the MDDQL parsing phase is a set of initial query terms which becomes the input to the query expansion phase. The query expansion process involves expanding the initial query using lexicons and ontologies. It also includes adding appropriate personal information as well as contextual information. For each query term, the first task is to identify the proper semantics of the

---

[3] The suffixes *-SU* and *–OB* are used to indicate the position of subjects and objects within the query or sentence.

Table 1. MDDQL Query Parsing Algorithm

Input: A query Q, an $A \subseteq L = Japanese$

Output: An *MDDQL* parse tree G_{MDDQL}

SET L=Japanese
SET V with <P: word-order-type, subject-object-verb>
SET input tape T to the query Q
SET a set of auxiliary stacks $\Delta = \{SU, OB, VP, PP, etc.\}$ *for the grammatical structures or*
  sets-of-states to be determined dynamically
SET $G_{MDDQL} = \{\}$

WHILE *not the end of the tape T*
    READ *word, e.g., "big"*
    IDENTIFY syntactic/semantic *part of word as* $\Delta (V)=SU$
    PUSH *word into stack* $\Delta (V)$
    MOVE *head on T to the right*
END OF WHILE

FOR ALL $\Delta \neq \{\}$
    CREATE vertices N(Δ **,C) and edges E(** Δ **,C) for a sub-graph G** $\Delta \subseteq G_{MDDQL}$ *as a*
      function of the nature of the stack and the ontological constraints C
    e.g., **G_{SU}** *: (<v_1: children (noun, subject, class), v_2: big (adjective, subject, property)>, e_1:*
      ""), when $\Delta = SU$, or
        G_{OB} *: (< v_4: dogs (noun, object, class), v_5: neighbors (noun, object, class)>, e_4: ""),*
          when $\Delta = OB$ or
        $G_{VP:}$ *< v_3: chasing (event, verb)>* **when** $\Delta = VP$
END FOR ALL

FOR ALL different pairs <G_1,G_2> of sub-graphs G $\Delta \subseteq G_{MDDQL}$
    CREATE connecting edges E(<G_1,G_2>, C) *with respect to the ontological constraints C*
    e.g., **< e_2: "" > connecting** *v_1: children (noun, subject, class) with v_3: chasing (event,*
      verb) and, therefore, connecting **G_{SU}** *with* **G_{VP}**
        <e_3: "" > connecting *v_3: chasing (event, verb) with v_4: dogs (noun, object, class)*
          and, therefore, connecting **G_{VP}** *with* **G_{OB}**
END FOR ALL

---

term, given the user's context. To do so, the word senses from a lexicon such as WordNet are used. For each term, synonym sets are extracted. The appropriate word sense is determined based on the context and other query terms (may also need user input) and a synonym from that synset is added to the query. To ensure precise query results, it is important to filter out pages that contain incorrect senses of each term. Thus, a synonym from the unselected synset with the highest frequency is added as negative knowledge to the query. Since ontologies contain domain specific concepts, appropriate hypernym(s) and hyponym(s) are added as mandatory terms to improve precision. In this phase, personal information and preferences relevant to the query is also added. For example, the user may limit the search to certain geographical area or domain. Such information helps narrow down search space and improve precision.

Phase 3 – Query Formulation: The output of the query expansion phase is the expanded set of query terms that includes the initial query terms, synonyms, negative knowledge, hypernyms, hyponyms, and personal preference information. This expanded set becomes the input to the query formulation phase. In this phase, the query is formulated according to the syntax of the search engine used. Appropriate boolean operators are used to construct the query depending upon the type of term added. For each query term, the synonym is added with an OR operator (e.g. query term OR synonym). Hypernym and hyponym are added using the AND operator (e.g. query term AND (hypernym OR hypernym)). Personal preference information is also added using the AND operator (e.g. query term AND preference). The negative knowledge is added using the NOT operator. The first synonym from the highest remaining synset not selected is included with the NOT operator (e.g. query term NOT synonym).

Phase 4 – Search Knowledge Sources: This phase submits the query to one or more web search engines (in their required syntax) for processing using the API provided by them. Our query construction heuristics work with most search engines. For example, AltaVista allows queries to use a NEAR constraint, but since other search engines such as Google and AlltheWeb do not, it is not used. Likewise, query expansion techniques in traditional information retrieval systems can add up to 800 terms to the query with varying weights. This approach is not used in our methodology because web search engines limit the number of query terms (e.g. Google has a limit of ten terms). The search query can also be submitted to internal knowledge sources within an organization that may contain relevant documents. Of course, this requires that knowledge repositories provide a well defined set of APIs for applications to use.

Phase 5 – Consolidate Results: In the final phase, the results from the search engine (URLs and 'snippets' provided from the web pages) are retrieved and presented to the user. The user can either accept the results or rewrite and resubmit the query to get more relevant results. This phase also integrates the search results from multiple language sources and takes care of the differences in formatting. The results are organized based on the knowledge sources used, target language, or domain.

4 System Architecture

The architecture of the proposed system is shown in Figure 1. It consists of the following components: a) MDDQL Query Parser, b) Query Expansion Module, c) Query Constructor, d) Query API Manager, and e) Results Integration Module. A proof-of-concept prototype is currently under development using J2EE technologies with client-server architecture. The user specifies search queries in natural language. The server contains Java application code and the WordNet database. The prototype will provide an interface to commercial search engines such as Google (www.google.com) and AlltheWeb (www.alltheweb.com). The MDDQL parser component is implemented using the Java programming language, where abstract data types have been defined for the construction and manipulation of the MDDQL query trees. A repository (knowledge base) for representing the parameters (dimensions), as well as a classification mechanism of a natural language into this parametric space is provided. The

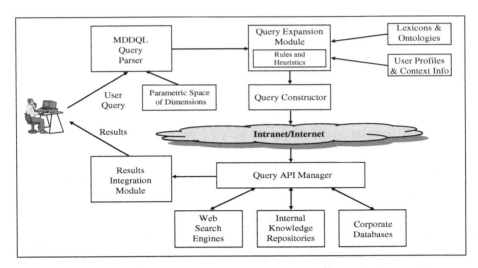

Fig. 1. System Architecture for Multi-Lingual Web Querying

heuristics within the query expansion module are being implemented as servlets and the rules and reasoning capability using Java Expert System Shell, Jess (http://herzberg.ca.sandia.gov/jess).

The prototype will also interface with ontology sources such as DAML and ResearchCyc and relational databases that store personal profiles and user preferences for query refinement. The query API manager component uses URL encoding to communicate with the knowledge sources and the API provided by the search engines. The results integration module returns the first twenty pages from the search engines in the format they provide. The results contain the title of the page, the snippet, and the URL for each page. Each of the components and their functionalities are briefly described below.

In order to verify the validity of our assumptions, and to clarify the internal workings of the system as presented in Figure 1, we describe in detail how a query is parsed, passed to the query expansion module, then to the query constructor, which will transform the query to be submitted to the query API manager.

Let us assume that a user submits the following Japanese query:
日本の 作家ノーベル賞 に 勝った (*Japanese writers who won the Nobel prize*) to the Google search engine, asking both pages in English and Japanese (the phrase in italics is not sent to the search engine, it is added here to help the reader understand the query). Since, Google relies on keywords, it will not be able to retrieve any links.

Obviously the phrase needs to be segmented into morphemes. The need for a segmentation tool does not arise for European languages, where at this stage a lexical analyzer like WordNet (for English) will suffice to help create the conceptual graph. There are many segmentation tools available for Japanese (e.g. Juman), with various levels of accuracy. In this example, we assume that the system being implemented can interface with such a tool and move on to actual parsing. The segmented query is: 日本の 作家 (Japanese writer) ノーベル 賞 (Nobel prize) に 勝った (they won).

Note that the initial query has not been translated into English. The intention is to postpone it as much as possible, since all translations are prone to ambiguities if the context is not clearly specified and the words are not chosen carefully from a lexicon.

According to the parsing algorithm described in section 3.1, the MDDQL parser will start by setting the language to Japanese, and define its parameters. For this scenario two parameters are considered: *the head-directionality* and the *topic-prominent*.

For maximum flexibility, the parser makes no assumptions about the underlying grammar of the language, but depending on the parameters it will adjust its behavior. The importance of this design decision is that it allows the system to dynamically vary the language it is tokenizing without changing the parser itself.

The head-directionality is a linguistic pattern of the Japanese language that manifests by the use of markers (postpositions added to noun phrases to emphasize their role -- subject or object) [14]. This parameter plays an important role in identifying the words in their dictionary form during parsing. The topic-prominent parameter, characterizes phrases such as the following: "*Japanese writers, they won the Nobel prize*" with an initial noun phrase (topic) followed by a complete clause as a comment on the topic. This type of phrase constructions is not accepted in English, and it is included in this example just to prove that translations can introduce verbiage to the query and complicate the semantic parsing.

In this instance the pronoun "they" would confuse a parser to correctly identify the subject phrase, while a human reader that understands English will easily grasp that the user is trying to find out more on the Japanese writers who won the Nobel prize, where the subject phrase is "Japanese writers", the object phrase is "Nobel prize" and the verb phrase is "won". Below, the algorithm given in section 3.1 is instantiated.

Input: 日本の 作家 (Japanese writer) ノーベル 賞 (Nobel prize) に 勝った (they won), an $A \subseteq L = Japanese$

A = {" 日本語 (Japanese)", "作家 (writer)", "勝利 (win)", "ノーベル (Nobel)"," 賞 (prize)", "本 (book)"}

Output: An *MDDQL* parse tree G_{MDDQL}

SET *L=Japanese; **SET** V with <P1: head-last case marker, P2: topic-prominent>*

The topic-prominent parameter helps correctly identify the subject phrase and disregard "they" from query, without loss of meaning. The head-directionality parameter helps add syntactic roles to query tree and identify the right word from the lexicon.

Generating the conceptual graph

Vertices: G_{SU} : (<v_1: writer (noun, subject, class), v_2: Japanese (adjective, subject, property)>, e_3: ""), **when** Δ = SU, or

G_{OB} : (< v_3: prize (noun, object, class), v_4: Nobel (proper noun, object, property)>, e_4: ""), **when** Δ = OB or

$G_{VP:}$: (< v_5: win (event, verb)> **when** Δ = VP

Connecting edges that respect the ontological constraints:

< e_1: ""> **connecting** v_1: writer (noun, subject, class) with v_5: win (event, verb) and, therefore, connecting G_{SU} with G_{VP}

<e_2: ""> **connecting** v_5: win (event, verb) with v_3: prize (noun, object, class) and, therefore, connecting G_{VP} with G_{OB}

<e_3: ""> **connecting** v_1: writer (noun, subject,class) with v_2: Japanese (adjective, subject, property)

<e_4: ""> **connecting** v_3: Nobel (proper noun, object, property) with v_4: prize(noun, object, class)

Due to the ontological constraints that the query parser abides by when building this graph, the outcome of the algorithm will be a tree; thus we have a conceptual tree. This tree is then extended by the *Query Expansion Module* and the extended tree is read and translated into a query by the *Query Constructor* with appropriate syntax.

Once the conceptual graph is created, the *Query Expansion Module* clones and translates each of the vertices into English. In this particular scenario the user asked for pages in both English and Japanese, but adding other languages in the initial query specification will only mean repeating the cloning and the translation process.

Translating such simple tokens is fast and adds less ambiguity in the translation process, and it also preserves the semantic relationships between concepts. During the translation of the vertices into another natural language, the system will interface with a set of chosen lexicons, ontologies, and a translation service to perform the mapping from the input language to the other natural languages requested. To this tree the *Query Expansion Module* will add a set of *a priori* global constraints that apply to all queries and local constraints based on the query context. These constraints are derived from the user's profile and they will enhance the queries precision.

In the scenario described so far, the global constraints refer to the language restrictions (English and Japanese). The local constraints will also become active since in the query's structure the key-concept "writer" arises. This user is a book reviewer, and he expects that his search will provide pointers to both authors' biographies, as well as titles of books they wrote. In the user's profile the association (semantic relationship) between the concepts "writer" and "book" is stored. The *Query Expansion Module* will detect this association and the concept "book" will be automatically added to the query tree. The conceptual graph will expand with:

a) a new vertex v_6: *book (noun, object, class)*, and
b) a new edge $<e_5$: *""> connecting v_1: writer (noun, object, property) with v_6: book (noun, object, class)*;

After the query tree is completed, the *Query Constructor* plays the role of a query factory that will read the query tree and generate queries for a set of heterogeneous resources (e.g. enumeration of the vertices for the search engines, or SQL queries for databases available via web services). The flexibility of this module is due to the high-level representation we have chosen to use for query representations.

The final task of the multi-lingual web querying system is to assemble the results obtained after the *Query Constructor* delegated the queries to different resources. The *Results Integration Module* will wrap the answers to the search by taking into consideration user preferences for content and formatting.

5   Conclusion and Future Work

Current MLIR techniques are not adequate for querying the Web. In this paper, we have presented a concept based methodology for multilingual querying on the Web. The MDDQL parsing algorithm discussed is language independent and hence the approach is flexible and scaleable. Our approach also uses contextual and semantic information in query refinement to improve precision. We have discussed the architecture of a system that implements our methodology. A proof-of-concept prototype is currently under development to demonstrate the feasibility of the approach. Our future work includes completing the prototype, experimental validation, and further refinement of the methodology. The validation process will entail collecting comparative data representing the number of hits obtained by submitting a translation of the query as a whole, disregarding any semantic aspect, and the hits provided by MLIR, in conjunction with a detailed registration of all the changes required for the MLIR system.

References

1. S. Amer-Yahia, P. Case, T. Rölleke, J. Shanmugasundaram, G. Weikum, "Report on the DB/IR Panel at SIGMOD 2005," 34(4), 71-74, SIGMOD Record, 2005.
2. Zhou, Y., Qin, J., Chen, H., and Nunamaker, J.F. "Multilingual Web Retrieval: An Experiment on a Multilingual Business Intelligence Portal," p. 43a, HICSS'05 - Track 1, 2005.
3. K. Sattler, I. Geist, E. Schallehn, Concept-based querying in mediator systems, Vol. 14, pp. 97–111, VLDB Journal, 2005.
4. Z. Liu, W. W. Chu: "Knowledge Based Query Expansion to Support Scenario Specific Retrieval of Medical Free Text," ACM Symp. on Applied Computing, 2005, pp. 13-17.
5. M. Sintek, S. Decker, Triple – A query, inference and transformation language for the Semantic Web. Proc of 1st Inter. Semantic Web Conference (ISWC), Sardinia, Italy, 2002.
6. B. Fonseca, P. Golgher, B. Possas, B. Ribeiro-Neto, N. Ziviani, Concept-based Interactive Query Expansion, CIKM 2005, pp. 696-703.
7. J. Wang, J. Teng, P. Cheng, W. Lu, and L. Chien, Translating Unknown Cross-Lingual Queries in Digital Libraries Using a Web-based Approach, JCDL'04, 2004, pp. 108-116.
8. W. Lu, L. Chien, H. Lee: Anchor Text Mining for Translation of Web Queries: A Transitive Translation Approach, ACM Trans. on Inf. Sys., Vol. 22, No. 2, 2004, pp. 242-269.
9. I. Ioannidis, G. Koutrika, Personalized Systems: From an IR & DB Perspective, Tutorial at VLDB Conference 2005, Trondheim, Norway, 2005
10. J. Allan, Challenges in Information Retrieval and Language Modeling: Report on a Workshop for Intelligent Information Retrieval, Univ. of Massachusetts Amherst, 2002.
11. V. Owei, An Intelligent Approach to Handling Imperfect Information in Concept Based Natural Language Queries, ACM Transactions on Information Systems, Vol. 20, No. 3, 2002, pp. 291–328.
12. A. Burton-Jones, V. Storey, V. Sugumaran, S. Purao. "A Heuristic-based Methodology for Semantic Augmentation of User Queries on the Web," 22nd International Conference on Conceptual Modeling, Chicago, Illinois, October 13 – 16, 2003, pp. 476 – 489.
13. E. Kapetanios, D. Baer, and P. Groenewoud. "Simplifying syntactic and semantic parsing of NL-based queries in advanced application domains," Data and Knowledge Engineering, Vol. 55, No. 1, 2005, pp. 38-58.
14. M. C. Baker. "The Atoms of the Language," Oxford Press, Oxford, 2001, pp. 182-184.

Using Semantic Knowledge to Improve Web Query Processing

Jordi Conesa[1], Veda C. Storey[2], and Vijayan Sugumaran[3]

[1] Departament de llenguatges i sistemes informàtics, Universitat Politecnica de Catalunya
Jordi Girona 1-3, 08034 Barcelona
jconesa@lsi.upc.edu
[2] Department of Computer Information Systems, J. Mark Robinson Collage of Business
Georgia State University, Box 4015 Atlanta, GA 30302
vstorey@cis.gsu.edu
[3] School of Business Administration, Oakland University, Rochester, MI 48309
sugumara@oakland.edu

Abstract. Although search engines are very useful for obtaining information from the World Wide Web, users still have problems obtaining the most relevant information when processing their web queries. Prior research has attempted to use different types of knowledge to improve web querying processing. This research presents a methodology for employing a specific body of knowledge, ResearchCyc, which provides semantic knowledge about different application domains. Semantic knowledge from ResearchCyc, as well as linguistic knowledge from WordNet, is employed. An analysis of different queries from different application domains using the semantic and linguistic knowledge illustrates how more relevant results can be obtained.

1 Introduction

The continued explosion of available information on the World Wide Web has lead to the need for processing queries intelligently to address more of the user's intended requirements, than previously possible [1]. Doing so, requires some notion of the context within which the query is being posed and the semantics of the query itself. In our context, *intelligent* means that the queries should be interpreted and extended in order to contextualize and disambiguate them.

Several knowledge repositories have been created to support agents (humans or programs) to increase the intelligence of their tasks. Examples include WordNet [2], Cyc [3], and ConceptNet [4]. Although all of these are useful for their intended purposes, they are limited as a general repository in several ways. Linguistic repositories, such as WordNet, do not capture the semantic relationships or integrity constraints between concepts. Semantic repositories such as Cyc do not represent linguistic relationships of the concepts (e.g. whether two concepts are synonyms). Some of the existing repositories are domain dependent, and only represent information about certain aspects of the domains, not the complete domain. Research on query extension has used knowledge repositories to develop tools that assist the user in processing queries that capture the user's intent [5-11]. Most query extension

C. Kop et al. (Eds.): NLDB 2006, LNCS 3999, pp. 106–117, 2006.
© Springer-Verlag Berlin Heidelberg 2006

approaches use only linguistic knowledge [12]. However, linguistic repositories lack semantic knowledge, so query expansion cannot deal with several issues: 1) knowledge related to the domain of the query, 2) common sense inferences, or 3) the semantic relationships in which the concepts of the query can participate. Grootjen and Weide [11] focus on creating a small lattice of concepts to support query expansion. In contrast, our approach focuses on grouping and using existing knowledge in large knowledge bases for query expansion in an efficient manner.

In this research, we consider semantic repositories to be repositories that represent semantic information about a domain. They are independent of syntax, word forms and languages, but tend to be domain and culture dependent. Semantic repositories need linguistic knowledge to identify relevant concepts from the repository that represent a given term used in the query. Therefore, the integration of linguistic and semantic information into one repository could be useful to increase the contexts where knowledge in these repositories can be used successfully. Table 1 shows examples of improvement in search results using semantic and linguistic knowledge.

The Cyc ontology is a repository developed to capture and represent common sense. ReseachCyc (http://research.cyc.com) is a huge semantic repository. It should be possible to use techniques from Cyc [13-15] to extend ResearchCyc with linguistic information from WordNet lexicon, and factual information from World Wide Web.

The objective of this research is to demonstrate that use of semantic and linguistic knowledge together improves the query refinement process. To do so, we study the problems associated with the web-query process and show how ResearchCyc in combination with WordNet helps improve query results in the context of web search.

This research makes several contributions. First, it demonstrates that semantic and linguistic knowledge together improves query expansion. Second, the research identifies and formalizes web-query problems and presents a query classification scheme that explains why, in some cases, the query expansion may not be done successfully, even if the repository used to support such a task is complete. Such information is used to identify the structure and knowledge that an ontology should have to increase the chances of improving different kinds of queries.

Table 1. Improvement in search results using semantic and linguistic knowledge sources

Query	Domain	Results	% Rel	Source	Results	% Rel
Pets	Animals	53,600,000	70	ResearchCyc	24,600,000	100
				ResearchCyc	10,400,000	95
	Buying animals in Atlanta			ResearchCyc + WordNet	260,000	95
Nike Georgia	Bulling Sport Stuff	2,180,000	0	ResearchCyc	1,550,000	10
Flute Bohemian Drink	Drink	57,900	25	ResearchCyc	153,000	82.5
Bonderdorfers Atlanta	Music	73	50	WordNet	49	90
Which universities offer online degrees?	Education		50	WordNet		90
Find cookie stores	Restaurant	2,900,000	20	ConcepNet + textual sources	950,000	90

2 Web Queries

The purpose of a web query is to search for information that best reflects the user's needed information. In this research, semantics is defined as the meaning, or essential message, of terms. To carry out useful research for dealing with semantics, symbols must be manipulated in ways that are meaningful and useful [19].

To process a web query, the *expected result* is E_R. This information, in general, belongs to several domains, *intended domains* D_I. Therefore, the expected result is contained in the knowledge defined for the intersection of all the intended domains $E_R \subseteq K(D_{I1}) \cap K(D_{I2}) \cap \dots \cap K(D_{IN})$, where $K(D)$ represents a function that returns the knowledge defined in the domain D as illustrated in Figure 1.

To perform a search, the user creates an *initial query* (Q_I) selecting some terms w_1, ..., w_k (called *query terms* Q_w) to describe what he or she is searching for. The problem arises with the ambiguity of the languages humans use. The user considers a query, Q_w, within a given context (i.e., the context of the *intended domains*). Since words have several senses in several domains, query search techniques are not able to determine which of the senses of a given query term is the one in which the user is interested. Given this ambiguity, the result of the query tends to contain results that deal with a number of domains D_{O1}, ..., D_{Om} greater than the *intended domains* $(m{\geq}n)$[1]. The resultant domains are called *obtained domains*, with each depending on a subset of the query terms $D_O(W)$, where $W{\subseteq}\{w_1, \dots, w_k\}$.

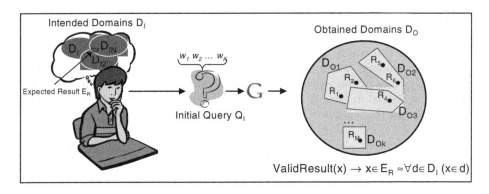

Fig. 1. Constraining the Search Domains for Web Queries

Suppose a user lives in Georgia, U.S.A., and wants to buy sports shoes with Nike brand. E_R is "Places in Georgia (USA) where I can find a pair of Nike shoes". E_R is composed of domain information that deals with sport stuff (sport shoes), commercial information (brand Nike sells sport stuff), and geographical information (which commercial organizations in Georgia sell Nike products). These three domains are the

---

[1] The number of resultant domains may be also smaller in the rare case that the user selects words that describe only a subset of the intended domains uniquely.

intended domains. Suppose the user defines a query that contains two words Q_w = "Nike Georgia". Then, some of the D_O will be D_{O1}(Nike)=Commercial Brand, D_{O2}(Nike)=Greek Mythology (Nike is the goodness of Victory in Greek Mythology), D_{O3}(Georgia)=Central-European Country, D_{O4}(Georgia)=State in the United States of America, D_{O5}(Georgia)=Football Team Georgia Bulldogs...The query results will be the WebPages that deal with the presented D_O.

2.1 Web-Query Problems

The ambiguity of the language used in the query, the possible partial knowledge of the user, and the difficulty in determining what the user really wants, lead to the following problems that affect the processing of web queries.

- **Identification of a good initial query:** There is no systematic way, or guidelines that support the user in identifying the best terms for a query. A good selection of Q_I is important. Terms that are too general may result in too many irrelevant D_O, and results. Using very specific words may result in missing some of the results that match E_R because they use a plain language.
- **Resolving language ambiguity:** Documents that deal with same domain can use different words for describing the same concepts. Therefore, for a given concept (*sport stuff*) some documents may use the words ("*sport stuff*"), other documents may use synonyms ("*sport material*"), and other words that deal with the same concept, but more generally ("*playing sport artifact*") or specifically ("*trainer*").
- **Identifying the relevant results:** It may be difficult to detect whether a given result of the query is valid. A result is valid if it belongs to the *expected result*. The problem is that the *expected result* is in the mind of the user. A result is also valid if it belongs to the intersection of the *intended domains*. Unfortunately, we do not know what those domains are, and, due to word ambiguity problems, we cannot conclude that the obtained domains are the expected ones. Hence, it is not possible to identify which results are relevant for the user and which are irrelevant.

Several research efforts have attempted to minimize these problems. Interactive approaches, such as query refinement, help the user identify better terms for a query [6, 16]. These techniques show the user information related to Q_W. The user then uses this information to learn more about the domain and identify better terms or concepts for the query. These techniques are also useful when the user is not certain about what he or she is searching for, and needs a conceptualization of the intended domains. For example, these techniques help the user to redefine an initial query about pets (namely, "Pet") to a less ambiguous query after the user realizes his or her interests are about buying domestic cats, "Buy Persian Cat Atlanta". Other approaches use linguistic repositories for minimizing the problem of query ambiguity by using synonyms, hypernyms and hyponyms. Nevertheless, there does not appear to be any technique that enables the user to identify when the results of the query are relevant.

2.2 Query Classification

Initial experiments using the ResearchCyc knowledge base for query expansion and refinement reveal that there are some queries that cannot be improved using

ResearchCyc or any other semantic repository. Recall the query where the user is searching for Nike sport shoes in Georgia. Nike is not a concept, but an instance in ResearchCyc. The extensional information of this repository indicates that it is a commercial organization with the name "Nike," and it has an affiliated called Michael Jordan. However, ResearchCyc does not give any information about what this organization sells, and therefore, the contained knowledge is useless. Thus, one of the contributions of this research is to identify classes of queries that could or could not take advantage of the knowledge in ResearchCyc. The classification takes into account the types of knowledge that are needed to improve a web query.

- **Intensional Query:** This type of query obtains intensional[2] information about E_R. This kind of query is directed by the necessity of the user increasing his or her knowledge. Only intensional terms should be used to define the query. For example, the query "Buy a Pet Cat" is intensional because the user is interested in learning something new about buying cats, such as which kinds of shops sell cats, guidelines for buying a cat, etc. Usually knowledge repositories use only intensional information to define their knowledge. Therefore, any knowledge repository that deals with the intended domains of an intensional query can be used successfully to improve such a query.
- **Extensional Query:** The purpose of this type of query is to obtain extensional information about E_R. The user is not interested in learning abstract knowledge, but specific knowledge. This kind of query tends to be motivated for more practical needs. In the query "Nike Georgia" the user may be interested in the shops in Georgia that sell Nike products, or the Nike factories located in the country of Georgia. This query is extensional because the user is not interested in general information about USA states or commercial companies. The user is interested in obtaining information about particular instances of those concepts (Nike is an instance of a commercial company and Georgia is an instance of the State in USA).

The user is not interested in the possible relationship types between the concepts, but in the real relationships between them. For instance, *Business* has a relationship type (in ResearchCyc) called *parentCompany* that relates one business to another business which is its parent company. In an intentional query the user may be interested in knowing that sometimes a business may have a parent company. However, in extensional queries, the user is only interested in this relationship when there is an instance of the relationship in which *Nike* is a participant.

To improve this kind of query knowledge repositories are needed that include both the intension of the intended domains, and their extension. The more extensional information the repository has, the better the results are obtained through query expansion. Unfortunately, the actual knowledge repositories do not take into account

---

[2] Intension vs. extension: is the distinction between ways in which the meaning of a term may be regarded:
  - The extension, or denotation, is the collection of things to which the term applies;
  - The intension, or connotation, is the set of things that have common features.
  In conceptual modeling intension is represented by concepts and extension by instances. Therefore, Person is the intension of the extension composed of all the persons that exist.

extensional knowledge; they only exemplify the intension knowledge. Therefore, the actual knowledge repositories are useless for improving this kind of query.

An intensional or extensional query may also contain other kinds of information, which helps to contextualize the query. In some cases, this additional knowledge allows discarding of domains that do not fit with the user's intended domains. For example, "Nike Georgia buy" is an extensional query ("Nike Georgia") that contains intensional information (buy) that allows delimiting the purpose of the user: buying. On the other hand, the query "Flute Bohemian Drink" is an intensional query ("Flute Drink") with extensional information ("Bohemian") that allows contextualizing our query. We are only interested in information regarding Flute and Drink related in any way with a Bohemian instance, which may be the instance of a geographical region (Czech Republic), a music movement, et cetera.

For queries that use intensional and extensional knowledge we need to use knowledge repositories that represent both of these types of knowledge for the intended domains. Table 2 summarizes the roles of the lexical, semantic and factual information in the query process.

Table 2. Roles of the different kind of information in the query process

<table>
<tr><td colspan="2" rowspan="2"></td><td colspan="3">Necessary to</td><td rowspan="2">Other effects</td></tr>
<tr><td>Find concepts related to query</td><td>Intensional queries</td><td>Extensional queries</td></tr>
<tr><td colspan="2">Synonymy</td><td>✓</td><td></td><td></td><td>– Increase the number of the intended domains
– Prioritize the intersection of the obtained domains</td></tr>
<tr><td rowspan="2">Relationships</td><td>Taxonomic</td><td></td><td>✓</td><td></td><td>– Produces the expansion or pruning of the obtained domains</td></tr>
<tr><td>Non Taxonomic</td><td></td><td>✓</td><td></td><td>– Allows inferring candidate domains
– Allows focusing of the query in the candidate domains</td></tr>
<tr><td colspan="2">Factual</td><td></td><td></td><td>✓</td><td>– Allows inferring candidate domains in intensional queries</td></tr>
</table>

3 Semantics in Query Processing

The use of semantic, linguistic and factual knowledge for web queries may require common sense knowledge. The following shows the kind of knowledge and structure an ontology should have to improve any kind of query (extensional or intensional). These types of knowledge could be combined to form an ontology that contains, for example, the semantic information of the ResearchCyc, the linguistic information from WordNet, and the factual information from the Web. The ontology could then be used to facilitate the processing of a web query. The semantic information is necessary to represent the intended domains, The linguistic information is necessary to identify the concepts that represent the query terms and to define the linguistic relationships (synonymy, antonymy, etc.) of such concepts. The factual information is necessary to represent the particular objects of the real world such as the cities of the

United States or the Pet stores of a given city. Since such an ontology should contain semantic, linguistic and factual knowledge, it should be composed of a set [17]:

- **Concepts.** A concept is something we have created in our mind in order to generalize the properties a set of objects have in common. A concept has an extension and an intension. The extension is the set of all its possible instances, and the intension is the set of common properties of all its instances. There are two kinds of concepts:
    - Classes. A class represents concept type; it can be specialized or generalized
    - Properties. A property relates objects, and describes their interactions or properties.
- **Individuals.** They are the extension of the concepts and represent a particular concept of a real world (tangible or intangible).
- **Classification relationships between an individual and a concept.** We denote as *InstanceOf(i,c)* the fact that an instance *i* is instance of a concept *c* (either an entity type or a relationship type).
- **Generalization relationships between concepts.** These binary relationships organize the concepts in a tree structure using generalization/specialization. These relationships specify that a concept (child) is a subtype of another concept (parent), and therefore, the extension of a child must be included in the extension of the parent. This relationship type is an inclusion integrity constraint between the parent and the child concepts. However, due to the important role of such relationships in the ontologies, these relationships are defined explicitly such as a relationship type.

The concepts and the generalization relationships are needed to conceptualize the intensional information about the domains to model. On the other hand, the individuals and the classification relationships are needed to represent the extensional information of our conceptualization. A concept of the ontology may represent either **semantic** or **linguistic** information. The rationale is that the ontology should represent the synonyms of each concept, when a concept is a compound name composed for two or more nouns and so on. For example, if there is a semantic concept in the ontology called *DomesticPet* the ontology should also contain linguistic information which indicate that its name is a noun comprised of two words: *Domestic* and *Pet*, and is the denotation of the word *Pet*. Although the heuristics are not necessary in an ontology, they enable inference. For example, ResearchCyc defines a heuristic for the concept *DomesticPet* which indicates that most pets have a pleasant personality. If the user is searching for a friendly animal, the prior information can be used to infer that he or she is interested in a *DomesticPet* because there is a generalization relationship between *Pet* and *Animal*, a synonymy relationship between *friendly* and *pleasant*, and a heuristic which indicates that *Pets* tend to be *friendly*.

Similarly, constraints are not needed but may be useful for detecting some concepts (or contexts) for which the user is interested. For example, suppose the user is interested in obtaining information about the Garfield cat, but does not remember which kind of animal Garfield is. The user's query: "Garfield Pet" may result in irrelevant web pages because Garfield is also a surname. The disjoint integrity constraint between the concepts Cat and Person (defined in the ResearchCyc ontology) may be used to determine that the user is not interested in persons, and therefore, modify the query to discard the web pages that deal with persons. Although most ontology languages facilitate representing instances, most of the ontologies used to support web queries neither represent the instances of the conceptualization they are modeling, nor the linguistic information about their concepts. As a result, they are not able to improve correctly the user requests that use extensional knowledge, and must use linguistic external repositories to identify which concepts in the ontology are related with the terms provided by the user.

4 Methodology

The proposed methodology uses semantic, linguistic and factual information from ResearchCyc and WordNet to process web queries. The two major aspects of the methodology are query expansion and query refinement. During query expansion, the query is "expanded" with new terms to improve the retrieval performance. The expansion is usually performed using synonyms of the initial query terms Q_w. Query expansion also takes into account the actions or properties of the initial terms (non-taxonomic relationships) and instances (in some cases). For example, the query *"Pet"* may be expanded as *Pet and Animal*. Query refinement is the incremental process of transforming a query into a new query that more accurately reflects the user's information need [16]. The goal is not to obtain better results but to change (shrink/grow) what the user are looking for (the expected result). To do so, the user is asked to disambiguate the query after which, the query may be reformulated automatically using the semantic knowledge of the ontology. This process uses generalization or specialization relationship types as well as non-taxonomic relationships and instances. For example, the query "Pet" may be refined by asking the user:

You are interested in Pets, but are you interested in any activity related with Pets?
1) buying/selling Pets, 2) Pet Stores in your area, 3) Providers of Animal Therapy

Supposing that the user is interested in Pet Stores in his/her area and he/she lives in Atlanta, then using the ResearchCyc knowledge the query may be automatically redefined as: *"Pet Store" and Atlanta and Georgia and buy*

The proposed methodology consists of four phases: a) Query Parsing, b) Query Expansion, c) Query Refinement, and d) Query Submission. The query parsing phase involves parsing the natural language query using POS tagging and identifying nouns and noun phrases. These terms form the initial query. The query expansion phase adds similar concepts to the query and negative knowledge as appropriate. The user identifies the correct word sense and the other word senses are added as negative knowledge since the user is not interested in them. The query refinement phase reformulates the query to better focus on the necessities of the user. This is accomplished by using the taxonomic and non-taxonomic relationships in ResearchCyc. The query submission phase creates the final query according to the syntax required by the search engine used and submits the query and provides the results back to the user. The steps in the methodology are given below. After each step, the user is asked if the query reflects his/her intension. If so, the final query is constructed using the appropriate syntax and submitted to the search engine.

Query Parsing Phase

Step 1: Parse the NL query submitted by the user using POS Tagger (such as QTag parser [18]. Identify the nouns and noun phrases which are used as initial query terms. This is done using ResearchCyc and/or WordNet.

Query Expansion Phase

Step 2: For each query term find related concepts or synonyms from ResearchCyc (and/or WordNet).

Step 3: For each concept find the word senses and let the user select the appropriate sense to use. Based on the selection, add the unrelated word senses as negative knowledge.

Query Refinement Phase

Step 4: Use the taxonomic relationship from ResearchCyc to refine the query.

Identify appropriate hypernym(s)/hyponym(s) to add or reformulate the query and let the user select the ones to use for query refinement.

Step 5: Use the non-taxonomic relationship from ResearchCyc to determine the purpose or specific action (action relationship) and reformulate the query accordingly.

Step 6: Add appropriate personal information to the query.

Query Submission Phase

Step 7: Construct the final Boolean query using appropriate syntax.

Step 8: Submit query to the search engine and provide the results back to the user.

Some of the above steps use relationship types, constraints and heuristics of ResearchCyc for query expansion and refinement. The following example shows how concepts in ResearchCyc can be used to reason about query terms and select appropriate sense and terms to add to the query. Consider the query *"Flute Bohemian Drink"* If we search in ResearchCyc for the term Flute, we obtain two entries: the concept of *ChampagneFlute* and the concept of *Flute* (the instrument). The ChampagneFlute concept has a supertype, namely, the concept of DrinkingGlass. Taking into account that the query contains also the word drink, and that the concept DrinkingGlass is a compost noun composed for the name "Drink", we can deduce automatically that the user is not interested in the instrument. If we search for the word Bohemian in ResearchCyc, we obtain two regions of the Czech Republic that represent historical areas of the Czech Republic. These two concepts are sub-regions of the Czech Republic, so we can deduce that the user is interested in the Flute glasses made in that country. Here the word drink has been necessary to disambiguate the flute concept, but after this, is not necessary to extend the query. Therefore, we can refine the query: "Champagne + Flute + glass + Czech".

5   Architecture and Implementation

The architecture for a system to implement this methodology is shown in Figure 2 and consists of: a) query parser module, b) query expansion module, c) query refinement module, and d) final query generation module. The *Query Parser Module* captures the user's query, parses it for nouns (noun phrases) and returns the part-of-speech for each term.   From this, a baseline query is created. The *Query Expansion Module* interfaces with WordNet and ResearchCyc knowledge sources and supports the query expansion steps. For each query term, it obtains the related concepts and the synsets and lets the user select the appropriate word sense to use. Based on the user's input, appropriate synonyms and negative knowledge are added to the query. In some cases, the word sense can be identified automatically when some of the terms in the query are relationship types that relate to other concepts in the query for only one of the possible senses. The *Query Refinement Module* interfaces with the Personal Information Database as well as ResearchCyc and WordNet. It adds personal information that is relevant to the query to restrict the search domains. Based on the user's selected synset, hypernyms and hyponyms for the selected sense of the term are obtained from ResearchCyc and WordNet. This module uses taxonomic and non-taxonomic relationships from ResearchCyc to reason about concepts and to add appropriate terms to the query. The Final Query Generation Module creates the augmented query using the appropriate syntax for the search engine. Boolean operators are used to construct the final query and adequate care is taken to ensure that the final query meets the length restrictions (e.g. Google has a 10-word limit). The Search Engine Interface enables the final query to be submitted to various search engines and forwards the results back to the user. A prototype is currently under development. The query parser module utilizes the QTag parser [18] to process the query. The query expansion and query refinement modules interact with ResearchCyc through its Java API. The reasoning capability is being implemented using Java Expert System Shell, Jess, (http://herzberg.ca.sandia.gov/jess). The prototype interfaces with Google and AlltheWeb search engines.

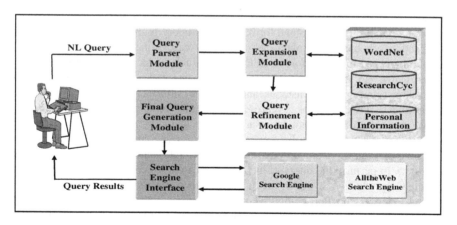

Fig. 2. System Architecture

6 Testing

Queries have been manually executed with the results shown in Table 3. The baseline query and the expanded query were executed in Google and the number of relevant hits in the top ten results identified (Relevance Score). The sample queries show that the addition of semantic and linguistic knowledge helps improve query results.

Table 3. Query Results with Semantic and Linguistic Knowledge

Base Query	Relevance Score (Google)	Expanded Query	Relevance Score (our method)
Nike Georgia	0	Nike Commercial Georgia USA Atlanta OR Columbus OR Augusta OR Macon OR Statesboro OR Valdosta OR Carrollton OR Albany OR "Fort Valley" OR Duluth OR Marietta OR Savannah OR "Stone Mountain – goddess	2
Pet	4	Pet + Store "+ Atlanta + Georgia + buy	9
Flute Bohemian Drink	3	Champagne + Flute + glass + Czech	8
Bass player Atlanta	3	bass player Atlanta Georgia -fish -singer -beer guitar hiring	6
Coach agency rules	4	coach agency rules sports government "code of conduct" -vehicle	7
Bridge component	1	bridge component span solid surface -game	8
Storm canal function	2	Storm canal function -"gale storm" - mathematical purpose	4
Country home collection	4	country home or house collection -music -state -"urban area"	9
Fog suspension	2	fog suspension -interruption causes	3

7 Conclusions

This research contributes to the improvement of web queries in several ways. First, it demonstrates that semantic and linguistic knowledge together improve query expansion. Second, the research identifies and formalizes web-query problems and presents a query classification scheme that explains why, in some cases, query expansion may not be successful, even if the repository used to support such a task is complete. The research illustrates that an ontology structure should contain concepts and generalization relationships to represent intensional (and linguistic) information, as well as individuals and classification relationships to represent extensional information. Although heuristics and integrity constraints are not necessary, their inclusion facilitates inferencing on new information to create more intelligent queries. Future research will identify heuristics for automating parts of the methodology (e.g. sense disambiguation) or inferring whether it is necessary to perform the query refinement. ResearchCyc contains linguistic, semantic and factual knowledge. However, the quantity of the semantic and factual knowledge is very low. Hence, the query improvement cannot be performed when the relevant knowledge for the query is missing in ResearchCyc. This research, therefore, integrates linguistic, semantic and factual information in only one repository, using merging [13, 15] and population [14] techniques defined over Cyc. The creation of such a repository may be useful in areas where information about the domain of an information system, and the cultural and law restrictions that exist over that domain may be obtained from a combination of semantic, linguistic and factual knowledge sources.

Acknowledgement. This work has been partly supported by the Ministerio de Educacion y Ciencia under project TIN 2005-06253.

References

1. McGuinness, D., *Question Answering on the Semantic Web*. IEEE Intelligent Systems, 2004. **19**(1): p. 82-85.
2. Fellbaum, V., *Introduction*, in *Introduction: Wordnet: An Electronic Lexical Database*. 1998, The MIT Press.
3. Cyc. *Cyc Ontology*. Available from: http://www.cyc.com.
4. Liu, H. and P. Singh, *ConceptNet: A Practical Commonsense Reasoning Toolkit*. BT Technology Journal, 2004. **22**.
5. Burton-Jones, A., et al., *A Heuristic-Based Methodology for Semantic Augmentation of User Queries on the Web*, in *ER 2003*. 2003. p. 476-489.
6. Hartmann, J., et al., *Ontology-Based Query Refinement for Semantic Portals*, in *Integrated Publication and Information Systems to Virtual Information and Knowledge Environments 2005*. 2005. p. 41-50.
7. Khan, M.S. and S. Khor, *Enhanced web document retrieval using automatic query expansion*. Jl. of the American Soc for Info. Science and Technology, 2004. **55**(1): p. 29-40.
8. Storey, V.C., V. Sugumaran, and A. Burton-Jones, *The Role of User Profiles in Context-Aware Query Processing for the Semantic Web*, Proc. of NLDB 2004, LNCS. p. 51-63.
9. Stojanovic, N., R. Studer, and L. Stojanovic, *An Approach for Step-By-Step Query Refinement in the Ontology-based Information Retrieval*, in *Proceedings of the 2004 IEEE/WIC/ACM International Conference on Web Intelligence*. 2004: Beijing, China.
10. Zhang, L., S. Ram, and D.D. Zeng, *Contextual Web Search Based on Semantic Relationships*, in *Proceedings of the 15th Workshop on Information Technology and Systems (WITS 2005)*. 2005: Las Vegas, Nevada.
11. Grootjen, F.A. and T.P.v.d. Weide, *Conceptual query expansion*. Data & Knowledge Engineering, 2006. **56**(2): p. 174-193.
12. Mandala, R., T. Tokunaga, and H. Tanaka, *Combining multiple evidence from different types of thesaurus for query expansion*, in *Proceedings of the 22nd Annual International ACM SIGIR Conference on Research and Development in Information Retrieval*. 1999: Berkeley, CA, USA. p. 191-197.
13. Masters, J., *Structured Knowledge Source Integration and its applications to information fusion, Fifth International Conference on Information Fusion*. 2002: Annapolis.
14. Matuszek, C., et al., *Searching for common sense: populating Cyc from the web*, in *Proceedings of the Twentieth National Conference on Artificial Intelligence*. 2005.
15. O'Hara, T., et al., *Inducing criteria for mass noun lexical mappings using the Cyc KB, and its extension to WordNet, Workshop on Computational Semantics*. 2003: Tilburg.
16. Vélez, B., et al., *Fast and Effective Query Refinement*, in *Proceedings of the 20th Annual International ACM SIGIR Conference on Research and Development in Information Retrieval*. 1997. p. 6-15.
17. Uschold, M., *Knowledge level modelling: concepts and terminology*. The Knowledge Engineering Review, 1998. **13**(1): p. 5-29.
18. Mason, O. *QTag - a Portable POS Tagger*. Accessed on Jan 7, 2005. Available from: http://www.english.bham.ac.uk/staff/omason/software/qtag.html.
19. Embley, D.W. "Toward semantic understanding—an approach based on information extraction ontologies," 15th Australasian Database Conference, New Zealand, 2004, p.3-12.

Using Semantic Constraints to Improve Question Answering

Jamileh Yousefi and Leila Kosseim

CLaC Laboratory
Department of Computer Science and Software Engineering
Concordia University
1400 de Maisonneuve Blvd. West
Montreal, Quebec, Canada H3G 1M8
j_yousef@cs.concordia.ca, kosseim@cs.concordia.ca

Abstract. In this paper, we discuss our experience in using semantic constraints to improve the precision of a reformulation-based question-answering system. First, we present a method for acquiring semantic-based reformulations automatically. The goal is to generate patterns from sentences retrieved from the Web based on syntactic and semantic constraints. Once these constraints have been defined, we present a method to evaluate and re-rank candidate answers that satisfy these constraints using redundancy. The two approaches have been evaluated independently and in combination. The evaluation on about 500 questions from TREC-11 shows that the acquired semantic patterns increase the precision by 16% and the MRR by 26%, the re-ranking using semantic redundancy as well as the combined approach increase the precision by about 30% and the MRR by 67%. This shows that no manual work is now necessary to build question reformulations; while still increasing performance

1 Introduction

Question reformulation (also called *surface pattern, paraphrase, answer pattern, . . .*) tries to identify various ways of expressing an answer given a natural language question. These reformulations are often used in a Question Answering (QA) system to retrieve answers in a large document collection. For example given the question *Who is the president of the U.S.?*, a reformulation-based QA system will search for formulations like *the president of the U.S. is <NP>* or *<NP>, the president of the U.S.* in the document collection and will instantiate *<NP>* with the matching noun phrase. The ideal reformulation should impose constraints on the answer so as not to retrieve incorrect answers (e.g. *the president of the U.S. is a nut lover*) but should also identify many candidate answers to increase the system's confidence in them.

Most work on reformulations have used patterns based on string constraints, syntactic constraints or named entity tags (e.g. person-name, organization, . . .). However, only a few have worked on semantically equivalent reformulations such

C. Kop et al. (Eds.): NLDB 2006, LNCS 3999, pp. 118–128, 2006.
© Springer-Verlag Berlin Heidelberg 2006

as *<NP>*, *also known as the leader of the United States* or *at the top of the US government is <NP>*.

We believe that stronger semantic constraints can be beneficial to find a more precise set of candidate answers. However writing semantic reformulations by hand is a labor-intensive and tedious task. Our goal is to learn semantically equivalent reformulation patterns automatically from natural language questions and use these constraints to re-rank our candidate answers to improve performance.

2   Related Work

Soubbotin et al. [1] along with [2] were among the first to use surface patterns as the core of their QA system. This approach searches the document collection for predefined patterns or exact sentences that could be the formulation of the potential answer. [1] wrote their patterns by hand and were among the best scoring team at the TREC-10 QA track [3]. Their work shows that if enough human resources are available, handcrafted rules can produce excellent results.

Given the success of this approach, many attempts have then been made to acquire reformulations automatically. [2] use simple word permutations to produce paraphrases of the question. More recently, [4] also uses simple word permutations and verb movements to generate paraphrases for their multilingual QA system.

In the work of [5, 6, 7], answer formulations are produced for query expansion to improve information retrieval. While in [7] reformulation rules to transform a question of the form *What is X?* into *X is* or *X refers to* are built by hand, [6, 5] learns to transform natural language questions into sets of effective search engine queries, optimized specifically for each search engine.

[8] use a machine learning technique and a few hand-crafted examples of question-answer pairs to automatically learn patterns along with a confidence score. However, the patterns do not contain semantic information. They include specific strings of words such as *was born on, was born in, ...* with no generalisation of the `is-born` relation. [9] does use semantic paraphrases, called *phrasal synonyms*, to enhance their TextMap QA system. However, many of these patterns are manual generalisations of patterns derived automatically by [8].

[10] use transformational grammar to perform syntactic modifications such as Subject-Aux and Subject-Verb movements. [11] learns the best query reformulations (or paraphrases) for their probabilistic QA system. Here again, the paraphrases are syntactic variations of the original question.

[12], however, do try to learn semantically equivalent reformulations by using the web as a linguistic resource. They start with one single prototypical argument tuple of a given semantic relation and search for potential alternative formulations of the relation, then find new potential argument tuples and iterate this process to progressively validate the candidate formulations.

In these systems and most similar approaches, automatic paraphrases are constructed based on lexical or syntactic similarity. When searching a huge document collection such as the Web, having only syntactic reformulations is acceptable because the collection exhibits a lot of redundancy. However, in a smaller collection, semantic reformulations are necessary.

3   Initial Hand-Crafted Patterns

Our work builds on our current reformulation-based QA system [13, 14], where reformulations were hand-crafted and only relied on named entities for semantic constraints. Given a question, the system needs to identify which answer pattern to look for. It therefore uses two types of patterns: *a question pattern* that defines what the question must look like, and a set of *answer patterns* to be looked for in the document collection. An answer pattern specifies the form of sentences that may contain a possible candidate answer.

For example, the question *Who is George Bush?* will be matched to the question pattern `Who Vsf PERSON?` which will trigger the search for any one of these answer patterns in the document collection:

```
<QT> <Vsf> <ANSWER>
<ANSWER> <Vsf> by <QT>
```

Where <ANSWER> is the candidate answer, <QT> is the question term (i.e. *George Bush*), and <Vsf> is the verb in simple form.

To develop the patterns, we used the 898 questions of TREC 8 & 9 as training set and used the 1000 questions of TREC 10 & 11 for testing. In total, 77 formulation templates were created, covering 90% of the questions of the training set. By coverage, we mean that at least one formulation template is applicable for a question. In the current implementation, both question and answer patterns are based on named-entity tags (e.g. `PERSON`), part-of-speech tags (e.g. `Vsf`), tags on strings (e.g. `QT`, `ANY-SEQUENCE-WORDS`) and specific keywords (e.g. `Who`, `by`). The templates generate 1638 actual answer formulations for the TREC 8 & 9 questions that are covered. So, on average, 2 answer formulations are produced per question.

4   Learning Semantic Answer Patterns

Our goal is to find many sentences from the Web that contain the correct answer and try to generalize them into syntactico-semantic patterns. First, we use a training corpus of question-answer pairs from which we learn how to generalise each type of questions. Each question-answer pair is analysed to extract its answer type, its arguments and its semantic relation. We then search the Web for sentences containing the arguments and the semantic relation and finally, we pass the sentences through a part-of-speech tagger and a noun phrase chunker to generalize them. Let us describe this process in detail.

4.1   The Training Corpus

We start with a training corpus of 1343 question-answer pairs taken from the TREC-8, TREC-9, and TREC-10 collection data [15, 16, 3]. Each question-answer pair is composed of one question and its corresponding answer. For example:

```
Where is the actress, Marion Davies, buried? Hollywood Memorial Park
When did Nixon die? April 22, 1994
Who is the prime minister of Australia? Paul Keating
```

We divided the training corpus according to the question type. We used the classification used in [17] to categorize questions into 7 main classes (what, who, how, where, when, which, why) and 20 subclasses (ex. what-who, who-person, how-many, how-long, ...).

Sentence Retrieval. For each question-answer pair, we define an argument set as the set of terms which a relevant document should contain. For example, consider the question-answer pair:

Q: *Who provides telephone service in Orange County, California?*
A: *Pacific Bell*

Any relevant document to this question-answer pair must contain the terms *"telephone service"*, *"Orange County, California"*, and *"Pacific Bell"*. Therefore to search documents on the Web, we formulate a query made up of all the arguments found in the question-answer pair. The argument set is made up of all the base noun phrases in the question (found using the BaseNP chunker [18]).

In the TREC 8-11 collections, the answers are typically a noun phrase. However, some supporting documents may only contain part of this noun phrase. To increase the recall of document retrieval, we search for a combination of question arguments and each sub-phrase of the answer. We restrict each sub-phrase to contain less than four[1] words and to contain no stop word. Finally, we assign a score to each sub-phrase according to its length (measured in words) relative the the length of the candidate answer. For example, the sub-phrases and the score assigned for the previous question-answer pair are: {`Pacific Bell` 1, `Pacific` $\frac{1}{2}$, `Bell` $\frac{1}{2}$}. The sub-phrase score will be used later to rank the extracted candidate answers from the retrieved sentences.

Once the argument set is built, we construct a query using all the arguments extracted from the question, and the original candidate answer or one of its sub-phrases. We send the query to Google and then we scan the first 500 retrieved documents to identify sentences that contain all of the question arguments and at least one answer argument.

Semantic Filtering of Sentences. We then filter the set of sentences retrieved by Google, according to the validity of the semantic relation that they contain. To do this, we need to find sentences that contain equivalent semantic relations holding between question arguments and the answer. We assume that the semantic relation generally appears as the main verb of the question. For

---

[1] This limit was set arbitrarily.

example, the verb *'provide'* is considered as the semantic relation in the following question-answer pair:

Q: *Who provides telephone service in Orange County, California?*
A: *Pacific Bell*

To check semantic equivalence, we examine all verbs in the selected sentences for a possible semantic equivalence using WordNet. We check if the main verb of the sentence is a synonym, hypernym, or hyponym of the original verb in the question.

At first, we only attempt to validate verbs but if the semantic relation is not found through the verbs, then we also validate nouns and adjectives because the semantic relation may occur as a nominalisation or another syntactic construction. For this, we use the Porter stemmer [19] to find the stem of the adjectives and nouns and then we check if it is equivalent to the stem of the original verb or one of its synonyms, hypernyms, or hyponyms.

For example, with our running example, both these sentences will be retained:

Sentence 1 *Pacific Bell, major provider of telephone service in in Orange County, California ...*
Sentence 2 *Pacific Bell Telephone Services today offers the best long distance rate in Orange County, California.*

Generating the Answer Pattern. Once we have identified a set of semantically equivalent sentences, we try to generalize them into a pattern using both syntactic and semantic features. Each sentence is tagged and syntactically chunked (with [18]) to identify POS tags and base noun phrases. To construct a general form for answer patterns, we replace the noun phrase corresponding to the argument in the answer by the corresponding named-entity tag (e.g <ORGANIZATION>) and the noun phrases corresponding to the question arguments by the tag <QARGx> where x is the argument counter. We replace the other noun phrases that are neither question arguments nor answer arguments with the syntactic tag <NPx>, where x is the noun phrase counter. To achieve a more general form of the answer pattern, all other words except prepositions are removed. For example, the following sentence chunked with NPs:

```
[California's/NNP Baby/NNP Bell,/NNP SBC/NNP Pacific/NNP Bell,/NNP]
/NP still/RB provides/VBZ nearly/RB all/DT of/IN [the/DT local/JJ
phone/NN service/NN]/NP]/NP in/IN [Orange/NNP County,/NNP
California./NNP]/NP
```

will generate the following pattern:
    <ORGANIZATION> <VERB> <QARG1> in <QARG2> | senseOf(provide)

The constraint senseOf(provide) indicates the semantic relation to be found in the candidate sentences through a verb, a noun or an adjective.

In total 98 patterns were created automatically, compared to the 77 hand-made patterns in the original system.

Evaluation. We tested our newly created patterns using the 493 questions-answers from the TREC-11 collection data [20] and our own QA system [13, 14]. The system was evaluated with the original 77 hand-crafted patterns and with the 98 learned ones. Then the answers from both runs were compared. Table 1 shows the result of this comparison based on precision, number of questions with at least one correct answer in the top 5 candidates and mean reciprocal rank (MRR). The evaluation shows an increase in precision of about 16% with the generated patterns (from 0.497 to 0.577). This shows that the semantic constraints have filtered out some bad candidates that the original patterns accepted. The MRR, which takes the order of the candidates into account, increased by 26% from 0.321 to 0.404. In addition, since the patterns are generated automatically, no manual work is now necessary.

Table 1. Results of the generated patterns compared with the original hand-crafted patterns (TREC-11 data)

System	Nb of questions	Nb of questions with a correct answer in the top 5 candidates	Precision of candidate list	MRR
Original System (Hand-Crafted Patterns)	493	86	0.497	0.321
Generated Patterns	493	101	0.577	0.404
Improvement		17%	16%	26%

A further analysis of the results, however, showed that although the semantic constraints imposed by the new patterns filtered out noisy candidates, quite a few bad answers still remained. This is because at least one document contained the semantic relation and the question arguments in the same sentence. Our next goal was then to improve these results by filtering out noisy candidates and re-rank the remaining candidates better.

5 Semantic Candidate Re-ranking

To re-rank the candidates, we used a redundancy technique, but this time, based on the satisfaction of the semantic constraints. That is, we evaluate how many times the candidate answer satisfies the semantic constraint then re-rank the list of candidates according to this proportion. If the semantic relation appears in the same sentence as the question arguments by chance, it should thus be given a lower rank or be removed completely. Let us describe this process in detail.

Sentence Retrieval. We first run the QA system on the Web and retrieve its top 200 answer candidates[2]. This first run can be done with the newly acquired semantic patterns or the original hand-crafted ones. In fact, section 5 presents the results for both methods.

---

[2] This number was set arbitrarily.

For example, with our question *Who provides telephone service in Orange County, California*, the system retrieves the following candidates:

```
Southwestern Bell
Pacific Bell
```

Similarly to our approach for learning reformulations, we build a set of argument tuples composed of the candidate answers and the argument expressed in the question. In order to achieve this task, we decompose the original question into two parts: the main semantic relation expressed (ex. *provides*) and the argument(s) of the relation (ex. *telephone service* and *Orange County, California*). A set of argument tuples is then created from the noun phrases of the question and the candidate found by the QA system. In our example, the following tuples are created:

```
('telephone service','Orange County,California','Southwestern Bell')
('telephone service','Orange County,California','Pacific Bell')
```

Once we have built the set of argument tuples, we search for them in the document collection to identify the possible semantic relations relating them, and make sure that the relation that relates them in the documents is equivalent to what we were originally looking for in the question (senseOf(provide)).

In our experiment, we submitted all the tuples to the Web to find paragraphs that contained these tuples. Then we extracted only the paragraphs where both tuple elements are at a distance of N words[3] or less. We used a context window size of N words between the tuple elements and N words on each side of them in the extracted paragraphs and then examined the words in these context windows for a possible similar semantic relation. This is shown in Figure 1.

Fig. 1. Example of a context window

Examining the Semantic Relation. Finally, we evaluate the relations expressed in the context windows to identify if at least one is semantically equivalent to the original semantic relation expressed in the question. To verify the semantic relation, we use the same procedure as for learning patterns (see section 4.1). We first check if any verb found in any context window is a synonym, a hypernym or a hyponym of the original verb in the question. If no verb has an equivalent semantic relation, we then back-off to validating nouns and adjectives. Any tuple that does not have a similar semantic relation in the question and in the documents is discarded. Thus if a candidate had been selected in the first QA run, but no further evidence is found in the re-ranking phase, it is filtered out.

---

[3] In our experiment, N was set to 5.

Re-Ranking Candidate Answers. The remaining candidates are re-ranked according to the proportion of passages in the collection containing the same relation. For example, when we submitted the tuple (`'telephone service'`, `'Orange County, California'`, `'Pacific Bell'`), we found 110 passages containing the elements of the tuple. Among these, only 24 contained the tuples and the relation `senseOf(provide)` within 5 words of each other. We therefore gave a rank of (24/110) to the candidate `Pacific Bell`. By applying this procedure to all the argument tuples, all candidates can be easily re-ranked.

Evaluation. We evaluated the semantic re-ranking alone again with the TREC-11 data. Table 2 shows the results. Here again, both the precision is higher (from 0.497 to 0.656) and the MRR is higher (from 0.321 to 0.537). A higher MRR means that the candidates found are better ordered in the list so as t0 move the correct answers up in the list. In fact, with the TREC-11 data, 42% of correct answers were moved up in the candidate list by 3.8 positions on average while 4% were actually ranked worse by 5.7 positions and 5% of good answers were lost during the process.

Table 2. Results of the semantic re-ranking (TREC-11 data)

System	Nb of questions	Precision	MRR
Original System	493	0.497	0.321
Semantic Re-Ranking	493	0.656	0.537
Improvement		32%	67%

6   Evaluation of the Combined Approach

Finally, we evaluated the combined approach: automatically acquired semantic patterns (section 4) and semantic re-ranking (section 5). Again, we used the TREC-11 collection for testing. The results are reported in Tables 3 and 4.

As Table 3 shows, the combined approach (A+B) yields a precision that is higher than the original system (0.638 versus 0.497) yet does not rely on manual expertise to hand-craft patterns. The MRR also increased from 0.321 to 0.554. It is therefore more advantageous when doing QA on a different domain or a new language. A further analysis of the results for each type of question (see Table 4) reveals that all question types benefit from this approach.

Table 3. Results of each type of approach (TREC-11 data)

	Nb of questions	Nb of questions with a correct answer in the top 5 candidates	Precision	MRR
Original System	493	86	0.497	0.321
Generated Patterns (A)	493	101	0.577	0.404
Semantic Re-Ranking (B)	493	86	0.656	0.537
Combined (A+B)	493	99	0.638	0.554

Table 4. The results of the combined approach based on question categories (TREC-11 data)

Question Type	Frequency	Original system MRR	Original system Precision	Combined (A+B) MRR	Combined (A+B) Precision
who	52 (10.4%)	0.301	0.571	0.447	0.710
what	266 (53.2%)	0.229	0.500	0.546	0.612
where	39 (7.8%)	0.500	0.533	0.786	0.786
when	71 (14.2%)	0.688	0.687	0.615	0.720
how + adj/adv	53 (10.6%)	0.194	0.277	0.477	0.545
which	12 (2.4%)	0	0	0	0
why	0 (0.0%)	0	0	0	0

It is worth mentioning that the combined approach (A+B) does not seem to do better at precision than re-ranking (B) alone (0.638 versus 0.656). While this difference is not statistically significant, it appears because the new patterns acquire a different set of candidate answers. In addition, since we used the live Web to perform the experiments, each time we run the system, a different set of answers can be retrieved. The semantic re-ranking (B) was evaluated with the list of candidates extracted from the original system; while the combined approach (A+B) was evaluated as a brand new run. This is why (A) found 101 candidates, while (A+B) found 99.

7   Conclusion and Future Work

We presented a method for acquiring reformulation patterns automatically based on both syntactic and semantic features then used these semantic constraints to re-rank the list of candidate answers using redundancy.

The experimental evaluation shows that using new semantic patterns increases precision by 16% and MRR by 26% compared to hand-crafted rules. The semantic re-ranking improves the results more significantly (about 30% for precision and 67% for MRR); while using the two approaches together is comparable to re-ranking alone, but removes the need for human intervention.

As opposed to several other approaches that use the Web for answer redundancy; our approach is less strict as it looks for reinforcement of the semantic relation between the arguments, rather than looking only for lexically similar evidence. In this respect, our approach is much more tolerant and allows us to find more evidence to support answers. On the other hand, as we look for evidence anywhere in a window of words, rather that a strict string match, we are more sensitive to mistakes. We are only interested in finding a word that carries a similar sense without doing a full semantic parse of the sentence. Negations and other modal words may completely change the sense of the sentence. When looking in a very large corpus such as the Web, this may lead to more noise. However, if we perform the QA task on a much smaller corpus, such as in closed-domain QA, looking for semantic equivalences may be more fruitful.

The current implementation only looks at semantic relations holding between two or three arguments. However, it can easily be extended to consider variable-size relations. However, as more constraints are taken into account, the precision of the candidate list is expected to increase, but recall is expected to decrease. A careful evaluation would be necessary to ensure that the approach does not introduce too many constraints and consequently filters out too many candidates.

Another interesting question is to what degree the results are bound to the thresholds we have used. For example, we have arbitrarily taken the first 500 hits from Google to generalise answer patterns. It is not clear if or how changing this value will affect the results.

This work tried to improve the quality of our QA system, but without looking at performance issues. In a real-time QA system, quality is important but if a question takes too long to be analysed, the system is practically unusable. Further work is thus necessary to measure such things as response time and scalability to a real application.

Acknowledgments. This project was financially supported by the Natural Sciences and Engineering Research Council of Canada (NSERC) and Bell University Laboratories (BUL). The authors would like to thank the anonymous referees for their valuable comments.

References

1. Soubbotin, M., Soubbotin, S.: Patterns of potential answer expressions as clues to the right answers. [3] 175–182
2. Brill, E., Lin, J., Banko, M., Dumais, S., Ng, A.: Data-Intensive Question Answering. In: Proceedings of The Tenth Text Retrieval Conference (TREC-X), Gaithersburg, Maryland (2001) 393–400
3. NIST: Proceedings of TREC-10, Gaithersburg, Maryland, NIST (2001)
4. Aceves-Prez, R., Villaseor-Pineda, L., y Gmez, M.M.: Towards a Multilingual QA System based on the Web Data Redundancy. In: Proceedings of the 3rd Atlantic Web Intelligence Conference, AWIC 2005. Lecture Notes in Artificial Intelligence, No. 3528, Lodz, Poland, Springer (2005)
5. Agichtein, E., Lawrence, S., Gravano, L.: Learning search engine specific query transformations for question answering. In: Proceedings of WWW10, Hong Kong (2001) 169–178
6. Agichtein, E., Gravano, L.: Snowball: Extracting Relations from Large Plain-Text Collections. In: Proceedings of the 5th ACM International Conference on Digital Libraries. (2000)
7. Lawrence, S., Giles, C.L.: Context and Page Analysis for Improved Web Search. IEEE Internet Computing **2** (1998) 38–46
8. Ravichandran, D., Hovy, E.: Learning surface text patterns for a question answering system. In: Proceedings of the 40th ACL conference, Philadelphia (2002)
9. Hermjakob, U., Echihabi, A., Marcu, D.: Natural language based reformulation resource and wide exploitation for question answering. [20]
10. Kwok, C.C.T., Etzioni, O., Weld, D.S.: Scaling question answering to the web. In: World Wide Web. (2001) 150–161

11. Radev, D.R., Qi, H., Zheng, Z., Blair-Goldensohn, S., Zhang, Z., Fan, W., Prager, J.M.: Mining the web for answers to natural language questions. In: CIKM. (2001) 143–150
12. Duclaye, F., Yvon, F., Collin, O.: Using the Web as a Linguistic Resource for Learning Reformulations Automatically. In: Proceedings of the Third International Conference on Language Resources and Evaluation (LREC'02), Las Palmas, Spain (2002) 390–396
13. Kosseim, L., Plamondon, L., Guillemette, L.: Answer formulation for question-answering. In: Proceedings of The Sixteenth Canadian Conference on Artificial Intelligence (AI'2003), Halifax, Canada, AI-2003 (2003)
14. Plamondon, L., Lapalme, G., Kosseim, L.: The QUANTUM Question-Answering System at TREC-11. [20]
15. NIST: Proceedings of TREC-8, Gaithersburg, Maryland, NIST (1999)
16. NIST: Proceedings of TREC-9, Gaithersburg, Maryland, NIST (2000)
17. Plamondon, L., Lapalme, G., Kosseim, L.: The QUANTUM Question Answering System. In: Proceedings of The Tenth Text Retrieval Conference (TREC-10), Gaithersburg, Maryland (2001) 157–165
18. Ramshaw, L., Marcus, M.: Text chunking using transformation-based learning. In: Proceedings of the Third ACL Workshop on Very Large Corpora, MIT (1995) 82–94
19. Porter, M.: An algorithm for suffix stripping. Program **14** (1980) 130–137
20. NIST: Proceedings of TREC-11, Gaithersburg, Maryland, NIST (2002)

An Abstract Model of Man-Machine Interaction Based on Concepts from NL Dialog Processing

Helmut Horacek

Fachrichtung Informatik, Universität des Saarlandes,
Postfach 15 11 50, D-66041 Saarbrücken, Germany
horacek@ags.uni-sb.de

Abstract. Developing human-computer (man-machine) interaction system components is time consuming, error-prone, and it is hard to produce high-quality interfaces with good usability. A fundamental reason for this unsatisfactory situation lies in the way the development process is organized, which widely works on a syntactic level in terms of sets of widgets, rather than on a semantic level that captures the task-relevant flow of information. As a step towards the development of human-computer interaction system components on principled grounds, we present an abstract model of human-computer interaction based on concepts borrowed from natural language processing, prominently operational models of human dialogs. Major ingredients of this model are speech act specifications and information state-based update rules capturing the effects of these speech acts, adapted to particularities of human-computer communication. The model is a crucial prerequisite for automatically building man-machine interfaces on the basis of high-level specifications.

1 Introduction

Human-computer interaction components increasingly appear to be a bottleneck in the development of interactive software systems. Building these interfaces tends to be time consuming and, even worse, can be quite error-prone. Moreover, it is very hard to produce high-quality interfaces with good usability, since this process requires not only technical know-how in terms of mastering dedicated specification languages, but also some sort of conceptual imagination, in terms of anticipating effects of the actions of the interface on its users. In our view, a fundamental reason for this unsatisfactory situation lies in the way the development process is organized, which widely works on a syntactic level in terms of sets of widgets, rather than on a semantic level capturing the task-relevant flow of information. Thus, we believe that specifying interfaces on a more abstract level is easier, since it discharges developers from using low-level technicalities.

As a step towards the development of human-computer interaction systems on principled grounds, we present an abstract model of human-computer interaction based on concepts borrowed from natural language processing, prominently operational models of human dialogs. Major ingredients of this model are speech act specifications and information state-based update rules capturing the force

C. Kop et al. (Eds.): NLDB 2006, LNCS 3999, pp. 129–140, 2006.

of these speech acts, adapted to particularities of human-computer communication. The model is a crucial prerequisite for automatically building man-machine interfaces on the basis of high-level specifications.

This paper is organized as follows. First, we expose the motivations for our investigations in more detail. Then we compare and contrast man-machine interaction with human communication, to identify relevant factors for our model. We follow with an overview of operational approaches modeling task-oriented human dialogs. A central section is devoted to the description of our model. Next, we discuss model extensions and steps towards its incorporation in the interface development process. Finally, we illustrate this model by a case study.

2 Motivation

An essential hope to make the development of human-computer interaction components easier and less error-prone lies in using descriptions of components, functionality, and behavior of these interfaces that capture the semantics of the communication involved. An important impact of such a specification technique lies in avoiding the need for technical expertise. This would make the interface development process accessible to the domain experts as well, which is beneficial since these people have a better understanding of the required system functionality and, perhaps, a better sense in judging usability. Another impact of such a specification technique aims at improving the development process of human-computer interaction systems in at least the following factors:

- *Consistency*
  The consistency of a user interface is an important contribution to its quality and also to its usability. In principle, abstract models have the potential of supporting a developer significantly in this respect, when generalities can be expressed at an appropriate place. For example, navigation options can be specified once for some entire application fragment so that these options are percolated systematically to all relevant places.
- *Completeness*
  The development of a human-computer interaction component may turn out to be problematic when applications get larger and taking into account all possible constellations gets increasingly harder for the designer. Consequently, it may easily happen that some situation is forgotten, which is very expensive to uncover by extensive testing.
- *Adaptivity*
  The demand of using an application program under varying devices is best met by a separation into *abstract* and *physical* description levels of an interface, which is typically underlying linguistic approaches [1, 5]. Such a separation essentially corresponds to factoring out device-independent issues from those which at least potentially depend on given presentation facilities.

The systematicity in abstract models is likely to support the design of interfaces in all these factors. In the following, we will put emphasis on this issue.

3 Man-Machine Interaction and Human Communication

There is no doubt that human-computer interaction and natural language communication between humans are fundamentally different. However, if we restrict the analysis to task-oriented dialogs, and if we abstract from the surface form of communication, these two forms of interaction also have a number of things in common. These commonalities concern the coordination of interaction, its incremental development, and the effects of interaction for the underlying goal:

- Well-coordinated forms of interaction are governed by the concept of *turn taking*, that is, both conversants generally make their contributions in an alternating fashion. However, an asynchronous initiative to overcome an occasional impasse is also reasonable in human-computer interaction.
- Exchanging information has the goal of establishing a *common ground*, thereby incrementally accumulating specifications, modifying them and making them more precise, and ultimately achieving fulfilment of the given task.
- Communication is never without context of the previous interaction. Thus, the notion of a *discourse history* plays a central role, so that reference to previous and still relevant interaction contributions can be made.

However, there are a number of discrepancies which are based on the different media and capabilities, which essentially lead to several forms of asymmetry in the role of the conversants and the interaction contributions they make:

- *Processing mode*
  The technical possibilities of the communication channels used govern the processing mode, which is always *sequential* in human communication. In man-machine interaction, a lot can be parallelized, depending on the device used (e.g., asking several items in one shot, as optional requests), and a process can run in the background (e.g., a database search).
- *Initiative*
  In human conversations, the initiative is passed back and forth between the dialog participants, depending on their role. In human-computer interaction, the somehow limited interpretation capabilities of the machine puts it in some sense in the role of the dialog leader – the machine essentially presents a set of options, in a variety of forms, from which the user has to choose.
- *Explicitness and avoidance of ambiguity*
  The bottleneck in the human communication channel is compensated by the exceptional cognitive capabilities of human conversants to keep the amount of information conveyed small: information may be conveyed implicitly, due to the exploitation of expectations and inference capabilities; and superficial ambiguities are tolerated, when they can be resolved on grounds of plausibility. In addition, human communication is enhanced by measures affecting the addressee's attention, including a variety of techniques supporting discourse coherence, and the avoidance of repetitions, which are felt boring by humans. In contrast, when communicating with a machine, specifications are entirely explicit and mostly uniform.

The relevance of *turn taking*, *information provision*, and *discourse history* lends us towards consulting operational models of human dialog, to support the design of human-computer interfaces. Thereby, applying computer-linguistic techniques for describing and organizing human communication can be *simplified*, since consistency is superior to variation in that 'genre', and *extended*, to handle certain parallel or regular repeating forms of information conveyance.

4   Methods for Modeling Natural Language Dialog

Traditionally, human dialogs are modeled by automata, which specify legal continuations for each situation. However, these automata are considered insufficient on principled reasons, since they lack flexibility and do not express underlying generalities. More recent approaches are based on an "information state", which comprises dialog relevant information, such as shared knowledge and subdialog structures. According to Traum and Larsson [9], the purpose of dialog modeling with information states includes the following functionalities:

- updating the dialog context on the basis of interpreted utterances
- providing context-dependent expectations for interpreting observed signals
- interfacing with task/domain processing, to coordinate dialog and non-dialog behavior and reasoning
- deciding what content to express next and when to express it

An information state-based theory of dialog has the following components:

- a description of the *information component*, such as common ground, obligations, commitments, and *formal representations* of these components
- a set of *dialog moves* that will trigger the update of the information state
- a set of *update rules*, that govern the updating of the information state in terms of the system's reaction type and content, as well as the new information state, in terms of added or dropped obligations, common knowledge
- an *update strategy* for deciding which rule(s) to apply at a given point

When it comes down to more details, there are not many standards about the information state, and its use for acting as a system in a conversation needs to be elaborated. Approaches pursued typically address certain text sorts or phenomena such as some classes of speech acts, in abstract semantics. Elaborations have been made for typical situations in information-seeking and task-oriented dialogs, including grounding [8], obligations [4], and negotiation [6].

The most important components of the information state used in several approaches are a structured representation of the discourse history, which is conceived as a `stack` of currently pending moves, a stack of obligations introduced resp. satisfied by discourse contributions, social commitments, and discourse intentions, which cover essential functionalities. In the following, we provide specific interpretations of these concepts.

5 An Abstract Model of Human-Computer Interaction

The fundamental difference in the interaction mode between human and man-machine communication manifests itself in the asymmetry of communicative means and in the composed discourse contributions made by the system, typically consisting of a number of options. In order to meet the intended functionality of interaction in such a setting, we use the following central concepts:

- *Discourse objects*
  represent abstractions of domain objects, in terms of partial descriptions of the properties of domain objects, according to a structured representation.
- *System functionalities*
  represent purely functional views of subcomponents of the application system such that these functionalities are accessible by appropriate procedures.
- *Communicative acts*
  constitute information transfer between system and user, with a specific perspective, distinguished according to categories of the communicative acts.
- *Discourse history*
  constitutes a representation of the active part of interaction, to enable references to discourse objects and reasoning about communicative acts.

Discourse objects are the basic elements about which the communication evolves. They play the role of binding several pieces of information that are possibly communicated at different times. Hence, these objects are incrementally made more precise over the course of communication, also including corrections, representing the *common ground* of the overall interaction, so that they eventually meet the access conditions of some system functionalities. In addition, accurate domain object representations comprise restrictions on value ranges for their attributes, as well as constraints between values belonging to diverse attributes or even domain objects. The restrictions and constraints have an impact on the communication about discourse objects. More formally, these objects are conceived as a conjunction of predicates that are compatible with domain object definitions, comprising a category $cat(x)$ and properties $prop_i(x, y_i)$ for some object x with properties $prop_i$ and values y_i. In addition to these structural components, there are constraints among the values of domain objects which are subject to a selective verification in the course of the communication process. Some of these constraints may be expressed statically as part of the domain ontology, while others may be encapsulated in system functionalities.

The system functionalities are conceived as a set of actions performed by the application system, reduced to their input/output behavior. The input is defined in terms of a set of discourse objects. The output expresses changes imposed on discourse objects or creation of new ones, accompanied by the state of the action performed, which may be either an *accept* or a *reject*, including an optional *inform* act with details about this state. We require the set of available system functionalities to be organized, in terms of dependency relations holding among them. These dependencies are evaluated, to assess the state of task accomplishment. Specifically, the successful accomplishment of a system functionality – or

Table 1. Communicative acts and categories of possible reactions

system act	user response	user act	system response
request(information)	answer	answer	accept, reject+inform
request(action)	confirm	confirm	implicit acknowledgement
offer(information)	accept(=ask for it)	ask for it	composition of acts
offer(action)	accept(=request it)	request it	composition of acts, reject+inform

a set of system functionalities with each member being dependent on another one – on which no others are dependent is conceived as a *task completion*, which initiates a pop operation on the discourse history stack. This way, the system functionalities in some sense represent the intentional structure of Grosz and Sidner's discourse model [3], which essentially is the task structure underlying a given conversation. Finally, system functionalities attribute states to the discourse objects involved, indicating their local or global use. The impact of this categorization is that discourse objects attributed with global state survive task completion, for subsequent reuse. All these specifications are consulted for updating the state of the discourse and for constructing a system response.

Due to the asymmetry of the roles of the conversants in human-computer interaction, communicative acts generally fall into two clusters, comprising acts that the user can perform, and acts that the system can perform, respectively. User acts comprise *answers* – to requests for information, *confirms*, as a way of explicitly expressing agreement to an indicated issue, and *accepts* of offers of some sorts, including offers of information provision, thus making a selection, and offers of actions, thus requesting the activation of some system functionality. System acts comprise *requests*, including *asking* for information, and *offers* to provide some information resp. to perform some action, *requesting* an action, typically an explicit confirmation, and *accepts*, *rejects*, and *informs*, as responses to user requests made via an accept, in dependency of the results obtained by the system functionalities addressed. These communicative acts are illustrated in Table 1, together with the appropriate reaction on behalf of the other conversant. In more formal terms, communicative acts comprise a category of the act performed, a source and an addressee (here: system to user or vice-versa), and a content specification. Communicative acts may be subcategorized according to the category of their content, such as *request* for *information* and for an *action*.

The discourse history contains a stack of communicative acts performed, including *obligations*, that is, expectations imposed on the addressee of a communicative act, and *commitments*, that is, the converse impact, affecting the producer of a communicative act. The discourse history is incrementally updated when (1) a communicative act is performed by the system, (2) a communicative act is performed by the user, or (3) a system reaction is determined. New states are pushed on the stack, unless a rule specifies a pop action. Since there is exactly one update rule for each situation, the update strategy is deterministic. The update rules are illustrated in Table 2. They comprise rules for making explicit the force imposed by a communicative act, and rules for selecting a system response.

Table 2. Update rules operating on the discourse history

Rule trigger	Force of the rule (and some proconditions)
(1a) $Ask(s, u, x)$	introduces a user obligation to answer eventually
(1b) $Answer(u, s, x)$	requires an obligation for x, adds new information to the common ground, and propagates constraints
(1a) $Request(s, u, Perform(u, x))$	introduces a user obligation to perform act x
(1b) $Confirm(u, Perform(u, x))$	requires an obligation to perform act x, adds this information to the common ground and retracts the associated obligation
(1a) $Offer(s, u, x)$	introduces a user obligation to accept x eventually and a system commitment to satisfy the offer – x is known information or a system functionality
(1b) $Accept(u, x)$	requires an active user obligation regarding an offer, drops the obligation and activates x
(1c) $Accept(s, x)$	retracts all user obligations within the scope of x, pops previous user communicative act from the stack, and preceeding system communicative act, unless corrections of specifications are permitted
(1c) $Reject(s, x)$	retracts preceeding common ground update, pops previous user communicative act from the stack
(1c) $Inform(s, u, x)$	effects are not modeled; used for error messages
(2) $Check - Inform(s, x)$	activated by an answer by the user; if check is successful, choose *Accept* otherwise *Reject*
(2) $Perform - Action(s, x)$	tries to perform action x, given common ground if check is unsuccessful, choose *Reject* and *Inform* otherwise *Accept*, retract system commitment and all user obligations related with the last offer; if a system functionality and those depending on it are completed, pop related interactions from the stack

The latter include *Check-Inform*, which verifies the validity of an answer, and *Perform-Action*, which tries to perform the action requested, (labeled by (2) in Table 2). Communicative acts are subcategorized into system requests and offers (1a), user reactions (1b), and system reactions to these (1c).

The effect of some update rules deviates from typical human conversations:

– ask and offer may be implicitly rejected by the user, through accepting some other offer, which is inconceivable in human conversations (see the retraction of user obligation by $Accept(s, x)$ in Table 2)
– an assertion by the user is made indirectly, through confirming a system request which precisely specifies the content of this assertion (see the second pair of system-user communicative acts in Table 2)
– issues may be reintroduced as options to be overwritten when some information provision is rejected, instead of carrying out a local subdialog (see the option associated with $Accept(s, x)$ in Table 2)

6   Embedding of the Model and Extensions

The model described in the previous section represents an abstract view on the basic functionality of human-computer interaction. Still, the model has a number of limitations and it covers only one perspective in the task of supporting the development of an interaction component. In the following, we briefly discuss extensions of the model, in terms of coverage and additional perspectives:

1. the concretization of the interface, complementing the abstract view
2. the degrees of expressive variety and coverage
3. issues in the dynamics involved in developing an interface component

The abstract view of communication, expressed in terms of communicative acts and their purely logical composition, is completely neutral concerning their physical realization. Especially larger compositions of communicative acts made by the system, which are very typical for man-machine interaction, provide no clues for a suitable realization, apart from the hierarchical dependencies of the referred domain objects and their properties. Hence, it is necessary to capture not only the functionality *across* several communication contributions, which the abstract model is aiming at, but also the functions of each component *within* a single, composed interaction contribution. This task can be accomplished by applying a functional theory to discourse, such as Rhetorical Structure Theory (RST) [7]. RST-based representations conceive composed interaction contributions as rhetorical structure trees, where the role of each component is expressed by a relation in which it stands to the remaining part of the interaction contribution. The underlying structure, as well as the semantics of the relations involved, provide useful indications for organizing the realization of the overall interaction contribution, that is, for rendering the manifestations of each communicative act on a computer screen. For example, contrastive items should be placed either besides each other, or one above resp. below the other, whereas offers leading to background information and related material should be placed in peripheral positions on the screen. Such correspondences between functional and physical relations have been elaborated in several approaches aiming at an automated document design [1], including adaptivity to various devices [5].

Another aspect of model extensions concerns the repertoire of interaction categories, both in terms of variety and regularities of interaction patterns. A simple example for a communicative act not yet considered by our model would be a *warning* as a specialization of an *inform* act, which would also have impact on the rendering task – making the appearance of this communicative act quite salient. A more involved example concerns the offer to correct information given within already answered questions, which may be effective if the question belongs to a composed system interaction, which is still incompletely addressed by the user. Yet another extension is the adequate treatment of expensive system functionalities – in the basic form of the model, the proper interaction is suspended until the system component referred produces its result. The resulting waiting time may sometimes be unavoidable, such as for a credit card information check or other kind of transaction-related verification processes. However, when satisfying requests such as database queries, elaborating the answer to such a query may be done asynchronously, so that the main interaction can continue. In abstract terms, this communicative situation can be treated as a multi-party communication, where the asynchronous process jumps in again when considered appropriate for reporting its result or for invoking further specification requests. Another advanced communicative situation, which is typical for human-computer interaction, is the regularity underlying sequences of communicative acts, which are entirely predictable in terms of their content, even though these sequences are rarely activated in their full length. Such regularities comprise long lists of items, which are partitioned into sublists each exposing a sequence of communicative acts, or some regular pattern, as in guided tours. Moreover, it may prove beneficial to capture regularities across situations, such as navigating to a specific communicative state, for example the initial state. Describing the generalities underlying such interaction patterns in a compact and operational form was never a topic in theories to human communication – hence, elaborating these issues may be a fruitful source for creative findings.

Finally, the interface development process needs to be organized around the components of the abstract model of communication and its concrete counterparts. This process can be supported in a number of ways:

– *Overview of the state of specifications made*
  A basic support is the inspection of the course of development pursued, which is useful in selective forms, including reference lists for domain object attributes, comparisons across composed communicative acts, and lists of discourse expectations, in terms of obligations at each interaction state.
– *Listing options*
  One useful support lies in providing evidence about available options for expanding specifications, including references to relevant portions of domain representations and applicable system functionalities.
– *Checking completeness*
  A valuable service lies in examining the state of definitions, in terms of issues still to be accomplished: compositions of the system's communicative acts to fulfil its own commitments, covering all obligations imposed by the user's possible reactions, or by the results of system component functionalities.

An important factor in the interface development lies in the dependency between available system functionalities and composed communicative acts. Specifically, if system funcionalities are broken down into subfunctionalities, more local and early checks are possible, which is not the case otherwise. For example, if system functionalities are available to check the validity of a single or a pair of items embedded in a composed interaction, such checks can be performed locally, and invalid specifications can be refused without requiring specifications of the other items involved in the composed interaction. Hence, if the design of the application system and the design of its interface are pursued in parallel, a desired behavior on the side of the interface may have an impact on the design of the application system so that exhibiting this behavior is possible.

7   A Case Study – Flight Booking

In this section, we illustrate the application of our model by an example scenario – getting a flight booked, as specified and selected by the user, with the embedded purpose of getting information about available flights. We assume a domain model (see the upper part of Figure 1), and a set of system functionalities:

- *Checking flight connections*
  This procedure takes two airports as input and verifies with the database whether or not a flight connection between them exists.
- *Picking available flights*
  This procedure takes a set of flight specifications as input, that is, partial instantiations of flight objects, and returns a list of still available flights satisfying the specifications given, if existing. In addition, there are a number of conditions that these specifications must fulfil, such as specification of airports, otherwise the procedure is not invoked.
- *Checking personal data and performing flight booking*
  This procedure takes the selected flight and the booking-relevant user data as input (name and credit card information), as well as the price of the flight selected and tries to deduct this amount from the user's account and, if all this is successful, to perform the transaction specified.

In order to achieve the intended purpose, the agents involved have several communicative acts at their disposal, according to the following categories:

- *Ask(information)* – the system and *Answer(information)* – the user
  These categories apply to a number of domain specifications, including the airports, dates, and return option for the flight itself, and name and credit card information on the side of the personal data.
- *Accept(information)* and *Reject(information)* – the system
  These categories apply to the answers provided by the user.
- *Offer(information resp. action)* – the system and *Accept(offer)* – the user
  These categories apply to a three kinds of situations: (1) the request for flight information, (2) the choice of a flight, and (3) the request for booking.
- *Ask(perform)* – the system and *Confirm(perform)* – the user
  These categories apply to the agreement to the purchase action, which is typically required in an explicit form due to legal reasons.

These communicative acts are invoked in compositions as given in the overview in the middle part of Figure 1, including connections with possible interaction. A sequence of interactions and the top part of the stack of the dialog history are shown in the lower part of that Figure. In this example, the system functionality *Checking personal data and performing flight booking* is dependent on the system functionality *Picking available flights*, which determines the price. Hence, accomplishing the latter does not lead to a pop operation on the discourse history stack, while accomplishing the former does so. Moreover, the availability of the system functionality *Check flight connections* enables a local information check on the user's airport specifications without the need to search the flight database, that is, addressing the system functionality *Picking available flights*.

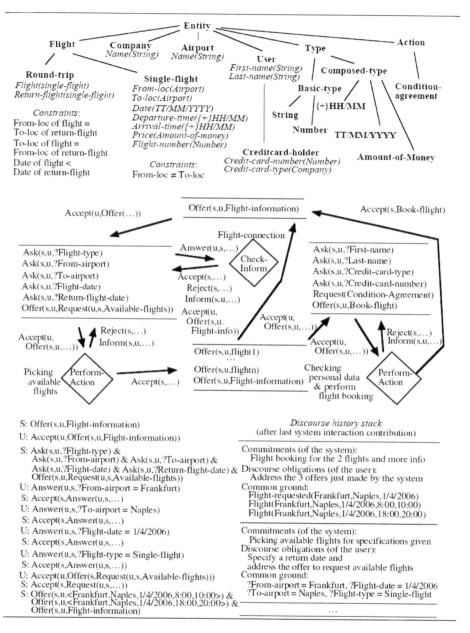

Fig. 1. Excerpt of the domain ontology for flight booking (top), an overview of the communication, including reference to system functionalities (in diamonds) (middle), and a dialog fragment (left bottom) and its associated dialog history stack (right bottom)

8   Conclusion

In this paper, we have elaborated an abstract model of human-computer interaction based on concepts borrowed from natural language dialog processing. We have adapted speech act specifications and information state-based update rules capturing the force of these speech acts, to particularities of human-computer communication, accommodating some basic interaction categories. Essentially, our model consists of an interplay between interpretations of communicative acts and accesses to system functionalities to determine system reactions, in dependency of the pieces of information established as common ground.

The model constitutes a step towards the development of human-computer interaction system components on principled grounds, going beyond the usual task models, in terms of elaborating various factors of interaction. The model serves as a crucial prerequisite for automatically building man-machine interfaces on the basis of high-level specifications, advancing over a similarly motivated approach [2] in terms of the human-orientedness in specifying the interaction. An essential hope in this approach is that the interface developer is discharged from technicalities and supported by conceptual information, so that he is in a good position to take usability issues into account in the development process.

References

1. Bateman John and Joerg Kleinz and Thomas Kamps and Klaus Reichenberger. Towards Constructive Text, Diagram, and Layout Generation for Information Presentation, *Computational Linguistics*, 27(3), pp. 409-449, 2001.
2. Jürgen Falb and Roman Popp and Thomas Röck and Helmut Jelinek and Edin Arnautovic and Hermann Kaindl. Using Communicative Acts in High-Level Specifications of User Interfaces for their Automated Synthesis. *Proceedings 20th IEEE/ACM International Conference on Automated Software Engineering (ASE'05)* (tool demo paper), ACM Press, pp. 429–430, 2005.
3. Barbara J. Grosz and Candace L. Sidner. Attention, intention, and the structure of discourse. *Computational Linguistics*, 12(3), pp. 175–204, 1986.
4. Jörn Kreutel and Colin Matheson. Incremental Information State Updates in an Obligation-Driven Dialogue Model. L. J. of the IGPL, 11(4), pp. 485–511, 2003.
5. A. Lampert and Cecile Paris. Information assembly for adaptive display. In the Proceedings of 2004 Australasian Language Technology Workshop (ALTW2004); Macquarie University. CD ROM. December 8th, 2004.
6. Staffan Larsson. Issue-Based Dialogue Management. PhD thesis, Gothemburg University, 2002.
7. Bill Mann and Sandra Thompson. Rhetorical Structure Theory: Toward a functional theory of text organization. *Text*, 8(3), pp. 243–281, 1988.
8. Colin Matheson, Massimo Poesio, and David Traum. Modelling Grounding and Discourse Obligations Using Update Rules. *Proceedings of the 1st Annual Meeting of the North American Association for Computational Linguistics (NAACL2000)*, 2000.
9. David Traum and Staffan Larsson. The Information State Approach to Dialogue Management. *Current and New Directions in Discourse and Dialogue*. Kluwer, 2003.

The PHASAR Search Engine

Cornelis H.A. Koster, Olaf Seibert, and Marc Seutter

Radboud University Nijmegen, Department of Computer Science
Postbus 9102, 6500 HC Nijmegen, The Netherlands

Abstract. This article describes the rationale behind the PHASAR system (Phrase-based Accurate Search And Retrieval), a professional Information Retrieval and Text Mining system under development for the collection of information about metabolites from the biological literature. The system is generic in nature and applicable (given suitable linguistic resources and thesauri) to many other forms of professional search. Instead of keywords, the PHASAR search engine uses Dependency Triples as terms. Both the documents and the queries are parsed, transduced to Dependency Triples and lemmatized. Queries consist of a set of Dependency Triples, whose elements may be generalized or specialized in order to achieve the desired precision and recall. In order to help in interactive exploration, the search process is supported by document frequency information from the index, both for terms from the query and for terms from the thesaurus.

The professional retrieval process as found e.g. in Bio-Informatics can be distinguished into two phases, viz. Search and Analysis. The *search* phase is needed to find the relevant documents (achieving recall), the *analysis* phase for identifying the relevant information (achieving precision). Analysis can be performed visually and manually, partly automatically and partly interactively.

Both processes are complicated by the fact that the searcher has to guess what words will be used in the documents to express the relevant facts about the topic of interest. For the search process, many online databases are available, but plowing through the many hits provided by a word-based search system is hard work. Analysis is a heuristic process, demanding all the searcher's knowledge, experience and skills, for which presently only primitive keyword- or pattern-based support is available. The searcher may become very skilled in search and analysis, but the process is only partially automated and when searching for another topic the whole manual process must be repeated.

In this paper we describe the ideas behind a novel search engine based on linguistically derived phrases, designed to support the search and analysis processes involved in retrieving information from the Biomedical literature. In section 1 we describe our approach to searching, which combines linguistic techniques with Information Retrieval. In section 2 we illustrate a possible way-of-working by means of an example. In section 3 we briefly describe the status of the implementation of PHASAR and the Medline/P collection used in the project. Finally, in section 4 we reflect on what has been achieved and what challenges are still ahead.

C. Kop et al. (Eds.): NLDB 2006, LNCS 3999, pp. 141–152, 2006.

1   The PHASAR Approach

Many years of TREC challenges and evaluations have produced diminishing improvements in the precision and recall from best-practice query-based retrieval systems. In particular, the use of phrases in query-based retrieval has never led to the hoped-for breakthrough in accuracy. Due to the ubiquity of word-based Search Engines like Lycos and Google, searchers have come to consider a combination of a few words as a natural and precise way to formulate a query, and they have learnt to cope with the deluge of hits that the query may cause by looking at only a few of them.

In designing the PHASAR system, we tried to "rethink" the support of phrase-based search and retrieval and the corresponding way-of-working.

1.1   Professional Search

Professional search may be distinguished from what could be termed *incidental search* by the following characteristics:

1. the search is performed by professionals, in their own area of competence
2. it is worth investing some (expensive) time and effort
3. the search is over a very large collection of documents, including many which may be relevant
4. the information need is clear but complex, the user can recognize relevant answers
5. the information need may have to be answered by gathering (passages from) many documents
6. repetitions of the search process with small modifications in the query are routine.

Contrast this with incidental search, which may have a vicarious and opportunistic character; where the searcher may easily be side-tracked; where out of a million hits only the first ten are ever considered; where the main problem is in formulating the information need, which can often be answered by a single document.

1.2   From Specifying the Question to Specifying the Answer

In the traditional view of Information Retrieval, the searcher has to formulate his information need, and the task of the search algorithm is to find those documents (best) answering the information need. Taking this approach too literally may lead to a quest for complete, consistent and formal specifications of the information need, which are not only hard to construct but for which also no effective search algorithm exists short of a reasoning agent with a complete model of the world. This works well only for severely limited application areas (no world model needed) and for limited query formalisms (where a weak but efficient inference mechanism suffices, like the Vector Space Model). We take a different point of view: The searcher has to indicate what formulations in the documents are expected to be relevant to his information need. He has to guess what the answers will look like, rather than the question (a form of query-by-example).

1.3 Dependency Triples as Terms

The Information Retrieval community has for a long time had high expectations of the use of phrases as index terms instead of keywords, but in practice the benefits were found hard to realize (see [Strzalkowski, 1999], in particular [Sparck Jones, 1999]). Rather than single words, word pairs [Fagan, 1988, Strzalkowski, 1995] or sequences of words (word n-grams; chunks; complete noun phrases) we shall use *dependency triples* as terms in the document representation and the search process. A dependency triple (DT) is a pair of (lemmatized) words (the *head* and the *modifier*) occurring in the document in a certain *relation*, which we denote by [head RELATION modifier].

Dependency triples (aka *dependency relations*) have already been used successfully in Question Answering [Bouma et al, 2005, Cui et al, 2005] for the precise matching of answers from a database to questions, but we propose to use DT's directly in a search interface querying large collections of free text without special preprocessing. They are closely related to the Index Expressions of [Grootjen and van der Weide, 2004].

The following table illustrates the major syntactic dependency relations.

relation	examples
subject relation	[penicillin SUBJ reduce]
	[it SUBJ improve]
object relation	[cause OBJ reduction]
	[interrupt OBJ it]
attributive relation	[cancer ATTR lung]
	[cancer ATTR alveolar]
preposition relation (various prepositions)	[interact WITH medium]
	[interaction WITH medium]
	[relative TO period]

In order to obtain this representation, both documents and queries are syntactically analyzed (including NER and robust lexicalization) and transduced to dependency trees that are then unnested to dependency triples in which all word forms are lemmatized. In the transduction, all elements of the text that do not contribute to its *aboutness* (see [Bruza and Huibers, 1996, Arampatzis et al., 2000]) are elided: determiners, quantifiers, auxiliary verbs.

A query matches any document that contains *all of the words and triples derived from the query*. Besides this *by document* matching, it is also possible to invoke stricter matching rules, matching by passage, sentence or phrase, which raise precision and reduce recall. The most precise matching strategy, phrase matching, amounts to the matching of *factoids*, taking the non-composed phrases of the documents as factoids.

1.4 Linguistic Normalization

Natural language admits great variability in the expression of a given piece of information. A writer or speaker hates to use the same formulation every time when referring to some person, object or fact, and will go out of his way to bring variation to his formulations. This holds not only in literature, but also for journalistic and even for scientific texts. This linguistic variability has to be countered in some way in full-text retrieval.

Rather than letting the searcher predict all possible variations in the form of the answer, we systematically apply normalizations to reduce the linguistic variation in both the documents and the queries:

- morphological normalization by lemmatization
- syntactical normalizations, e.g. standardizing the word-order and transforming passive formulations into active ones
- lexico-semantical normalization using multiple thesauri
- elimination of all elements from the text that do not contribute to the aboutness, such as time, degree and modality.

Ideally, *all phrases that are equivalent formulations of the same factoid should be conflated to one same phrase.*

1.5 The Fruit Machine Model

Although our intended users are professionals, they are in most cases not professional linguists. The user interface should therefore be such that they are not burdened with arcane linguistic notions or notations. On the other hand, they can be expected to have a general understanding of basic linguistic notions, like the structure and function of subject, verb, object and complements in a sentence.

In the PHASAR system, a query is in its most extensive form a basic sentence in natural language, in English an SVOC sentence. The user interface expects any or all of its four elements (subject, verb, object and eventual complement) in a box of its own on the screen, resulting in a display of four boxes that looks like a *fruit machine*, a Las Vegas slot machine.[1]

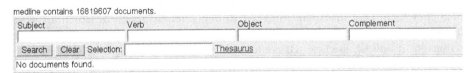

The query can be a word, a collocation, a phrase or a sentence, that has to be distributed appropriately over the four boxes. Any box can be left blank, and at most one box (under certain restrictions) may contain a question mark (the *joker*, see later).

---

[1] All screen shots presented here are taken from the prototype version 0.8 of the PHASAR system.

The query in the fruit machine can be modified by modifying its elements. Furthermore, there are explicit mechanisms to generalize or specialize the query (next sections). The user can return to a previous query by using the backward and forward buttons on the browser.

1.6   Generalizing the Query

Although phrases are highly precise indexing terms, they also have a very low probability of occurrence, and therefore a low recall – the problem of *sparseness*. In order to increase recall when the query is too restrictive, the query can be generalized by replacing some of its elements by a more general one:

- a list of terms joined by |
- a semantic type (SEM-type) taken from one of the thesauri (see 1.9), standing for all terms belonging to that type.

In this way, queries may be generalized from individual phrases to phrase patterns, which may match many different phrases in the documents. Furthermore, queries can be combined disjunctively in a profile (see 1.10) to raise recall, or conjunctively to raise precision.

1.7   Specializing the Query

In order to raise precision when there are too many irrelevant hits, the query can be specialized by specializing some of its elements. A phrase can be made as precise as you wish. Phrases consist of words, joined together in linguistically meaningful ways to achieve more precision. Each word in a phrase helps to disambiguate the others.

- adding another element, e.g. a preposition phrase as complement, or
- specializing an element, e.g. by adding a modifier to a noun (an adjective or another noun), and adverb to a verb.

This specialization process is supported by information from the index.

1.8   Support from the Index

The searcher has to know what is actually said in the documents, and how often, in order to get nearer to his answer. It is inefficient to get this information by browsing the documents, which takes too much time and effort. Therefore this information must be presented at a higher level of aggregation. Quantitative information about the documents is gathered by indexing after parsing, producing an index of words (lemmatized word forms) and DT's giving for each element the dependency relations in which it occurs in the text. As an example, the DT index of Medline for 'aspirin' starts with

triples with "aspirin" as head		triples with "aspirin" as modifier	
829	[aspirin SUBJ induce]	2065	[effect OF aspirin]
778	[aspirin SUBJ inhibit]	951	[dose OF aspirin]
532	[aspirin SUBJ reduce]	916	[therapy ATTR aspirin]
522	[aspirin SUBJ have]	781	[administration OF aspirin]
327	[aspirin PRED effective]	679	[treatment ATTR aspirin]
327	[aspirin SUBJ prevent]	453	[combination OF aspirin]
232	[aspirin SUBJ cause]	424	[kg OF aspirin]
216	[aspirin SUBJ treat]	383	[ingestion OF aspirin]
197	[aspirin SUBJ decrease]	250	[trial OF aspirin]
187	[aspirin SUBJ increase]	234	[acetylsalicylic_acid PRED aspirin]
158	[aspirin SUBJ produce]	225	[administer OBJ aspirin]

1.9   Support from Thesauri

An important mechanism for generalizing from single words to collections of words is furnished by domain-specific thesauri providing synonyms and hypernyms. We see such a thesaurus purely as a device for imposing a hierarchical *categorization* of semantical types (SEM-types) on the words occurring in the documents. Therefore we need shallow and broad hierarchies whose categories are of obvious importance to a certain domain, rather than deep and detailed semantical categorizations. Our use of thesauri is syntactical (what can be written?) rather than semantical (what does it mean?). Looking up the word 'aspirin' in a simplified UMLS thesaurus (reduced to four levels) provides the following information:

```
1. [109] aspirin [84], asa [25],
       * ORGANIC-CHEMICAL: [185638] go
          o CHEMICALS-&-DRUGS: [766632] go
             + ROOT: [2422116] go
2. [109] aspirin [84], asa [25],
       * PHARMACOLOGIC-SUBSTANCE: [249944] go
          o CHEMICALS-&-DRUGS: [766632] go
             + ROOT: [2422116] go
```

The numbers given in square brackets indicate how many Medline records contain a word with this SEM-type. On the basis of this combined qualitative and quantitative information, the searcher may choose to generalize the word 'aspirin' to one of the SEM-types 'ORGANIC-CHEMICAL:' or 'PHARMACOLOGIC-SUBSTANCE:'; or he may click on 'go' to inspect the thesaurus entry for one of the hypernyms of 'aspirin'.

The professional user knows the semantic ontology of his domain and need not be reminded of it, but he needs a way to specify easily whether the subject or object of his verb is a DRUG:, ILLNESS:, GENE:, PATHOGEN: or PERSON:. In this light, the reduced UMLS thesaurus is not particularly helpful.

A word or collocation may occur more than once in a thesaurus, or in multiple thesauri. We do not distinguish word senses, but we exploit the fact that the head of a triple tends to disambiguate the modifier and vice versa. We shall also need domain-dependent thesauri of verbs (CURE:, CAUSE:, etc.).

1.10   From Queries to Profiles

Experiences in Automatic Document Classification show that a profile, in the sense of a *weighted collection of terms* can give surprisingly high precision and recall. In fact, many successful classification techniques (for an overview see [Sebastiani, 2002]) result in a linear classifier, which is just such a weighted collection of terms. A profile of words can be learned automatically (provided enough training examples are available) but a profile of linguistically moti- vated search patterns can also be built by hand, (witness the work of Riloff, e.g. [Furnkranz et al, 1998, Riloff and Lorenzen, 1999]), which is the case in PHASAR.

As a side effect of the search process, we will allow the user to build a com- plex combination of search patterns, a *profile*, in which search patterns may be combined by *discourse operators*: not only logical operators like AND, OR and NOT but also textual operators like BEFORE and more subtle ones that will have to be the subject of further research. Furthermore we shall investigate how to use information from the browsing activities to assign weights to the patterns, so that we can impose a ranking on hits for browsing.

1.11   Browsing

Browsing long documents to inspect relevant phrases is tedious and time consum- ing. That is why some search machines supply each search result with one or two sentences extracted from the document, which helps greatly in determining its relevance. This problem also motivates much present research on summarization techniques and passage retrieval.

In the PHASAR browser, all terms from the query are weakly highlighted in the document, and sentences that match the complete query are strongly highlighted. Furthermore, the unit of viewing can be chosen by the user, be- ing either the whole document or only the passages or sentences matching the query. Highlighting and condensed viewing significantly improve the efficiency of browsing.

2   An Example Search

PHASAR is intended for professional search in a wide sense. Since it differs greatly from traditional search engines, a whole new way-of-working will have to be found, which must still be shaped in trial applications, along with its support tools. In this section we illustrate a proposed way-of-working by means of an example which was contrived to explain the interface rather than its application.

Assume that some doctor or journalist wishes to investigate the knowledge expressed in Medline abstracts about cancer, its causes and effects. He can start the search by supplying either a (noun)phrase or a sentence. For the heck of it he types 'aspirin causes cancer' into the fruit machine and hits the search button.

medline contains 16819607 documents.

Subject	Verb	Object	Complement
aspirin	causes	cancer	

Search | Clear | Selection: | | Thesaurus

[N:aspirin]	[V:cause]	[N:cancer]	[N:aspirin,V:cause]	[V:cause,N:cancer]
20452	755656	441958	232	1365

No documents found.

Of course there are zero hits. Nobody in his right mind would write something like that in a Medline abstract. It is an example of a *hyper-precise query*. But it will serve to start the search.

The fruit machine is presented showing this sentence, with under it the elements of the query, each with its document frequency in the collection. Clicking on one of the elements under the fruit machine will cause the relevant part of the pair indices to be shown, as was done for 'aspirin' in 1.8.

The user replaces the word 'aspirin' by a more likely choice, namely 'solvents'.

medline contains 16819607 documents.

Subject	Verb	Object	Complement
solvents	cause	cancer	

Search | Clear | Selection: | | Thesaurus

[N:solvent]	[V:cause]	[N:cancer]	[N:solvent,V:cause]	[V:cause,N:cancer]
26675	755656	441958	138	1365

No documents found.

Again no hits are obtained, although the elements of the query all appear in the Medline collection. He now realizes that he is not so much interested in general remarks containing the word 'solvent' but in the names of all solvents that are said in Medline to cause cancer. The term 'solvent' must be generalized to all terms in the semantic category of solvents, which unfortunately does not occur in the UMLS thesaurus.

Going on another tack, the searcher decides to find out what specific substances are said in Medline to cause cancer. He replaces the word 'solvents' in the subject field of the fruit machine by a *joker* (in the form of a question mark). Pressing the search-button gets him a list of the left-relations of the verb 'cause' occurring in the hits of the query 'causes cancer' (this sounds quite complicated but is actually quite natural: The query determines the subset of documents to look in, and the joker in the subject box indicates that left-relations of the verb are wanted). Through another use of the joker it is possible to obtain the right-relations of the object 'cancer'. The lists are shown together in the following table:

78	[it SUBJ cause OBJ cancer]	104	[cause OBJ cancer ATTR cervical]
72	[mutation SUBJ cause OBJ cancer]	74	[cause OBJ cancer ATTR liver]
63	[exposure SUBJ cause OBJ cancer]	54	[cause OBJ cancer ATTR bladder]
45	[infection SUBJ cause OBJ cancer]	42	[cause OBJ cancer ATTR prostate]
34	[smoking SUBJ cause OBJ cancer]	30	[cause OBJ cancer ATTR colorectal]
32	[agent SUBJ cause OBJ cancer]	25	[cause OBJ cancer OF tract]
29	[factor SUBJ cause OBJ cancer]	24	[cause OBJ cancer ATTR certain]
26	[gene SUBJ cause OBJ cancer]	24	[cause OBJ cancer ATTR stomach]
26	[virus SUBJ cause OBJ cancer]	21	[cause OBJ cancer SUBJ occur]
24	[type SUBJ cause OBJ cancer]	18	[cause OBJ cancer ATTR cervix]
21	[hpv SUBJ cause OBJ cancer]	16	[cause OBJ cancer ATTR breast]
19	[they SUBJ cause OBJ cancer]	15	[cause OBJ cancer ATTR kidney]

In the left list, the personal pronouns in first and last line are place holders for anaphora, the others are reasonable (although not very novel) causes of cancer. Maybe lower down the list is more surprising. The right list mainly enumerates forms of cancer. The searcher can again replace the joker by a word (or more generally a list of terms) and maybe try another joker to find the most promising directions for further specialization.

Returning to the query 'aspirin causes cancer', the searcher would at this point like to generalize the verb form 'causes' to a wider class of verb forms 'CAUSES:' but we do not as yet dispose of a suitable thesaurus of verbs to make this generalization. That is future work.

The searcher modifies the query into 'cancer causes pain' and submits it. This time he gets some hits:

medline contains 16819607 documents.

Subject	Verb	Object	Complement
cancer	causes	pain	

Search   Clear   Selection: _____   Thesaurus

[N:cancer]	[V:cause]	[N:pain]	[N:cancer,V:cause]	[V:cause,N:pain]
441958	755656	187382	928	3277

40 documents found.
First document   Next document   Previous document   Random document

Browsing through the documents found, he arrives at the following document, which is shown with deep highlighting for the sentence matched and, with less color difference, for the other matches with words from the query. Notice the effect of the passive-to-active normalization.

Abstract: Hundred patients with far-advanced cancer and pain were interviewed within a few days of admission to a special care unit. Eighty had more than one pain; 34 had four or more. A total of 303 anatomically distinct pains were recorded. Ninety-one patients had pain caused by the cancer itself. Twelve had treatment-related pain; and 19 had pain related to chronic disease or debility ('associated pain'). Thirty-nine patients had one or more pains unrelated to cancer or treatment; the most common of these was myofascial pain. In 41 patients only was all the pain caused directly by the cancer. Bone involvement and nerve compression were the most common forms of cancer-related pain; soft tissue and visceral pains also occurred frequently. Fifty-seven patients had pain for more than 4 months.

It is also possible to browse by passage and even by sentence, which makes good sense for larger documents than those in Medline.

Rather than starting with a hyper-precise query, the search will usually start with a single word, e.g. 'aspirin' or 'cancer', or (in other applications) with a proper name. The appropriate verbs may then be found by means of a joker.

The searcher continues to generalize or specialize the elements of the query until he is satisfied with the accuracy of the query pattern. He can combine this query pattern with others into a profile, and in various ways ply the tools of his trade.

3   Status of the Project

In this section we briefly describe the application for which the system was implemented, the implementation tools used and the present status.

The mining of information about metabolites from the medical literature provides a difficult test for the PHASAR technology. It is definitely professional search, satisfying the criteria given in section 1.1. Metabolites are roughly those side- and end products of biochemical processes which are not considered important enough to write papers about them, but that may be mentioned in passing. Therefore it is hard to find them in the literature by traditional means.

In the course of an interactive analysis of selected documents mentioning certain processes, reagents or metabolites, a profile is generated, consisting of (possibly weighted) query patterns joined by discourse operators, which can then be used for an exhaustive automatic analysis of a large body of literature. The profiles can afterwards be re-used for other metabolites or even to find (as yet unknown) candidate metabolite names. For each metabolite, all passages referring to its source, effects and interactions can be retrieved.

As a first corpus for experiments with PHASAR, a snapshot of Medline containing all abstracts which were on-line as of September 25, 2005 has been parsed, transduced to dependency trees, unnested into dependency triples and lemmatized (more than 16 million documents, 2.4 Giga words). The resulting terms were indexed using the indexing system MRS [Hekkelman and Vriend, 2005] which is in the public domain. The whole process took 792 CPU-hours on the LISA system of SARA[2] in Amsterdam. The next step will be to analyze and index all openly accessible full-text papers and journals.

The parser used was generated using the AGFL-system [Koster and Verbruggen, 2002] from the EP4IR grammar and lexicon of English, which are freely available in the public domain[3]. The EP4IR grammar version 2.4 was used as provided, but in order to adapt the lexicon to Biomedical applications it was extended with material from the Unified Medical Language System (UMLS) lexicon[4], which is also freely available.

The current version of the PHASAR system is a thin client/server system built using HTML, Javascript, Perl and C++. It is a prototype system available only to project members, intended for development of the interface, search tactics and thesaurus resources. It is running on one of the mirror servers of Medline.

---

[2] www.sara.nl

[3] http://www.cs.ru.nl/agfl

[4] http://www.nlm.nih.gov/research/umls/

4   Conclusion

The PHASAR system is a new kind of search engine, developed for supporting professional search processes in the BioMedical field. Although the present implementation of PHASAR is a prototype and comparative evaluation still has to start, the ideas behind PHASAR should be of interest to the whole Information Retrieval community. The system is now being benchmarked on tasks from BioInformatics and from other areas. We expect the system to perform more accurate searching than conventional search engines, at least in the hands of professionals, because of its use of phrases and linguistic techniques. Replacing browsing over documents by passage browsing and browsing over the index makes it an efficient tool for *exploratory search* over very large document collections. Its ability to reduce documents to sentences matching a pattern makes it a suitable tool for full-text mining.

Due to its generic character, it is applicable other application areas, such as:

- professional search by patent clerks and documentalists
- text-based research by linguists and musicologists
- forensic search and chat monitoring, and
- opinion mining and media analysis on the Internet.

A lot of work will have to be done in our project to develop PHASAR into a mature tool for BioInformatics:

- improving the linguistic resources: increasing the coverage of the lexicon and the accuracy of the grammar, implementing anaphora resolution
- constructing a number of comprehensive flat thesauri for the application domain, largely by conversion of existing resources
- elaborating the user interface and the way-of-working on the basis of user experiences
- testing and evaluating the technology in various benchmarks, and improving it wherever possible.

The PHASAR system can search or mine enormous collections of documents. As section 3 shows, the technology exists for parsing very many documents (in English) at reasonable speed. Although for parsing and indexing the present Medline collection a few hundred computers were used in parallel for a few hours, a single computer can keep up with the weekly increments in Medline.

The Medline collection contains about 17M (short) documents, less than one promille of the size of the Internet measured in web-pages [5]. But the parsing and indexing technology we have used can certainly be scaled up by three orders of magnitude. It is therefore feasible to construct and maintain a syntactically analyzed and indexed version of all documents in English accessible on the Internet and search them with PHASAR.

---

[5] according to `http://www.metamend.com/internet-growth.html`

References

[Arampatzis et al., 2000] A. Arampatzis, Th.P. van der Weide, C.H.A. Koster, P. van Bommel (2000), An Evaluation of Linguistically-motivated Indexing Schemes. *Proceedings of BCS-IRSG, 22nd Annual Colloquium on IR Research*, pg 34-45.

[Bouma et al, 2005] G. Bouma, J. Mur, G. van Noord, L. van der Plas, and J. Tiedemann (2005), Question Answering for Dutch using Dependency Relations. Proceedings of the CLEF 2005 Workshop.

[Bruza and Huibers, 1996] P. Bruza and T.W.C. Huibers, (1996), A Study of Aboutness in Information Retrieval. *Artificial Intelligence Review*, 10, p 1-27.

[Cui et al, 2005] Hang Cui, Renxu Sun, Keya Li, Min-Yen Kan and Tat-Seng Chua (2005), Question Answering Passage Retrieval Using Dependency Relations, In Proceedings SIGIR 2005.

[Fagan, 1988] J.L. Fagan (1988), *Experiments in automatic phrase indexing for document retrieval: a comparison of syntactic and non-syntactic methods*, PhD Thesis, Cornell University.

[Furnkranz et al, 1998] Furnkranz, J., Mitchell, T., and Riloff E., (1998), Case Study in Using Linguistic Phrases for Text Categorization on the WWW, AAAI/ICML Workshop on Learning for Text Categorization.

[Grootjen and van der Weide, 2004] F. A. Grootjen and T. P. van der Weide (2004), Effectiveness of Index Expressions. NLDB 2004, Springer LNCS 3136 pp. 171-181

[Hekkelman and Vriend, 2005] M.L. Hekkelman and G. Vriend (2005), MRS: A fast and compact retrieval system for biological data. Nucleic Acids Res. 2005 July 1; 33(Web Server issue): W766W769.// Also http://mrs.cmbi.ru.nl/.

[Koster and Verbruggen, 2002] C.H.A. Koster and E. Verbruggen (2002), The AGFL Grammar Work Lab, Proceedings FREENIX/Usenix 2002, pp 13-18.

[Melčuk, 1988] I. A. Melčuk. Dependency Syntax: Theory and Practice. State University of New York Press, Albany, NY, 1988.

[Riloff and Lorenzen, 1999] Riloff, E. and Lorenzen, J., (1999), Extraction-based Text Categorization: Generating Domain-specific Role Relationships Automatically, In [Strzalkowski, 1999].

[Sebastiani, 2002] F. Sebastiani (2002), Machine learning in automated text categorization, ACM Computing Surveys, Vol 34 no 1, 2002, pp. 1-47.

[Sparck Jones, 1999] K. Sparck Jones (1999), The role of NLP in Text Retrieval. In: [Strzalkowski, 1999] pp. 1-24.

[Strzalkowski, 1995] T. Strzalkowski (1995), Natural Language Information Retrieval, *Information Processing and Management*, 31 (3), pp. 397-417.

[Strzalkowski, 1999] T. Strzalkowski, editor (1999), *Natural Language Information Retrieval*, Kluwer Academic Publishers, ISBN 0-7923-5685-3.

Language Identification in Multi-lingual Web-Documents

Thomas Mandl, Margaryta Shramko, Olga Tartakovski,
and Christa Womser-Hacker

Universität Hildesheim, Information Science
Marienburger Platz 22, D-31141 Hildesheim, Germany
mandl@uni-hildesheim.de

Abstract. Language identification an important task for web information retrieval. This paper presents the implementation of a tool for language identification in mono- and multi-lingual documents. The tool implements four algorithms for language identification. Furthermore, we present a n-gram approach for the identification of languages in multi-lingual documents. An evaluation for monolingual texts of varied length is presented. Results for eight languages including Ukrainian and Russian are shown. It could be shown that n-gram-based approaches outperform word-based algorithms for short texts. For longer texts, the performance is comparable. The evaluation for multi-lingual documents is based on both short synthetic documents and real world web documents. Our tool is able to recognize the languages present as well as the location of the language change with reasonable accuracy.

1 Introduction

Language Identification is a research topic which is becoming increasingly important due to the success of the internet. The authors of internet pages do not always provide reliable meta data which indicates the language of the text on the page. Even worse, many internet documents contain text portions in different languages. Language identification is an important task for web search engines.

For users, it is rarely a problem to identify the language of a document as long as it is written in a language they understand. However, when a user encounters a page in an unknown language and wants to automatically translate it with an online tool, the source language usually needs to specified. Language is a barrier for user access. Therefore, it is an important factor which needs to be considered during web usage mining of multilingual sites [7]. Consequently, automatic language identification is necessary for web usage mining studies.

Access to web pages is often guaranteed by internet search engines which automatically crawl and index pages. Indexing methods are usually language dependent because they require knowledge about the morphology of a language [5]. Even indexing methods which do not rely on linguistic knowledge like n-gram based stemming can be optimized for languages by choosing an appropriate value for n [11]. In 2005, the first multi-lingual web collection for a comparative analysis of information retrieval approaches for web pages was released [13]. Systems working with this corpus need accurate language identification.

C. Kop et al. (Eds.): NLDB 2006, LNCS 3999, pp. 153–163, 2006.

Often, web search engines focus on content in one specific language and aim at directing their crawlers to pages in that language [10].

Multilingual documents containing text in different languages are a reality on the web. There may be short sentences like "optimized for internet explorer", foreign language citations or even parallel text. Many popular language identification methods deal inadequately with multi-lingual documents and their performance drops. So far, little research has been dedicated toward multi-lingual content. The current project and the tool presented in this paper aims at recognizing the extent to which multi-lingual content is present on the web and to which extent it can be automatically identified.

Language identification is closely related to the recognition of the character encoding. This aspect is not dealt with in this paper. The remainder of the paper is organized as follows. The following section introduces research on language identification. Section 3 describes the tool LangIdent, the implemented algorithms, the interface and the language model creation. Section 4 shows the evaluation results and the last section gives an outlook to future work.

2 Related Work

Language identification is a classification task between a pre-defined model and a text in an unknown language. Most language identification systems are either based on short and frequent words or character n-grams. This section provides a brief overview.

It is obvious that words often are unique for a language and that they can be used for language identification. On the other hand, for efficiency reasons, not all words of a language can be used for language identification nor are all words known. All languages integrate new words into their vocabulary frequently. Many character sequences can be words in more than one language.

Therefore, most approaches are based on common or frequent words [11, 3,4]. Typically, the most frequent words in a trainings corpus of a known language are determined. The number of words used varies, Souter et al. use 100 words [10] and Cowie et al. use 1000 [3]. Similar languages often share some common words and are therefore more difficult to be distinguished.

A novel and elaborated approach considers word classes and their order [8]. Closed word classes which rarely change in a language like adverbs or prepositions are listed for each language. At first the algorithm checks the presence of prepositions in the text. Depending on the result and previous empirical experience, another word class is called and tested. In that manner, a word class can be called upon which discriminates well between previous hypotheses [8].

For short texts, word based language identification can easily fail, when a few words are present and these are not stored in the language model. Therefore, character n-grams have been used for identification as well and n varies between 2 and 5. This approach primarily focused on the occurrence of characters or n-grams unique for a specific language [14]. Current approaches store the frequency of the most frequent n-grams and compare them to the n-grams encountered in a text [2]. Excellent results can be achieved by combining words and n-grams [12].

Most of the approaches for mapping a document to one language model use traditional algorithms from machine learning which do not need to be mentioned here, except for the "out of place" method. It compares the ranks of the most frequent items in the document and the model. The distance between the rank in one list and the rank in the other list is calculated. The distances are summed up and provide a measure for the similarity between model and document. This method can be regarded as a simple approach to rank correlation. It has been applied by [2].

Most previous experiments have been carried out for Western European languages. Little research has been done for Ukrainian and Russian.

Research has focused on the identification of one language per document. The identification of multiple languages in documents has not been dealt with. The most prominent approach lies a floating window of n words on the text [10]. The language within the window is identified and all windows are projected onto the document.

3 Implementation of LangIdent

We developed LangIdent, a prototype for language identification. LangIdent allows the development of models from training data. It has been implemented in JAVA and has a graphical user interface, but can also be run in batch mode. More details can be found in [1].

3.1 Algorithms

Based on previous research, the system includes four classification algorithms:

- Vector space cosine similarity between inverse document frequencies
- "out of place" similarity between rankings
- Bayesian classification
- Word based method (count of word hits between model and language)

The first three methods are based on n-grams. The prototype includes words as well as n-grams. The multi-lingual language identification runs a window of k words through the text and matches the short window with the language models.

3.2 Language Model Development

The prototype allows the assembly of a language model form an example text. Words and n-grams are stored in the model and depending on the selection of the user during the classification phase, only one of them may be used.

Previous retrieval experiments with n-gram models showed that tri-grams work reasonably well for most languages [11]. Based on this experience, we implemented tri-gram models within LangIdent. For both the n-gram and the word based model, some parameters can be specified by the user.

Trigram-Parameters:

- absolute frequency
- relative frequency
- inverse document frequency
- transition probability

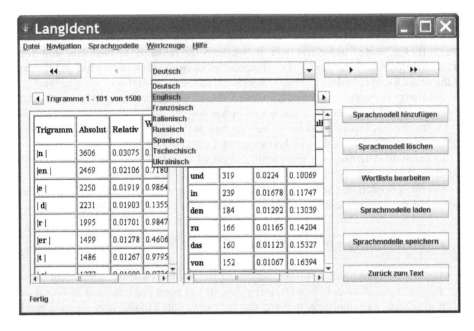

Fig. 1. Language Model displayed in LangIdent

For language models based on words, the same parameters are used, except for the last one. It is replaced by the cumulative probability.

The models can be explored within the prototype and even be manipulated manually. For example, if the user encounters a usually non-frequent word, a proper name or even a foreign language word which occurred often in the training corpus, this word can be deleted from the model. Figure 1 shows the interface for the language model selection and manipulation.

3.3 Multi-lingual Language Identification

Our algorithm for language identification in multi-lingual documents is based on the word-window approach [10]. However, it was modified to overcome some shortcomings. For short text passages in another language, word based approaches are not the optimal solution. This will also be shown by the evaluation for mono-lingual documents in the following section. As a consequence, we build a n-gram language model. We chose tri-grams and a windows size of eight words.

For each window, the most likely language is determined based on the transition probability between tri-grams. For windows in which a different language occurs, a language change is assumed. The position is determined based on the position of the first window in which the new language is encountered. The change is assumed to occur at the first position of that window plus two words.

4   Evaluation for Mono-lingual Documents

With the prototype LangIdent described above, models for eight language were developed (German, English, Spanish, French, Italian, Russian, Czech, Ukrainian). These models were evaluated. The text for the language model creation had a size of some 200 Kbyte from several online newspapers.

Table 1. Error rates for two word-based methods

English	word frequency	0.12
	word count	0.12
French	word frequency	0.62
	word count	21.9
German	word frequency	0
	word count	0.35
Italian	word frequency	0
	word count	3.55
Russian	word frequency	0.12
	word count	0.12
Spanish	word frequency	0.48
	word count	0.12

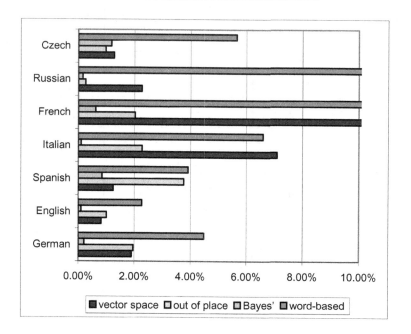

Fig. 2. Error rates for Document Size 100 Bytes

Table 2. Detailed error rates for four classification methods

Language	document size (chars)	Vector space	Out of place	Bayes'	Word-based
German	25	8.30%	6.64%	2.32%	20.04%
	50	1.90%	1.96%	0.21%	4.48%
	125	0.12%	0.12%	0%	0%
	250	0%	0%	0%	0%
	500	0%	0%	0%	0%
English	25	4.50%	6.72%	1.79%	12.40%
	50	0.82%	1.01%	0.10%	2.26%
	125	0%	0%	0%	0%
	250	0%	0%	0%	0%
	500	0%	0%	0%	0%
Spanish	25	5.37%	10.39%	5.55%	15.76%
	50	1.25%	3.76%	0.85%	3.91%
	125	0%	0.37%	0%	0.37%
	250	0%	0%	0%	0%
	500	0%	0%	0%	0%
Italian	25	20.26%	11.10%	1.94%	24.68%
	50	7.10%	2.27%	0.10%	6.60%
	125	0.48%	0.12%	0%	0.12%
	250	0%	0%	0%	0%
	500	0%	0%	0%	0%
French	25	29.45%	9.15%	3.53%	31.06%
	50	14.88%	2.02%	0.62%	10.32%
	125	3.14%	0.12%	0%	0.70%
	250	0.92%	0%	0%	0%
	500	0%	0%	0%	0%
Russian	25	5.77%	2.84%	2.16%	31.18%
	50	2.26%	0.26%	0.16%	12.55%
	125	0.61%	0%	0%	1.47%
	250	0%	0%	0%	0.24%
	500	0%	0%	0%	0%
Czech	25	4.07%	3.51%	4.02%	20.98%
	50	1.28%	0.98%	1.18%	5.65%
	125	0.62%	0.25%	0.25%	0%
	250	0%	0%	0%	0%
	500	0%	0%	0%	0%
Ukrainian	25	9.92%	6%	6.11%	31.32%
	50	6.46%	1.95%	2.20%	12.81%
	125	2.84%	0.49%	0.62%	1.85%
	250	1.71%	0.24%	0.73%	0.24%
	500	0%	0%	0%	0%

For word-based methods, the most frequent words with a cumulative probability of 40% were stored and for n-gram methods, the 1500 most frequent tri-grams were included into the model. The models were not further processed manually which would be possible within LangIdent.

First, an evaluation for the word-based method was carried out in order to determine the best settings. Subsequently, the best word-based approach was compared to the other methods.

4.1 Word-Based Method

There are two main approaches for the identification of a language with a word based model. Either the word hits between text and all language models are counted or the relative frequency of all word hits are added. Both methods are mentioned in the research literature.

In a preliminary test with six languages and text parts of size 250 Bytes it could be shown that the simple word count is superior. The results are presented in table 1. Consequently, the main evaluation relies solely on the word count.

4.2 Eight Languages and Document Size

The quality of language identification as well as for many other classification tasks heavily depends on the amount of evidence provided. For language identification, it depends on the number of characters available. As a consequence, the system was tested with text of varying length. Newspaper documents from all eight languages were split into sections of length between 25 and 500 characters. The recognition rate for shorter sections is important for an analysis of multi-lingual documents. The error rates for all languages can be found in table 2. The best results for are shaded. Figure 2 displays the error rates for document size 100.

It can be seen from figure 2 and table 2 that a Bayes classifier results in the best classification quality for most languages. Only for Czech and Ukrainian, out-of-place is superior. A look at the average performance over all languages considered confirms the assumption, that Bayes leads to the highest performance. The numbers are given in table 3.

Table 3. Average error rates for four classification methods

Document size (Chars)	Vector space	Out of place	Bayes'	Word-based
25	10.95%	7.04%	3.43%	23.43%
50	4.49%	1.78%	0.68%	7.32%
125	0.98%	0.18%	0.11%	0.56%
250	0.33%	0.03%	0.09%	0.06%
500	0%	0%	0%	0%

An informal analysis of wrongly classified text parts showed that often proper names and words in other languages led to the misclassification. However, it could be argues that in cases where a text snippet form a French newspaper contains mainly English words, it should indeed not be classified as a French text. However, not all errors can be manually assessed. The experiments are described in more detail [1].

5 Evaluation for Multi-lingual Documents

The evaluation of language identification for multi-lingual content is difficult. Different metrics need to be developed for this endeavor. Mainly two issues need to be considered:

- Identification of the languages present in the document
- Identification of the location of a language shift

Figure 3 shows the user interface of LangIdent for a successful recognition of multi-lingual parts of one document. The text layout is modified for the different languages.

5.1 Corpus Creation

For this evaluation, two corpora were assembled. One is a collection of real-world multi-lingual documents from the web. Some suitable 100 documents with two languages have been identified. Most multilingual texts contain more language due to the following reasons:

- Parallel text: the same text is present in two languages
- Citation: Text in one language contains a citation in another language

For the evaluation, we did not consider syntactic hints for language changes or layout changes. These texts were long on average. Length varies between 120 and 1500 characters and average length is 550 characters. In order to evaluate the performance of our approach for smaller portions of text, a synthetic corpus of short texts was created. The synthetic corpus of multi-lingual documents has been assembled from the data used for the mono-lingual experiments described above.

Three methods were used to create text which has similar features as the real world texts:

- XY: Two languages were subsequently pasted into a document (like a parallel text)
- XYX: One portion in one language is inserted into a document in another language (like a citation)
- XYZ: Three languages were subsequently pasted into a document

All eight languages mentioned above were used for the synthetic corpus. Altogether, 100 texts were created. Their average length is 130 characters for type XY and 280 for the other types.

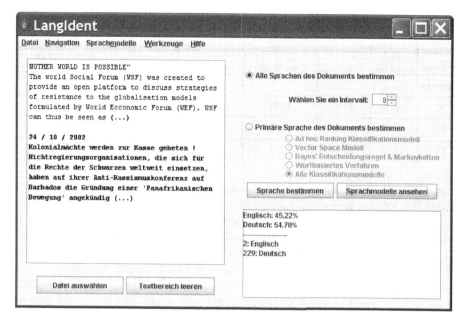

Fig. 3. A multi-lingual document in LangIdent

5.2 Evaluation Results

The languages present in the documents were generally well identified in both corpora. Results are shown in table 4.

Table 4. Accuracy of multiple language identification

Type	All languages in document correctly identified
Internet	97 %
XY	96 %
XYX	95 %
XYZ	97 %

Most errors are due to the presence of similar languages like Ukrainian and Russian or Italian and Spanish.

The identification of the location of the language change is a harder challenge. The evaluation measures the distance between actual change and detected change. Documents of type XYX and XYZ have two languages changes. The change detected with less accuracy is used as measure for the entire document. Table 5 displays the evaluation results.

Overall, the identification of language change locations in multilingual documents is possible with good accuracy. For more than 50% of the documents, language

Table 5. Accuracy of language change location detection

Type	Exact position	1 word off	2 words off	3 words off	4 words off	Cumulative for at most 2 words off
Internet	29 %	26 %	26 %	10 %	3.2 %	81 %
XY	38 %	40 %	16 %	2.0 %	-	94 %
XYX	20 %	55 %	10 %	10 %	-	85 %
XYZ	39 %	45 %	13 %	-	-	97 %

changes are detected with no or one word distance from the actual location. The recognition rate for real world documents is lower than for the synthetic corpus. This seems surprising at first, because the internet documents are longer. However, the language identification actually works on the shorter window. The method reaches a recognition rate for the change location of 81% for internet documents. This compares well to 80% for monolingual HTML documents in a recent experiment [8].

For future evaluation experiments, other evaluation measures need to be considered. Recall and precision of correctly identified sections might also be a valid measure. However, the final yardstick for the evaluation of languages identification programs depends on the application area. For information retrieval systems, the quality of the subsequent retrieval system will determine the adequacy of a language identification system.

6 Conclusion and Future Work

LangIdent allows the setting of many parameters. It enables further extensive evaluation. The evaluation of LangIdent for mono-lingual documents or for documents with a dominating language will continue and will be extended to the EuroGOV corpus of web documents. We are in the process of creating a set of manually identified pages for many languages as ground truth for the system.

For the EuroGOV corpus, several evidences for the language of a document are present. First, the top level domain provides first evidence. For example, pages of the de domain are often in German. In addition to the recognition results of LangIdent, the language of pages linking to the page under question and link label text are also available.

References

1. Artemenko, O.; Shramko, M.: Entwicklung eines Werkzeugs zur Sprachidentifikation in mono- und multilingualen Texten. Master thesis. University of Hildesheim. 2005. http://web1.bib.uni-hildesheim.de/2005/artemenko_shramko.pdf
2. Cavnar, W.B., Trenkle, J. M: N-Gram-Based Text Categorization. Symposion on Document Analysis and Information Retrieval. Univ. of Nevada, Las Vegas. 161-176.

3. Cowie, J., Ludovik, E., Zacharski, R.: An Autonomous, Web-based, Multilingual Corpus Collection Tool. Proc Intl. Conference on Natural Language Processing and Industrial *Applications*. Moncton. 1998. 142-148.
4. Grefenstette, G.: Comparing two language identification schemes. In: *JADT 1995, 3rd International conference on Statistical Analysis of Textual Data*, Rome.
5. Hollink, V., Kamps, J., Monz, C., de Rijke, M.: Monolingual Document Retrieval for European Languages. In: *Information Retrieval* 7 (1-2) 2004. 33-52
6. Kikui, G. Identifying the Coding System and Language of On-line Documents on the Internet. In: *Proc 16th Conf. on Computational linguistics. Denmark*, vol. 2 (1996), 652-657.
7. Kralisch, A., Mandl T.: Barriers of Information Access across Languages on the Internet: Network and Language Effects. In: *Proc Hawaii International Conference on System Sciences (HICSS-39)* 2006.
8. Lins, R., Gonçalves, P.: Automatic Language Identification of Written Texts. *Proc ACM SAC Symposium on Applied Computing*, March 2004, Nicosia, Cyprus. 1128-1133.
9. Martino, M. and Paulsen, R.: Natural language determination using partial words, Apr. 2001, U.S. Patent No. 6216102 B1.
10. Martins, B., Silva, M.: Language Identification in Web Pages. *Proc ACM SAC Symposium on Applied Computing*. March 13.-17. 2005. Santa Fe, New Mexico, USA. 764-768.
11. McNamee, P., Mayfield, J.: Character N-Gram Tokenization for European Language Text Retrieval. *Information Retrieval* 7 (1/2) 2004. 73-98.
12. Prager, J.: Linguini: Language Identification for Multilingual Documents. In: *Proc 32nd Hawaii International Conf on System Sciences*, 1999.
13. Sigurbjörnsson, B., Kamps, J., de Rijke, M.: Blueprint of a cross-lingual web retrieval collection. *Journal on Digital Information Management* vol. 3 (9-13) 2005.
14. Souter, C., Churcher, G., Hayes, J., Hughes, J., Johnson, S.: Natural Language Identification Using Corpus-Based Models. Hermes J. Linguistics vol. 13, 1994. 183-203.

DILUCT: An Open-Source Spanish Dependency Parser Based on Rules, Heuristics, and Selectional Preferences[*]

Hiram Calvo and Alexander Gelbukh

Natural Language Processing Laboratory,
Center for Computing Research, National Polytechnic Institute
Mexico City, 07738, Mexico
likufanele@likufanele.com, gelbukh@gelbukh.com

Abstract. A method for recognizing syntactic patterns for Spanish is presented. This method is based on dependency parsing using heuristic rules to infer dependency relationships between words, and word co-occurrence statistics (learnt in an unsupervised manner) to resolve ambiguities such as prepositional phrase attachment. If a complete parse cannot be produced, a partial structure is built with some (if not all) dependency relations identified. Evaluation shows that in spite of its simplicity, the parser's accuracy is superior to the available existing parsers for Spanish. Though certain grammar rules, as well as the lexical resources used, are specific for Spanish, the suggested approach is language-independent.

1 Introduction

The two main approaches to syntactic pattern analysis are those oriented to the constituency and dependency structure, respectively. In the constituency approach, the structure of the sentence is described by grouping words together and specifying the type of each group, usually according to its main word [12]:

[[The old man]ₙₚ [loves [a young woman]ₙₚ]ᵥₚ]ₛ

Here NP stands for noun phrase, VP for verb phrase, and S for the whole sentence. Such a tree can also be represented graphically:

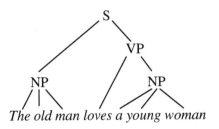

The old man loves a young woman

---

[*] This work was done under partial support of Mexican Government (SNI, CGPI-IPN, COFAA-IPN, and PIFI-IPN). The authors cordially thank Jordi Atserias for providing the data on the comparison of TACAT parser with our system.

C. Kop et al. (Eds.): NLDB 2006, LNCS 3999, pp. 164–175, 2006.

where the nodes stand for text spans (constituents) and arcs for "consists of" relationship. In dependency approach, words are considered "dependent" from, or modifying, other words [175]. A word modifies another word (governor) in the sentence if it adds details to the latter, while the whole combination inherits the syntactic (and semantic) properties of the governor: *old man* is a kind of *man* (and not a kind of *old*); *man loves woman* is a kind of (situation of) *love* (and not, say, a kind of *woman*). Such dependency is represented by an arrow from the governor to the governed word:

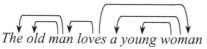

The old man loves a young woman

or, in a graphical form:

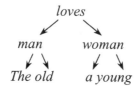

where the arcs represent the dependency relation between individual words, the words of the lower levels contributing details to those of the upper levels while preserving the syntactic properties of the latter. In spite of the 40-year discussion in literature, there is no consensus as to which formalism is better. Though combined formalisms such as HPSG [26] have been proposed, they seem to bear the heritage of the advantages as well as disadvantages of both approaches, the latter impeding their wide use in natural language processing practice. Probably the pertinence each approach depends on a specific task.

We had two-fold motivation for this work. One task we had in mind was the study of lexical compatibility of specific words, and in particular, compilation and use of a dictionary of collocations—stable or frequent word combinations, such as *eat bread* or *deep sleep* as opposed to **eat sleep* and **deep bread* [4]. Such combinations were shown to be useful in tasks ranging from syntactic analysis [31] and machine translation to semantic error correction [5] and steganography [2]. Dependency approach to syntax seems to be much more appropriate for such task.

Our second motivation was the construction of semantic representation of text, even if partial, for a range of applications from information retrieval and text mining [24, 23] to software specifications [16]. All known semantic approaches—such as conceptual graphs [27], Minimal Recursion Semantics [14], or semantic networks [21]—roughly resemble a set of predicates, where individual words represent predicates or their arguments (which in turn can be predicates). The resulting structures are in much closer direct correspondence with the dependency tree than with a constituency tree of the sentence in question, so that dependency syntax seems to be more appropriate for direct translation into semantic structures. Specifically, dependency structure makes it much easier matching—say, in information retrieval—paraphrases of the same meaning (such as active/passive voice transformation) or transforming from one such synonymous structure to another one.

In addition, we found that a dependency parser can be much easier made robust than a constituency parser. The known approaches to dependency parsing much easier cope with both incomplete grammars and ungrammatical sentences than the standard approaches to context-free parsing. Indeed, a standard context-free parser builds the structure incrementally, so that failure of constructing a constituent implies the impossibility to construct all the further constituents that should have contained this one. What is more, an incorrect decision on an early stage of parsing leads to completely or largely incorrect final result. In contrast, in dependency parsing the selection of a governor for a given word, or the decision on whether the given two words are connected with a dependency relation, is much more (though not at all completely) decoupled from the corresponding decision on another pair of words. This makes it possible to continue the parsing process even if some of such decisions could not be made successfully. The resulting structure can prove to be incomplete (with some relationships missing) or not completely correct (with some relationships wrongly identified). However, an incorrect decision on a particular pair of words usually does not cause a snowball of cascaded errors at the further steps of parsing.

In this paper we present DILUCT, a simple robust dependency parser for Spanish. Though some specific rules, as well as the lexical resources and the preprocessing tools used, are specific for Spanish, the general framework is language-independent. An online demo and the source code of the system are available online.[1] The parser uses an ordered set of simple heuristic rules to iteratively determine the dependency relationships between words not yet assigned to a governor. In case of ambiguities of certain types, word co-occurrences statistics gathered in an unsupervised manner from a large corpus or from the Web (through querying a search engine) is used to select the most probable variant. No manually prepared tree-bank is used for training.

We evaluated the parser by counting the number of correctly identified dependency relationship on a relatively small tree-bank. The experiments showed that the accuracy of our system is superior to that of existing Spanish parsers, such as TACAT [11] and Connexor. The rest of the paper is organized as follows. In Section 0 we discuss the existing approaches to dependency parsing that have influenced our work. In Section 0 we present our algorithm, and in Section 0 give the evaluation results. Section 0 concludes the paper.

2   Related Work

Dependency approach to syntax was first introduced by Tesnière [30] and further developed by Mel'čuk [21], who extensively used it in his Meaning ⇔ Text Theory [20, 28] in connection to semantic representation as well as with a number of lexical properties of words, including lexical functions [22, 3]. One of the first serious attempts to construct a dependency parser we are aware about was the syntactic module of the English-Russian machine translation system ETAP [1]. The parsing algorithm consists of two main steps:

1. All individual word pairs with potentially plausible dependency relation are identified.
2. So-called filters remove links incompatible with other identified links.
3. Of the remaining potential links, a subset forming a tree (namely, a projective tree except for certain specific situations) is chosen.

---

[1] www.likufanele.com/diluct

In ETAP, the grammar (a compendium of situations where a dependency relation is potentially plausible) is described in a specially developed specification language describing the patterns to be searched for in the sentence and the actions on constructing the tree that are to be done when such a pattern is found. Both the patters and the actions are expressed in semi-procedural way, using numerous built-in functions (some of which are language-dependent) used by the grammar interpreter. An average pattern–action rule consists of 10–20 lines of tight code. To our knowledge, no statistical information is currently used in the ETAP parser.

Our work is inspired by this approach. However, we made the following main design decisions different from those of ETAP. First, our parser is meant to be much simpler, even if at the cost of inevitable loss of accuracy. Second, we do not rely on complex and detailed lexical recourses. Third, we rely on word co-occurrences statistics, which we believe to compensate for the lack of completeness of the grammar.

Indeed, Yuret [31] has shown that co-occurrence statistics (more precisely, a similar measure that he calls *lexical attraction*) alone can provide enough information for highly accurate dependency parsing, with no hand-made grammar at all. In his algorithm, of all projective trees the one that provides the highest total value of lexical attraction of all connected word pairs is selected. However, his approach relies on huge quantities of training data (though training is unsupervised). In addition, it only can construct projective trees (a tree is called projective if it has no crossing arcs in the graphical representation shown in Section 0).

We believe that a combined approach using both a simple hand-made grammar and word co-occurrence statistics learned in an unsupervised manner from a smaller corpus provides a reasonable compromise between accuracy and practical feasibility.

On the other hand, the mainstream of current research on dependency parsing is oriented to formal grammars [15]. In fact, HPSG [25] was perhaps one of the first successful attempts to, in effect, achieve a dependency structure (necessary for both using lexical information in the parser itself and constructing the semantic representation) by using a combination of constituency and dependency machinery. As we have mentioned, low robustness is a disadvantage of non-heuristically-based approaches.

Of syntactic parsers with realistic coverage available for Spanish we can mention the commercially available XEROX parser[2] and Connexor Machinese Syntax[3] and the freely available parser TACAT.[4] We used the latter two systems to compare their accuracy with that of our system. Only Connexor's system is really dependency-based, relying on the Functional Dependency Grammar formalism [29], the other systems being constituency-based.

3 Algorithm

Following the standard approach, we first pre-process the input text—incl. tokenizing, sentence splitting, tagging, and lemmatizing—and then apply the parsing algorithm.

---

[2] which used to be on www.xrce.xerox.com/research/mltt/demos/spanish.html
[3] www.connexor.com/demo/syntax.
[4] www.lsi.upc.es/~nlp/freeling/demo.php.

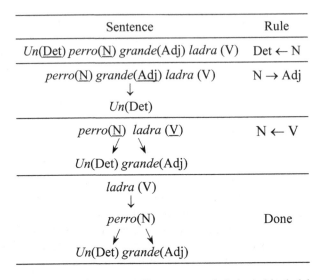

Sentence	Rule
Un(<u>Det</u>) *perro*(<u>N</u>) *grande*(Adj) *ladra* (V)	Det ← N
perro(<u>N</u>) *grande*(<u>Adj</u>) *ladra* (V) ↓ *Un*(Det)	N → Adj
perro(<u>N</u>) *ladra* (<u>V</u>) ↙ ↘ *Un*(Det) *grande*(Adj)	N ← V
ladra (V) ↓ *perro*(N) ↙ ↘ *Un*(Det) *grande*(Adj)	Done

Fig. 1. Applying rules to parse *Un perro grande ladra* 'a big dork barks

3.1 Preprocessing

Tokenization and sentence splitting: The text is tokenized into words and punctuation marks and split into sentences. We currently do not distinguish punctuation marks; thus each punctuation mark is substituted with a comma (in the future we will consider different treatment for different punctuation marks). Two compounds of article and preposition are split: *del* → *de el* 'of the', *al* → *a el* 'to the'.

Compound prepositions represented in writing as several words are jointed into one word, for example: *con la intención de* 'in order to', *a lo largo de* 'throughout', etc. Similarly treated are a few adverbial phrases such as *a pesar de* 'in spite of', *de otra manera* 'otherwise', etc., and several pronominal phrases such as *sí mismo* 'itself'. The list of such combination is small (currently including 62 items) and closed. Though we currently do not perform named entity recognition, we plan this for the future.

Tagging: The text is POS-tagged using the TnT tagger [6] trained on the Spanish corpus CLiC-TALP.[5] This tagger has a performance of over 94%. We also correct some frequent errors of the TnT tagger, for example:

Rule	Example
Det Adj V → Det S V	*el inglés vino* 'the English(man) came'
Det Adj Prep → Det S Prep	*el inglés con* 'the English(man) with'

Lemmatizing: We use a dictionary-based Spanish morphological analyzer [18].[6] In case of ambiguity the variant of the part of speech (POS) reported by the tagger is selected, with the following exceptions:

---

[5] clic.fil.ub.es.
[6] www.Gelbukh.com/agme.

Tagger predicted	Analyzer found	Example
Adjective	Past participle	*dado* 'given'
Adverb	Present participle	*dando* 'giving'
Noun	Infinitive	*dar* 'to give'

If the analyzer does not give an option in the first column but does give one in the second column, the latter is accepted. If an expected nouns, adjective, or participle is not recognized by the analyzer, we try removing a suffix removal, e.g., *flaquito → flaco* 'little (and) skinny → skinny.' For this, we try removing a suspected suffix and check whether the word is recognized by the morphological analyzer. Examples of the suffix removal rules are:

Rule	Example
-cita → -za	*tacita → taza*
	'little cup → cup'
-quilla → -ca	*chiquilla → chica*
	'nice girl → girl'

3.2 Rules

Parsing rules are applied to the lemmatized text. Following an approach similar to [1,8], we represent a rule as a sub-graph, e.g., N ← V. Application of a rule consists in the following steps:

1. A substring matching the sequence of the words in the rule is searched for in the sentence.
2. Syntactic relations between the matched words are established according to those specified in the rule.
3. All words that have been assigned a governor by the rule are removed from the sentence in the sense that they do not participate in further comparisons at step 1.

For example, for the sentence *Un perro grande ladra* 'a big dog barks' see Figure 1. As it can be seen from the example, the order of the rule application is important. The rules are ordered; at each iteration of the algorithm, the first applicable rule is applied, and then the algorithm repeats looking for an applicable rule from the first one. The processing stops when no rule can be applied. Note that one of consequences of such an algorithm is its natural treatment of repeated modifiers. For example, in the phrases *el otro día* 'the other day' or *libro nuevo interesante* 'new interesting book' the two determiners (two adjectives, respectively) will be connected as modifiers to the noun by the same rule Det ← N (N → Adj, respectively) at two successive iterations of the algorithm. Our rules are not yet fully formalized (this is why we call our approach semi-heuristic), so in what follows we will give additional comments to some rules. Currently our grammar includes the rules sown in Table 1.

Table 1. Grammar rules for parsing

Rule	Example
Auxiliary verb system and verb chains	
estar	*andar* ← Ger	*estar comiendo* 'to be eating'
haber	*ser* ← Part	*haber comido* 'to have eaten'
haber ← *estado* ← Ger	*haber estado comiendo* 'have been eating'
ir$_{pres}$ *a* ← Inf	*ir a comer* 'to be going to eat'
ir$_{pres}$ ← Ger ← Inf	*ir queriendo comer* 'keep wanting to eat'
V → *que* → Inf	*tener que comer* 'to have to eat'
V → V	*querer comer* 'to want to eat'
Standard constructions	
Adv ← Adj	*muy alegre* 'very happy'
Det ← N	*un hombre* 'a man'
N → Adj	*hombre alto* 'tall man'
Adj ← N	*gran hombre* 'great man'
V → Adv	*venir tarde* 'come late'
Adv ← V	*perfectamente entender* 'understand perfectly'
Conjunctions (see explanation below)	
N Conj N V(pl) ⇒ [N N] V(pl)	*Juan y María hablan* 'John and Mary speak'
X Conj X ⇒ [X X] (X stands for any)	*(libro) nuevo e interesante* 'new and interesting (book)'
Other rules	
N → *que* V	*hombre que habla* 'man that speaks'
que → V	*que habla* 'that speaks'
N X *que* (X stands for any)	*hombre tal que* 'a man such that'; *hombre , que* 'man, which'
Det ← Pron	*otro yo* 'another I'
V → Adj	*sentir triste* 'to feel sad'
N , Adj	*hombre , alto* 'man , tall'
N , N	*hombre , mujer* 'man , woman'
N → Prep → V	*obligación de hablar* 'obligation to speak'
V , V	*comer , dormir* 'eat , sleep'
V Det ← V	*aborrecer el hacer* 'hate doing'

Coordinative conjunctions always have been a pain in the neck of dependency formalisms and an argument in favor of constituency approaches. Following the idea of Gladki [19], we represent coordinated words in a constituency-like manner, joining them in a compound quasi-word. In the resulting "tree" we effectively duplicate (or multiply) each arc coming to, or outgoing from, such a special node. For example, a fragment [*John Mary*] ← *speak* (*John and Mary speak*) is interpreted as representing two relationships: *John* ← *speak* and *Mary* ← *speak*; a fragment *merry* ← [*John Mary*] ← *marry* (*Merry John and Mary marry*) yields for dependency pairs: *merry* ← *John* ← *marry* and *merry* ← *Mary* ← *marry*. We should note that currently this machinery is not yet fully implemented in our system.

Accordingly, our rules for handling conjunctions have are rewriting rules rather than tree construction rules. The first rule forms such a compound quasi-word out of two coordinated nouns if they precede a plural verb. The rule eliminates the conjunction, since in our implementation conjunctions do not participate in the tree structure. Basically what the rule does is to assure that the verb having such a compound subject is plural, i.e., to rule out the interpretation of *John loves Mary and Jack loves Jill* as *John loves [Mary and Jack] loves Jill.*

3.3 Prepositional Phrase Attachment

This stage is performed after the stage of application of the rules described in the previous section. For any preposition that have not yet been attached to a governor, its compatibility with every noun and every verb in the sentence is evaluated using word co-occurrence statistics (which can be obtained by a simple query to an Internet search engine). The obtained measure is combined with a penalty on the linear distance: the more distant is a potential governor from the preposition in question the less appropriate it is for attachment. More details on the statistical technique of prepositional used here can be found in [9].

3.4 Heuristics

The heuristics are applied after the stages described in the previous sections. The purpose of the heuristics is to attach the words that were not assigned any governor in the rule application stage. The system currently uses the following heuristics, which are iteratively applied in this order, in a manner similar to how rules are applied:

1. An unattached *que* 'that, which' is attached to the nearest verb (to the left or to the right of the *que*) that does not have another *que* as its immediate or indirect governor.
2. For an unattached pronoun is attached to the nearest verb that does not have a *que* as its immediate or indirect governor.
3. An unattached N is attached to the most probable verb that does not have a *que* as its immediate or indirect governor. For estimating the probability, an algorithm similar to the one described in the previous section is used. The statistics described in [10] are used.
4. For an unattached verb *v*, the nearest another verb *w* is looked for to the left; if there is no verb to the left, then the nearest one to the right is looked for. If *w* has a *que* as direct or indirect governor, then *v* is attached to this *que*; otherwise it is attached to *w*.
5. An unattached adverb or subordinative conjunction (except for *que*) is attached to the nearest verb (to the left or to the right of the *que*) that does not have another *que* as its immediate or indirect governor.

Note that if the sentence contains more than one verb, at the step 4 each verb is attached to some another verb, which can result in a circular dependency. However, this does not harm since such a circular dependency will be broken in the last stage of processing.

3.5 Selection of the Root

The structure constructed at the steps of the algorithm described in the previous sections can be redundant. In particular, it can contain circular dependencies between verbs. The final step of analysis is to select the most appropriate root. We use the following simple heuristics to select the root. For each node in the obtained digraph, we count the number of other nodes reachable from the given one through a directed path along the arrows. The word that maximizes this number is selected as the root. All its incoming arcs are deleted from the final structure.

4 Evaluation

We present in this section a comparison of our parser against a hand-tagged gold standard. We also compare our parser with two widely known parsers for Spanish. The first one is Connexor Machinese Syntax for Spanish, a dependency parser, and TACAT, a constituency parser. We have followed the evaluation scheme proposed by [7], which

Table 2. Triples extracted for the sentence: El más reciente caso de caridad burocratizada es el de los bosnios, niños y adultos

Spanish triples	gloss	3LB	Connexor	DILUCT	TACAT
adulto DET el	'the adult'	x			
bosnio DET el	'the bosnian'	x	x	x	
caridad ADJ burocratizado	'bureaucratized charity'	x		x	x
caso ADJ reciente	'recent case'	x		x	x
caso DET el	'the case'	x		x	x
caso PREP de	'case of'	x	x	x	x
de DET el	'of the'	x			x
de SUST adulto	'of adult'	x			
de SUST bosnio	'of bosnian'	x		x	
de SUST caridad	'of charity'	x	x	x	x
de SUST niño	'of children'	x			
niño DET el	'the child'	x			
reciente ADV más	'most recent'	x			x
ser PREP de	'be of'	x		x	x
ser SUST caso	'be case'	x		x	x
recentar SUST caso	'to recent case'		x		
caso ADJ más	'case most'			x	
bosnio SUST niño	'bosnian child'			x	
ser SUST adulto	'be adult'			x	
de ,	'of ,'				x
, los	', the'				x
, bosnios	', Bosnian'				x

suggests evaluating parsing accuracy based on grammatical relations between lemmatized lexical heads. This scheme is suitable for evaluating dependency parsers and constituency parsers as well, because it considers relations in a tree which are present in both formalisms, for example [Det *car the*] and [DirectObject *drop it*]. For our purposes of evaluation we translate the output of the three parsers and the gold standard into a series of triples including two words and their relationship. Then the triples of the parsers are compared against the triples from the gold standard.

We have chosen the corpus Cast3LB as our gold standard because it is, until now, the only syntactically tagged corpus for Spanish that is widely available. Cast3LB is a corpus consisting of 100,000 words (approx. 3,700 sentences) extracted from two corpora: the CLiCTALP corpus (75,000 words), a balanced corpus containing literary, journalistic, scientific, and other topics; the second corpus was the EFE Spanish news agency (25,000 words) corresponding to year 2000. This corpus was annotated following [13] using the constituency approach, so that we first converted it to a dependency treebank. A rough description of this procedure follows. For details, see [10].

1. Extract patterns from the treebank to form rules. For example, a node called NP with two children, Det and N yields the rule NP → Det N
2. Use heuristics to find the head component of each rule. For example, a noun will always be the head in a rule, except when a verb is present. The head is marked with the @ symbol: NP → Det @N.
3. Use this information to establish the connection between heads of each constituent
4. Extract triples for each dependency relation in the dependency tree-bank.

As an example, consider Table 2. It shows the triples for the sentence taken from Cast3LB. *El más reciente caso de caridad burocratizada es el de los bosnios, niños y adultos.* 'The most recent case of bureaucratized charity is the one about the Bosnian, children and adult.' In some cases the parsers extract additional triples not found in the gold standard. We extracted 190 random sentences from the 3LB tree-bank and parsed them with Connexor and DILUCT. Precision, recall and F-measure of the different parsers against Cast3LB are as follows.

	Precision	Recall	F-measure
Connexor	0.55	0.38	0.45
DILUCT	0.47	0.55	0.51
TACAT[7]	–	0.30	–

Note that the Connexor parser, though has a rather similar F-measure as our system, is not freely available and of course is not open-source.

5   Conclusions

We have presented a simple and robust dependency parser for Spanish. It uses simple hand-made heuristic rules for the decisions on admissibility of structural elements and on word co-occurrence statistics for disambiguation. The statistics is learned from a

---

[7] Results for TACAT were kindly provided by Jordi Atserias.

large corpus, or obtained by querying an Internet search engine, in an unsupervised manner—i.e., no manually created tree-bank is used for training. In case if the parser cannot produce a complete parse tree, a partial structure is returned consisting of the dependency links it could recognize. Comparison of the accuracy of our parser with two the available systems for Spanish we are aware of shows that our parser outperforms both of them. Though a number of specific rules of the grammar are specific for Spanish, the approach itself is language-independent. As future work we plan to develop similar parsers for other languages, including English, for which the necessary preprocessing tools—such as POS tagger and lemmatizer—are available. As other future work direction we could mention in the first place improvement of the system of grammar rules. The current rules sometimes do their job in a quick-and-dirty manner, which results in just the right thing to do in most of the cases, but can be done with greater attention to details. Finally, we plan to evaluate the usefulness of our parser in real tasks of information retrieval, text mining, and constructing semantic representation of the text, such as conceptual graphs.

References

1. Apresyan, Yuri D., Igor Boguslavski, Leonid Iomdin, Alexandr Lazurski, Nikolaj Pertsov, Vladimir Sannikov, Leonid Tsinman. 1989. *Linguistic Support of the ETAP-2 System* (in Russian). Moscow, Nauka.
2. Bolshakov, Igor A. 2004. A Method of Linguistic Steganography Based on Collocationally-Verified Synonymy. *Information Hiding 2004, Lecture Notes in Computer Science*, 3200 Springer-Verlag, pp. 180–191.
3. Bolshakov, Igor A., Alexander Gelbukh. 1998. Lexical functions in Spanish. Proc. *CIC-98, Simposium Internacional de Computación*, Mexico, pp. 383–395; www.gelbukh.com/CV/Publications/1998/ CIC-98-Lexical-Functions.htm.
4. Bolshakov, Igor A., Alexander Gelbukh. 2001a. A Very Large Database of Collocations and Semantic Links. Proc. NLDB-2000: 5th Intern. Conf. on Applications of Natural Language to Information Systems, France, 2000. *Lecture Notes in Computer Science* N 1959, Springer-Verlag, pp. 103–114;
5. Bolshakov, Igor A., Alexander Gelbukh. 2003. On Detection of Malapropisms by Multistage Collocation Testing. *NLDB-2003, 8th Int. Conf. on Application of Natural Language to Information Systems*. Bonner Köllen Verlag, 2003, pp. 28–41.
6. Brants, Thorsten. 2000. TNT—A Statistical Part-of-Speech Tagger. In: Proc. *ANLP-2000, 6th Applied NLP Conference*, Seattle.
7. Briscoe, Ted. John Carroll, Jonathan Graham and Ann Copestake. 2002. Relational evaluation schemes. In: *Procs. of the Beyond PARSEVAL Workshop, 3rd International Conference on Language Resources and Evaluation,* Las Palmas, Gran Canaria, 4–8.
8. Calvo, Hiram, Alexander Gelbukh. 2003. Natural Language Interface Framework for Spatial Object Composition Systems. *Procesamiento de Lenguaje Natural*, N 31;
9. Calvo, Hiram, Alexander Gelbukh. 2004. Acquiring Selectional Preferences from Untagged Text for Prepositional Phrase Attachment Disambiguation. In: *Proc. NLDB-2004, Lecture Notes in Computer Science*, N 3136, pp. 207–216.
10. Calvo, Hiram. Alexander Gelbukh, Adam Kilgarriff. 2005. Distributional Thesaurus versus WordNet: A Comparison of Backoff Techniques for Unsupervised PP Attachment. In: *Computational Linguistics and Intelligent Text Processing* (CICLing-2005). *LNCS* 3406, Springer-Verlag, pp. 177–188.

11. Carreras, Xavier, Isaac Chao, Lluis Padró, Muntsa Padró. 2004. FreeLing: An Open-Source Suite of Language Analyzers. *Proc. 4th Intern. Conf. on Language Resources and Evaluation (LREC-04)*, Portugal.
12. Chomsky, Noam. 1957. *Syntactic Structures*. The Hague: Mouton & Co.
13. Civit, Montserrat, and Maria Antònia Martí. 2004. Estándares de anotación morfosintáctica para el español. *Workshop of tools and resources for Spanish and Portuguese*. IBERAMIA 2004. Mexico.
14. Copestake, Ann, Dan Flickinger, and Ivan A. Sag. 1997. *Minimal Recursion Semantics. An introduction*. CSLI, Stanford University.
15. Debusmann, Ralph, Denys Duchier, Geert-Jan M. Kruijff, 2004. Extensible Dependency Grammar: A New Methodology. In: *Recent Advances in Dependency Grammar. Proc. of a workshop at COLING-2004*, Geneve.
16. Díaz, Isabel, Lidia Moreno, Inmaculada Fuentes, Oscar Pastor. 2005. Integrating Natural Language Techniques in OO-Method. In: Alexander Gelbukh (ed.), *Computational Linguistics and Intelligent Text Processing* (CICLing-2005), *Lecture Notes in Computer Science*, 3406, Springer-Verlag, pp. 560–571.
17. Gelbukh, A., S. Torres, H. Calvo. 2005. Transforming a Constituency Treebank into a Dependency Treebank. Submitted to *Procesamiento del Lenguaje Natural* No. 34, Spain.
18. Gelbukh, Alexander, Grigori Sidorov, Francisco Velásquez. 2003. Análisis morfológico automático del español a través de generación. *Escritos*, N 28, pp. 9–26.
19. Gladki, A. V. 1985. *Syntax Structures of Natural Language in Automated Dialogue Systems* (in Russian). Moscow, Nauka.
20. Mel'čuk, Igor A. 1981. Meaning-text models: a recent trend in Soviet linguistics. *Annual Review of Anthropology* 10, 27–62.
21. Mel'čuk, Igor A. 1988. Dependency Syntax: Theory and Practice. State U. Press of NY.
22. Mel'čuk, Igor A. 1996. Lexical Functions: A Tool for the Description of Lexical Relations in the Lexicon. In: L. Wanner (ed.), *Lexical Functions in Lexicography and Natural Language Processing*, Amsterdam/Philadelphia: Benjamins, 37–102.
23. Montes-y-Gómez, Manuel, Alexander F. Gelbukh, Aurelio López-López. 2002. Text Mining at Detail Level Using Conceptual Graphs. In: Uta Priss *et al.* (Eds.): *Conceptual Structures: Integration and Interfaces*, 10th Intern. Conf. on Conceptual Structures, ICCS-2002, Bulgaria. *LNCS*, N 2393, Springer-Verlag, pp. 122–136;.
24. Montes-y-Gómez, Manuel, Aurelio López-López, and Alexander Gelbukh. 2000. Information Retrieval with Conceptual Graph Matching. *Proc. DEXA-2000, 11th Intern. Conf. DEXA, England, LNCS*, N 1873, Springer-Verlag, pp. 312–321.
25. Pollard, Carl, and Ivan Sag. 1994. *Head-Driven Phrase Structure Grammar*. University of Chicago Press, Chicago, IL and London, UK.
26. Sag, Ivan, Tom Wasow, and Emily M. Bender. 2003. *Syntactic Theory. A Formal Introduction* (2nd Edition). CSLI Publications, Stanford, CA.
27. Sowa, John F. 1984. *Conceptual Structures: Information Processing in Mind and Machine*. Addison-Wesley Publishing Co., Reading, MA.
28. Steele, James (ed.). 1990. *Meaning-Text Theory. Linguistics, Lexicography, and Implications*. Ottawa: Univ. of Ottawa Press.
29. Tapanainen, Pasi. 1999. *Parsing in two frameworks: finite-state and functional dependency grammar*. Academic Dissertation. University of Helsinki, Language Technology, Department of General Linguistics, Faculty of Arts.
30. Tesnière, Lucien. 1959. *Eléments de syntaxe structurale*. Paris: Librairie Klincksieck.
31. Yuret, Deniz. 1998. *Discovery of Linguistic Relations Using Lexical Attraction*, PhD thesis, MIT.

Fine Tuning Features and Post-processing Rules to Improve Named Entity Recognition*

Óscar Ferrández, Antonio Toral, and Rafael Muñoz

Natural Language Processing and Information Systems Group,
Department of Software and Computing Systems,
University of Alicante, Spain
{ofe, atoral, rafael}@dlsi.ua.es

Abstract. This paper presents a Named Entity Recognition (NER) system for Spanish which combines the learning and knowledge approaches. Our contribution focuses on two matters: first, a discussion about selecting the best features for a machine learning NER system. Second, an error study of this system which lead us to the creation of a set of general post-processing rules. These issues are explained in detail and then evaluated. The selection of features provides an improvement of around 2.3% over the results of our previous system while the application of the set of post-processing rules provides an increment of performance which is around 3.6%, reaching finally 83.37% f-score.

1 Introduction

Nowadays, we have been witnesses of a huge growth of digital information. This growth requires the automation of processes like searching, retrieving and maintaining information. The access to digital information by the users for locating information that is of interest to them is becoming daunting as the digital information grows larger.

One of the difficulties that impedes the complete automation of the task of locating relevant information is the fact that the contents are presented mainly in natural language, and it is a well-known problem due to the ambiguities of natural language are very hard to be solved by a machine.

In order to achieve this purpose, the Natural Language Processing (NLP) applications, characterized by a deep analysis of the information, adopt a privileged position. Applications like Information Extraction, Information Retrieval, Question Answering and other text processing applications are able to select, classify, retrieve and exploit the information so that they provide the sought-after information for the users. Moreover, Information Extraction techniques are a population method which gets information from natural language sources and stores the relevant data in a database.

---

* This research has been partially funded by the Spanish Government under project CICyT number TIC2003-07158-C04-01.

C. Kop et al. (Eds.): NLDB 2006, LNCS 3999, pp. 176–185, 2006.

Many of the aforementioned NLP applications may use a preprocessing tool called Named Entity Recognition (NER). This subtask aims to detect and classify named entities in documents such as person, organization and location names or dates, quantities, measures, etc. The use of a NER module helps these applications by providing relevant and classified snippets of information.

This paper describes a NER System for the Spanish language that combines several classifiers such as Hidden Markov Model, Maximum Entropy and Memory-based learner in order to solve the classification of the entities. Besides, a rule-based module is presented in order to lessen the errors committed during classification by the machine learning algorithms. A fine tuning study about the features that machine learning algorithms need plus an effective post-processing rules phase allow us to significantly improve our previous results.

The rest of this paper is organized as follows. Next section presents a brief background about NER. Section three introduces our system and the modules it is made of. The experiments carried out are explained and discussed in section four. Finally, section five outlines our conclusions and future work proposals.

2 Background and Motivation

The term Named Entity (NE) was introduced in the 6th Message Understanding Conference (MUC-6) [8]. In fact, the MUC conferences were the pioneer events that have contributed in a decisive way to the research in this area. Another meaningful conferences that continued to develop this research field were CoNLL [13] and ACE[1], gathering up the best current systems.

Mainly, two different approaches have been developed by the researchers in order to solve the Named Entity Recognition task: one is based on knowledge techniques which normally use handcrafted linguistic resources such as grammars, regular expressions, gazetteers or dictionaries. The other approach involves supervised learning techniques. Although the knowledge-based approach has better results for restricted domains, these systems heavily rely on manually defined rules and dictionaries. Moreover, an approach based on machine learning methods has the advantage of acquiring knowledge automatically from a pool of properly annotated samples. Therefore, this approach facilitates the portability of NER systems to new domains or languages just finding an adequate corpus.

For each approach several systems have been developed. We emphasize two knowledge-based systems like Arevalo et al. [1] and Maynard et al. [9]. Regarding supervised learning techniques we point out several systems using different machine learning algorithms like Carreras et al. [4] using AdaBoost algorithm, Zhou et al. [15] using Hidden Markov Model, Borthwick et al. [3] using Maximum Entropy and Florian et al. [7] which carries out a classifiers combination.

Finally, there are systems that combine both of the approaches that have been previously pointed out. There are different ways in which the different approaches can be combined. The two main manners in which these systems can

---

[1] http://www.nist.gov/speech/test/ace/

be built up are parallel and sequential combination. An example of a parallel approach is a voting combination, in which modules following different approaches are executed and their results combined by a voting strategy. Regarding combinations in a sequential way, an example is [2] in which NER is performed with a learning-based module and its results are processed by a set of knowledge rules.

3   System Description

Our Spanish Named Entity Recognition System is made up of two modules: a NER module based on machine learning and a rule-based NER module. An overview of our system is depicted in Figure 1.

Concerning machine learning NER, we have used the architecture of our system NERUA [6], which was developed combining three classifiers by means of a voting strategy. This system carries out the recognition of entities in two phases: detection of entities and classification of the detected entities. The three classifiers integrated in NERUA are [11] for Hidden Markov Model algorithm, [12] for Maximum Entropy and [5] for Memory-based learner algorithm. The outputs of the classifiers are combined using a weighted voting strategy which consists of assigning varying weights to the models corresponding to the correct class they determine. For this research, we have used NERUA but we have carried out a fine tuning features study in order to improve the information given for the classifiers, removing noisy features and incorporating new meaningful features. This study is shown in the following subsection.

Regarding the rule-based module, we have used DRAMNERI [14]. This is a NER system belonging to the knowledge paradigm which was developed with the aim to be as customizable as possible so that it can be adapted to different domains or subtasks within NER. In the case of this research, it has been adapted to deal with the task of applying rules to an already NER tagged text.

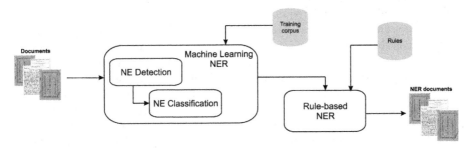

Fig. 1. System architecture

3.1   Fine Tuning Features

For the detection and classification phases, the Memory-based learner and Maximum Entropy classifiers make use of a set of features in order to classify the entities in the correct forecasted classes. However, Hidden Markov Model does not use these sets of features. Because of this, we have developed the method shown in [10] for supplying feature information to the tags used in this model.

In order to improve the performance of the classifiers of our previous system, a large number of features were extracted from the training corpus like a pool of potentially useful features. Many of these features are inspired by the best Named Entity Recognisers up to now, e.g. [4, 7]. We have divided our features into several groups: orthographic (about the orthography of the word), contextual (about the context of the word), morphologic (about morphological characteristics), statistic (about statistical characteristics) and handcrafted-list (test whether or not the word is contained in some handcrafted list of general entities obtained from several web pages). We describe all the features in detail as follows:

- **a**: anchor word (e.g. the word to be classified)
- **cntxt**: word context at position ± 1, ± 2, ± 3
- **cap**: capitalization of the word and context
- **allcap**: whole word and context are in upper case
- **lower**: whole word and context are in lower case
- **internal**: word and context have internal upper case letters
- **digits**: word and context are only made up of digits
- **contdig**: word and context contain digits
- **ispunct**: word and context are punctuation marks
- **contpunct**: word and context contain punctuation marks
- **hyphen**: word and context are hyphenated
- **stopword**: word and context are stop-words
- **initial**: word and context are initials (e.g. B.O.E. or D.O.G.V.)
- **url**: word and context represent an URL
- **length**: number of characters of the word and context
- **prefix**: the first three and four characters of the word and context
- **suffix**: the last three and four characters of the word and context
- **middle**: half substring of the word and context
- **postag**: PoS tag of the word and context
- **lemma**: lemma of the word and context
- **stem**: stem of the word and context
- **dict**: word and context are in handcrafted dictionaries of entities (locations, persons and organizations)
- **trigg**: word and context are in handcrafted dictionaries of trigger words
- **connec**: context is contained in a dictionary of connectives.
- **WNword**: the WordNet semantic prime of the word from the Spanish Word-Net
- **Verbword**: the nearest verb that comes with the entity
- **firstpos**: word is the first word of the sentence
- **firstword**: first word of the whole entity
- **secondword**: second word of the whole entity
- **clx**: words within the entity are upper-cased (c), lower-cased (l) or made up of other symbols (x), e.g. Charles de Gaulle: clc

When we finished the thorough study of the potentially useful features, we focused on selecting the best sets of features, which thus, maximise the performance of the system. In order to do this, we have followed a bottom-up strategy. This strategy iteratively adds one feature at a time and checks the effect of this feature in the results according to the information gain of this feature.

By applying this selection procedure we have created different sets. On one hand, we focused on creating the sets which obtained the best results (DL). On the other, we were interested in the generation of sets which do not contain features derived from language dependent data (e.g. PoS-taggers), which are referred as IDL. The generated sets and the features they contain are:

- IDL sets for the detection phase
  - IDL1d: a, cntxt, cap, allcap^2, firstpos, url^2, ispunct^2, contpunct^2, digits^2, contdig^2, internal^2, ishyphen^2, lower^2.
  - IDL2d: IDL1 + prefix^2, suffix^2, middle^2.
- IDL sets for the classification phase
  - IDL1c: a, cntxt, firstpos, firstword, secondword, clx, url^2, ispunct^2, contpunct^2, digits^2, contdig^2, internal^2, ishyphen^2, lower^2.
- DL sets for the detection phase
  - DL1d: a, cntxt, cap, connec, firstpos, url^2, ispunct^2, contpunct^2, digits^2, contdig^2, internal^2, ishyphen^2, lower^2, lemma^2, stem^2, dict, trigg.
  - DL2d: DL1 + postag.
  - DL3d: DL1 but the context is not considered for dict.
- DL sets for the classification phase
  - DL1c: a, cntxt, firstpos, trigg^2, dict^2, firstword, secondword, clx, WNword, lemma, url^2, ispunct^2, contpunct^2, digits^2, contdig^2, internal^2, ishyphen^2, lower^2.
  - DL2c: DL1c + postag^3.

3.2 Post-processing Rules

In order to improve the results of the machine learning module, we have made an in-depth analysis of its errors. By doing this, we have found out that some of these errors follow patterns which could be matched by means of regular expressions. Therefore, our hypothesis is that by processing the output of the machine learning module by applying a set of general rules derived from the error analysis commented before, the results could be improved.

A knowledge-based Named Entity Recogniser (DRAMNERI) was adapted to perform this task. Next, we present the rules that we extracted from the error analysis. In section 4 we analyse how these rules affect the performance obtained.

- Rule 1 deals with quotation marks(' and "). We found out that in entities inside quotation marks, these are included within the entity in the training corpus. However, the machine learning module does not include the quotation marks as part of the entity in some cases. This rule detects this situation and includes the quotation marks within the entity.
- Rule 2 deals with abbreviations inside parenthesis. We discovered that three-letter country abbreviations (e.g. ESP), which should be tagged as locations, are incorrectly tagged by the machine learning module.

---

^{2} only the word (not the context).
^{3} word and context of size 1.

Besides, abbreviations within parenthesis are not always classified. However, in some cases, this abbreviation is the acronym of an entity that has been just previously introduced (e.g. Virus de Inmunodeficiencia Humana (VIH)). Therefore, it is straight-forward to classify the entity within the parenthesis with the category of the previous classified entity.

- Rule 3 treats URLs. These are matched by using a generic regular expression. If a URL is matched but it is not classified as an entity, then we assign it the miscellaneous category.
- Finally, rule 4 is about connectives within entities. There are entities that take the general form capitalised_word + connective_word + capitalised_word. In some cases, the machine learning module detects this as two different entities. The connectives considered have been 'de' and 'de la' for the entity categories organization and location. Therefore, if an entity of one of these classes appears followed by one of these connectives, and just after that, another entity of the same class, we join both entities.

4   Experiments and Discussion

The aim of the experiments carried out is to check if our study on fine tuning features and the post-processing rules derived from an error analysis can improve the results of a learning-based NER system. In this section we present the data collection and the evaluation measures used and later we explain the experiments carried out and show the respective results which are also commented.

4.1   Data Collection and Measures Used

The Spanish corpora used for the fine tuning features, error analysis and evaluation has been the provided corpus for the CoNLL-2002 shared task and the tags used for classification (PER, LOC, ORG and MISC) are the ones proposed by CoNLL-2002. The training corpus contains 264,715 tokens, from which 18,797 are entities. The development corpus has 52,923 tokens and 4,351 entities. Finally, the test dataset contains 51,533 tokens from which 3,558 are entities.

The measures used for the evaluation of the system were precision, recall and $F_{\beta=1}$. The script used to carry out the evaluations was the one provided by the CoNLL-2002 organization (*conlleval*).

4.2   Fine Tuning Features Experiments

The feature sets obtained from the fine tuning study (see section 3.1), have been applied to the test corpus achieving similar results. The final results for the detection and classification phases are shown in Tables 1 and 2 respectively. These tables also show the results for our system (previous voting) without the fine tuning features.

For the detection phase we have followed the well-known BIO model, which consists of assigning a tag depending on whether the word is at the beginning of an entity (B tag), inside an entity (I tag) or outside an entity (O tag). It should be noted that Maximum Entropy algorithm was not used in this phase. The reason was that the classification of all words into BIO tags is an inefficient and expensive task for this classifier and moreover, produces poor-quality results.

Regarding HMM, we have carried out a tag transformation in the same way that we did in [6] incorporating the most significant features in accordance with the information gain measure. Like in the others feature sets created in the fine tuning features study, we have two kinds of feature sets: sets which features use language dependent tools (DLh: cap^4, $dict^4$) and sets without these features ($IDLh$: cap^4, $allcap^4$).

In both phases, detection and classification, we distinguish between the results obtained for the sets with features that use language dependent tools and for the sets without these features. We consider having the last feature sets is important, because these sets can be directly applied to other languages.

Although HMM algorithm achieves the lowest results, this algorithm has the advantage of its reduced processing time in comparison with the other classifiers. Moreover, in almost all cases HMM is worth for the voting strategy as it improves the results of each classifier.

Table 1. Detection phase results for classifiers with dependent and independent language sets of features

	BIO(%)				BIO(%)		
DL-classifiers	Prec.	Rec.	$F_{\beta=1}$	IDL-classifiers	Prec.	Rec.	$F_{\beta=1}$
HMM_{DLh}	90.53	91.93	90.93	HMM_{IDLh}[5]	90.68	91.17	90.92
MBL_{DL1d}	92.80	92.86	92.83	MBL_{IDL2d}	93.12	92.55	92.84
MBL_{DL3d}	92.83	92.78	92.81	MBL_{IDL1d}	92.89	92.82	92.90
MBL_{DL2d}	92.77	93.16	92.97				
Voting (develop)	92.32	91.97	92.15	Voting (develop)	91.23	91.19	91.21
Voting (test)	93.44	93.86	93.65	Voting (test)	93.15	93.19	93.17
Previous voting (test)	93.34	93.24	93.29	Previous voting (test)	92.81	93.10	92.96

The results regarding fine tuning features are promising. Although the improvement about the detection phase is almost insignificant, we obtain around 2.3% better results for the whole process of recognition both for IDL and DL configurations. It is also important to note that the difference in percentage between the DL configuration (80.44%) and the IDL (79.28%) is quite low (1.44%).

4.3   Post-processing Rules Experiments

We have applied these rules to two different outputs from the machine learning NER system. One is the output when applying a set of features which include language dependent ones. The other does not have any language dependent feature. In both cases, we applied each rule at a time in order to be able to see how each of them affects the results from the machine learning module. The

---

[4] only the word (not the context).
[5] This classifier is also used for DL Voting.

Table 2. Classification phase results for classifiers with dependent and independent language sets of features

	LOC(%)	MISC(%)	ORG(%)	PER(%)	overall(%)		
DL-classifiers	$F_{\beta=1}$	$F_{\beta=1}$	$F_{\beta=1}$	$F_{\beta=1}$	Prec.	Rec.	$F_{\beta=1}$
MBL$_{DL1c}$	77.11	62.09	79.34	87.19	78.59	78.99	78.79
ME$_{DL2c}$	79.71	63.18	80.19	87.99	80.09	80.50	80.30
ME$_{DL1c}$	79.41	64.40	80.09	88.52	80.18	80.58	80.38
Voting (test)	79.60	64.05	80.12	88.59	80.23	80.64	80.44
Voting (develop)	74.08	53.25	77.19	84.65	76.23	76.49	76.36
Previous voting (test)	78.46	57.00	78.93	86.52	78.09	79.10	78.59
IDL-classifiers	$F_{\beta=1}$	$F_{\beta=1}$	$F_{\beta=1}$	$F_{\beta=1}$	Prec.	Rec.	$F_{\beta=1}$
MBL$_{IDL1c}$	76.51	57.95	79.04	85.83	77.46	78.09	77.78
ME$_{IDL1c}$	78.08	60.56	79.26	87.99	78.88	79.52	79.20
HMM	72.24	48.34	71.97	65.96	68.17	68.72	68.44
Voting (test)	78.10	61.86	79.29	87.84	78.96	79.60	79.28
Voting (develop)	70.13	51.97	73.48	81.05	73.64	74.54	74.09
Previous voting (test)	77.29	56.39	78.13	84.72	77.00	78.00	77.50

Table 3. Results applying rules into dependent language approach

	Develop			Test		
Rules	Prec.(%)	Rec.(%)	$F_{\beta=1}$(%)	Prec.(%)	Rec.(%)	$F_{\beta=1}$(%)
without rules	76.23	76.49	76.36	80.23	80.64	80.44
R1	76.73	76.98	76.85	80.48	80.86	80.67
R1+R2	75.84	76.08	75.96	82.71	83.10	82.90
R1+R2+R3	75.81	76.06	75.93	82.69	83.13	82.91
R1+R2+R3+R4	76.07	76.13	76.10	83.34	83.41	83.37
R1+R4	76.89	77.00	76.95	81.06	81.06	81.06

results for the language dependent output can be seen in table 3 while the results for the language independent output are presented in table 4.

As it can be seen in both tables, the application of post-processing rules significantly improves the results that the machine learning module obtains. In both cases the improvement is around 3.6% for the test corpus. All the rules provide an improvement in the F-value for this corpus. This is not the case, however, for the development corpus. In this case, R2 produces an important decrement of the F-value (-1.16% DL, -0.74% IDL). This is due to the fact that country acronyms are not tagged consistently (they are classified as organization in the development corpus while they are tagged as location in the test corpus).

Regarding the test corpus, it should be noted as well that the rules that have more impact are R2 (+2.69% DL, +2.76% IDL) and R4 (+0.55% DL, +0.46% IDL) due to the fact that the machine learning system does not accurately classify connective words within an entity (R4) and because of the tagging inconsistency regarding country acronyms (R2).

Table 4. Results applying rules into independent language approach

Rules	Develop			Test		
	Prec.(%)	Rec.(%)	$F_{\beta=1}$(%)	Prec.(%)	Rec.(%)	$F_{\beta=1}$(%)
without rules	73.64	74.54	74.09	78.96	79.60	79.28
R1	74.00	74.89	74.44	79.34	79.97	79.65
R1+R2	73.46	74.33	73.89	81.59	82.23	81.91
R1+R2+R3	73.48	74.36	73.92	81.58	82.26	81.92
R1+R2+R3+R4	73.64	74.40	74.02	82.12	82.48	82.30
R1+R3+R4	74.21	74.98	74.59	79.86	80.22	80.04

5   Conclusions and Future Work

The main contributions of this research are the improvement of machine learning NER systems by the study and tuning of features, the creation of a set of general rules that help to lessen the handicaps of machine learning approach and the development of a set of features which attributes do not depend on dictionaries or language specific tools.

Regarding the error analysis and the respective rules developed, we can conclude that the learning paradigm can benefit from the knowledge-based one for the weakness of the first can be detected by an error analysis and in some cases be successfully overcomed by simple techniques from the knowledge paradigm such as regular expressions.This approach has improved in a 3.6% the results obtained by our previous machine learning NER system [6].

Another important conclusion from this research is that the final score for language independent configuration (82.30%) is only 1.28% worst than the language dependent one (83.37%). We think that this minimal loss can be assumed for the advantages that a language independent system provides.

Although one feature set we have developed and evaluated is language independent, we have not tested it for another language. Therefore, it would be interesting to study how this set behaves when applying it to other languages so that we can see the applicability of each feature to different languages.

We also consider the automatic generation of linguistic resources. As it has been said, the difference between the language dependent configuration and the language independent one is small. Thus, it is not worth to handcraft linguistic resources because of the cost it implies. Anyway, this small improvement could be obtained by an automatic acquisition of resources.

References

1. Montserrat Arevalo, Montserrat Civit, and Maria Antonia Martí. Mice: A module for named entity recognition and clasification. *International Journal of Corpus Linguistics*, 9(1):53–68, March 2004.
2. Toine Bogers. Dutch named entity recognition: Optimizing features, algorithms, and output. Master's thesis, Tilburg University, September 2004.

3. Andrew Borthwick, John Sterling, Eugene Agichtein, and Ralph Grishman. Exploiting diverse knowledge sources via maximum entropy in named entity recognition. In *Proceedings of the 6th Workshop on Very Large Corpora, WVLC-98*, Montreal, Canada, 1998.

4. Xavier Carreras, Lluís Màrques, and Lluís Padró. Named entity extraction using adaboost. In *Proceedings of CoNLL-2002*, pages 167–170. Taipei, Taiwan, 2002.

5. Walter Daelemans, Jakub Zavrel, Ko van der Sloot, and Antal van den Bosch. TiMBL: Tilburg Memory-Based Learner. Technical Report ILK 03-10, Tilburg University, November 2003.

6. Óscar Ferrández, Zornitsa Kozareva, Andrés Montoyo, and Rafael Muñoz. Nerua: sistema de detección y clasificación de entidades utilizando aprendizaje automático. In *Procesamiento del Lenguaje Natural*, volume 35, pages 37–44, 2005.

7. Radu Florian, Abe Ittycheriah, Hongyan Jing, and Tong Zhang. Named entity recognition through classifier combination. In *Proceedings of CoNLL-2003*, pages 168–171. Edmonton, Canada, 2003.

8. Ralph Grishman and Beth Sundheim. Message understanding conference-6: a brief history. In *Proceedings of the 16th conference on Computational linguistics*, pages 466–471, Copenhagen, Denmark, 1996.

9. Diana Maynard, Valentin Tablan, Cristian Ursu, Hamish Cunningham, and Yorick Wilks. Named entity recognition from diverse text types. In R. Mitkov, N. Nicolov, G. Angelova, K. Bontcheva, and N. Nikolov, editors, *Recent Advances in Natural Language Processing, RANLP 2001*, Tzigov Chark, Bulgaria, 2001.

10. M. Rössler. Using markov models for named entity recognition in german newspapers. In *Proceedings of the Workshop on Machine Learning Aproaches in Computational Linguistics*, pages 29–37. Trento, Italy, 2002.

11. Ingo Schröder. A case study in part-of-speech tagging using the icopost toolkit. Technical Report FBI-HH-M-314/02, Department of Computer Science, University of Hamburg, 2002.

12. Armando Suárez and Manuel Palomar. A maximum entropy-based word sense disambiguation system. In *Proceedings of the 19th International Conference on Computational Linguistics, COLING 2002*, pages 960–966, August 2002.

13. Erik F. Tjong Kim Sang. Introduction to the conll-2002 shared task: Language-independent named entity recognition. In Dan Roth and Antal van den Bosch, editors, *Proceedings of CoNLL-2002*, pages 155–158. Taipei, Taiwan, 2002.

14. Antonio Toral. DRAMNERI: a free knowledge based tool to Named Entity Recognition. In *Proceedings of the 1st Free Software Technologies Conference*, 2005.

15. GuoDong Zhou and Jian Su. Named entity recognition using an hmm-based chunk tagger. In *ACL '02: Proceedings of the 40th Annual Meeting on Association for Computational Linguistics*, pages 473–480, Philadelphia, Pennsylvania, 2002.

The Role and Resolution of Textual Entailment in Natural Language Processing Applications

Zornitsa Kozareva and Andrés Montoyo

Departamento de Lenguajes y Sistemas Informáticos
Universidad de Alicante
{zkozareva, montoyo}@dlsi.ua.es

Abstract. A fundamental phenomenon in Natural Language Processing concerns the semantic variability of expressions. Identifying that two texts express the same meaning with different words is a challenging problem. We discuss the role of entailment for various Natural Language Processing applications and develop a machine learning system for their resolution. In our system, text similarity is based on the number of consecutive and non-consecutive word overlaps between two texts. The system is language and resource independent, as it does not use external knowledge resources such as WordNet, thesaurus, semantic, syntactic or part-of-speech tagging tools. In this paper all tests were done for English, but our system can be used with no restrains by other languages.

1 Introduction

Natural Language Processing applications, such as Question Answering, Information Extraction, Information Retrieval, Document Summarization and Machine Translation need to identify sentences that have different surface forms but express the same meaning. The semantic variability task is very important and its resolution can lead to improvement in system's performance. For this reason, researchers [15], [16], [7] draw attention of the semantic variability problem.

Major components in the modelling of semantic variability are paraphrase rules, where two language expressions can replace each other in a sentence without changing its meaning. Paraphrase rules range from synonyms, such as "purchase" and "buy", to complex expressions, such as "to kick the bucket" and "to die", "X assassinates Y" and "Y is the murderer of X". There are numerous paraphrase rules in a language and it is a laborious task to collect them all manually. This perception led in the last few years to a substantial effort in the direction of automatic discovery of paraphrase rules [3], [14], [4].

More general notion needed for applications that handle semantic variability is that of entailment rules [7]. An entailment rule is a directional relation between two language expressions, where the meaning of one can be entailed from the meaning of the other. According to the entailment definition of [7] for the sentence "Jane bought a car" entails the meaning of the sentence "Jane owns a car", but not vice versa. Entailment rules provide a broad framework for representing and recognizing semantic variability and are a generalization

C. Kop et al. (Eds.): NLDB 2006, LNCS 3999, pp. 186–196, 2006.

of paraphrases, which correspond to bidirectional entailment rules (e.g. "X purchase Y " "X buy Y"). A text t is said to textually entail a hypothesis h if the truth of h can be most likely inferred from t [10]. Textual entailment recognition is a complex task that requires deep language understanding.

2   Entailment in NLP

Textual Entailment Recognition was proposed by [7] as a generic task that captures major semantic inference needs across many natural language processing applications. The textual entailment task requires to recognize, given two text fragments, whether the meaning of one text can be inferred from the other text.

The aim of current Question Answering (QA) system is to return brief answers in response to natural language questions. Given the question "Who is Albert Einstein?", the QA module has to find answers from large text collections related to this question. However, a question might be formulated using certain words and expressions while the corresponding answer in the corpus might include variations of the same expressions. Entailment can be seen in QA as identifying texts that entail the expected answer.

Given some static templates, Information Extraction (IE) systems try to extract the most salient elements in a text and identify the existing relations among these silent elements. A silent element can refer to a name of a person, organization, location etc., while the relations among them can be expressed in various ways: "Jane bought a car" or "A car is owned by Jane". In IE, textual entailment represent different text variants that express the same target relation.

The primary task of Information Retrieval (IR) is to retrieve set of relevant documents corresponding to given query search. The user who formulates the query is expecting to find documents containing these terms. However, a document may not contain all query terms and still to be relevant. A document about "orange" may be relevant to a query about "tropical fruit" yet the words "tropical" or "fruit" may be absent in that document. Entailment in IR are needed to help identifying when a document is relevant regardless of the occurrence or absence of the query tokens in the document. For IR, the entailment task can be seen as a query expression that should be entailed from relevant retrieved documents.

In Summarization entailment can be used to compute the informativity of one text segment compared to another one [20]. This is used to avoid redundancy, when one segment entails another segment, only the entailing segment should be included in the summary. Multi-document summarization systems need to deduce that different expressions found in several documents express the same meaning. For this application, entailment can be seen as omitting redundant sentence or expression from the summary that should be entailed from other expressions in the summary.

For Machine Translation (MT) this problem is expressed by identifying which of the produced translations is acceptable translations of a given source sentence. The translations may vary in word choice or in word order even when they use the same words. Human MT are time consuming and expensive to produce, this lead current research to focus on the automatic MT evaluation. It consists of comparing the output of a MT system and one or more reference translations. The entailment task for MT can be seen as the evaluation of a correct translation that should be semantically equivalent to the gold standard translation, and thus both translations have to entail each other.

So far, we mentioned the role of textual entailment for various Natural Language Processing applications, and how their resolution can lead to improvement in the system's performance. Thus, in this paper we propose and develop a textual entailment system that is entirely based on machine learning. To our knowledge it is the first system that uses machine learning for the resolution of textual entailment. Our system does not use external resources such as WordNet, thesaurus, semantic, syntactic or part-of-speech tagging tools, which makes it resource independent. This system is evaluated on a standard textual entailment evaluation test. The obtained results are analyzed and future work is discussed.

3   System Overview

The entailment resolution system we develop, considers the number of common words or sequences of words between the entailing text (T) and the hypothesis (H). To each (T, H) pair a set of features is associated. Based on these features an instance-based machine learning algorithm assesses the entailment relation as true or false. In Figure 1, we show the modules of our system.

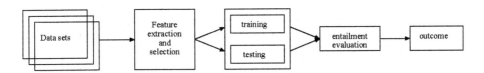

Fig. 1. Modules of the entailment system

3.1   Attributes

The characteristics we modelled for our machine-learning entailment system include some well known machine translation and text summarisation benchmark evaluation measures. The idea behind these measures is to evaluate how close an automatic machine translation is to a human one. This task is similar to the textual entailment task we are resolving, therefore we considered the usage of these attributes as proper for out textual entailment approach.

- Unigrams: The first attributes look for common unigram matches between (T, H) pair. The measures $unigramT = \frac{1}{m}$ and $unigramH = \frac{1}{n}$, where m corresponds to the number of words in T, n corresponds to the number of words in H and 1 stands for unigrams[1], detect common unigrams for the both texts. According to these measures, two sentences are not similar, when there is no common

---

[1] unigram means one word.

unigram, i.e. $unigramT = 0$ and $unigramH = 0$. For the sentences *Andres drinks tea.* and *John buys tea and donut.*, the only common unigram is *tea*.

• Bigrams: The more common n-grams two texts have, the more similar they are. Unigrams search for one consecutive common word, while bigrams discover two such consecutive common words. For this reason, bigrams are more reliable than unigrams. The measures are $bigramT = \frac{2}{m}$ and $bigramH = \frac{2}{n}$, where m is the number of words in T, n is the number of words in T and 2 stands for two consecutive common words between T and H. We do not apply word lemmatization to the data sets, so the occurance of more than two consecutive word matches is not frequent.

The measures we discussed so far are based on position-independent n-gram matches and are not sensitive to word order and sentence level structure. This may lead to errors and insufficient information for the correct similarity assignment between texts. Therefore, we introduce measures such as longest common subsequence and skip-grams.

• LCS: Longest common subsequence (LCS) measure looks for non-consecutive word sequences of any length. The intuition is that the longer the LCS is, the more similar the entailment text and the hypothesis are. LCS estimates the similarity between text T with length m and hypothesis H with length n, as $\frac{LCS(T,H)}{m}$ and $\frac{LCS(T,H)}{n}$. These measures are known as ROUGE-L [13]. LCS does not require consecutive matches but in-sequence matches that reflect the sentence level word order. It automatically includes the longest in-sequence n-gram and therefore no predefined n-gram length is needed. By this measure we reflect the proportion of ordered words found in T and also present in H. An important characteristic of LCS is that it captures the sentence level structure in a natural way.

• Skip-grams: The skip-gram co-occurance statistics measure is known as ROUGE-S [13]. The skip-grams represent any pair of words in sentence order that allow arbitrary gaps. For the entailment text T and hypothesis H, we calculated bi, tri and four skip-grams. We did not go to upper n-gram level due to the high computational cost and the fact that the skip-grams with order higher than four occur rarely.

The measures are $skip\_gramT = \frac{skip\_gram(T,H)}{C(m,number\_of\_skip\_gram)}$ and $skip\_gramH = \frac{skip\_gram(T,H)}{C(n,number\_of\_skip\_gram)}$, where $skip\_gram(T,H)$ refers to the number of common skip grams found in T and H, $C(x, number\_of\_skip\_gram)$ is a combinatorial function, where x is the number of words in the entailment text T (or the hypothesis H) and $number\_of\_skip\_grams$ corresponds to the number of common n-grams between $(T,H)^2$.

In comparison with LCS values which look for one longest common subsequence, the skip-grams find common non-consecutive words. In the example

S_1: John loved Mary.
S_2: John loves Mary.
S_3: Mary loves John.

---

[2] (e.g. $number\_of\_skip\_grams$ is 1 if there is a common unigram between T and H, 2 if there is a common bigram etc.).

the skip-gram measures identify that the similarity between the sentences S_2 and S_1 is stronger than the similarity between the sentences S_3 and S_1. However, the previous measures fail in measuring this similarity correctly. The results given by the *skip_gram* measures are more intuitive than *LCS*, *unigram* or *bigram*.

• Negations: The whole entailment relation is changed when a negation is present. Two texts may be very similar, containing numerous common words, but when one of the texts has a negation, the entailment relation is transformed from true to false, or vice versa. To handle such cases, we introduced binary negation attributes for the T and H texts.

A negation present in T and not present in H, transforms the (T, H) pair from true to false, or respectively from false to true. The same occurs when a negation is found in H and not in T, as in the following example "John knows Kate" and "John does not know Kate". The binary negation attributes are robust to cases where there is no negation at all or both text contain it. For such cases the entailment relation outcome of the (T, H) pair depends on the values of the other attributes. In our experimental setup a pair (T, H) with one or more negations has more weight than a pair with zero negations.

After we described the features of our machine learning system, we constructed feature vectors $\phi_i = \{f_1, f_2, ..., f_n\}$, where i corresponds to the number of instances in the data set and f_n is the number of features. We did not know from all the designed attributes, which would be the most informative ones for the resolution of the textual entailment task. Therefore, we applied a feature selection algorithm.

3.2   Feature Selection Algorithm

An important issue for every machine learning algorithm is the feature selection process. There are various feature selection algorithms, but for out system we used the algorithm described in Figure 2.

Given:
  − a set of all the designed features $F=\{f_1, f_2, ..., f_n\}$;
  − a set of selected features $SF=\emptyset$;

1. select a feature f_i from F;
2. construct a classifier with the selected feature using 10-fold cross validation only on the training data set;
3. determine the feature f_i leading to the best accuracy;
4. remove f_i from F and add it to SF;
5. go to 1 until no improvement is obtained.

Fig. 2. Feature selection algorithm

The output of the algorithm is the set of *unigramT*, *bigramT*, *LCS* for T, *skip − gramT*, *skip − gramH* and the two negation attributes. These attributes were determined as the most informative ones and were used for the final evaluation of our system.

3.3 Machine Learning Module

The machine learning algorithm we worked with is called Memory-based learning developed by [6]. It stores every training example in the memory. During testing, a new case is classified by extrapolating the most similar stored examples. The similarity between a new instance X and all examples Y in the memory is computed by the distance metric $\triangle(X, Y) = \sum_{i=1}^{n} \delta(x_i, y_i)$, where $\delta(x_i, y_i) = |\frac{x_i - y_i}{max_i - min_i}|$. To every test examples is assigned the category of the most similar training examples (k-nearest neighbors). We used the Memory-based learning algorithm with its default parameter settings[3].

4 Experiments

In order to estimate the performance of our developed entailment system, several experiments were conducted. We used the development and test data sets provided by the First Textual Entailment Recognition Challenge (RTE)[4] [8]. The examples in these data sets have been extracted from real Information Extraction, Information Retrieval, Question Answering, Machine Translation, Comparable Documents, Paraphrase Acquisition and Reading Comprehension applications.

The development set consisted of 567 text-hypothesis pairs, which we used as training examples and for testing we had another set of 800 text-hypothesis pairs. The provided data sets were prepared only for the English language. The next subsections describe the evaluation measures and the obtained results from the conducted experiments.

4.1 Entailment Evaluation Measures

The returned classifications by our machine learning system were compared to the manually annotated test data set, and evaluated through the official RTE evaluation site[5]. The RTE evaluation script calculates accuracy, precision, recall and f-score measures for the whole system and individually for each one of the NLP tasks. A system is ranked according to its accuracy.

4.2 Results and Error Analysis

Every machine learning based system consists of training and testing phase. Once the most informative attributes were found by the feature selection algorithm and the classifier was trained, the set of 800 examples was tested. The achieved results are shown in Table1. In the same table are placed the performances of several systems participating in the RTE challenge. For each system, we listed systems' complete accuracy, precision and recall, as well as the accuracy scores for each one of the seven NLP tasks. Each system is denoted with the name

---

[3] the k-nearest neighbor is equal to 1.

[4] http://www.pascal-network.org/Challenges/RTE/

[5] http://132.70.1.54:64080/cgi/rte_eval.pl

of the first author and in the brackets can be found the reference number to the authors' paper. For two systems the precision and recall scores were not available, so we denoted them with X to indicate that they are missing.

Taking into consideration that the examples in the test data represent different levels of entailment reasoning, such as lexical, syntactic, morphological and logical, the obtained 54.13% accuracy using only word overlaps are very promising. The highest results per individual NLP application were for Comparable Documents 60.67% and for Paraphrase Acquisition 60.00%. While other systems had varying precision and recall measures, we obtained quite stable scores and significantly similar results for the various NLP tasks. Compared to the other systems, we achieved high score for the Paraphrase Acquisition task. This was due to the bidirectional n-gram measures we modelled and especially to the skip-gram measures.

Table 1. Entailment recognition for various NLP applications

Systems	Acc.	Prec.	Rec.	CD	IE	MT	QA	RC	PP	IR
ourEnt	**54.13**	**54.11**	**54.25**	**60.67**	**53.33**	**53.33**	**52.31**	**53.57**	**60.00**	**45.56**
Pérez[19]	49.50	X	X	70.00	50.00	37.50	42.31	45.71	46.00	48.89
Wu[23]	51.25	X	X	71.33	55.00	40.00	40.77	47.14	56.00	46.67
Andreevska[2]	51.90	55.00	18.00	63.00	52.00	47.00	45.00	48.00	50.00	53.00
Akhmatova[1]	51.88	61.19	10.25	58.67	50.83	49.17	47.69	52.14	52.00	51.11
Zanzotto[18]	52.40	52.65	49.75	76.51	46.67	52.10	39.53	48.57	54.00	44.44
Kouylekov[12]	56.60	55.00	64.00	78.00	48.00	50.00	52.00	52.00	52.00	47.00

From the RTE challenge, the system of Pérez [19], was the only one entirely relying on word overlaps. Their approach calculated the BLEU measure between a text T and a hypothesis H. They evaluated the entailment relation by a hand-made threshold. The z' statistical test [9] showed that the 5% difference between our system and the one developed by [19], is significant. The disadvantage of their system comes from the BLEU measure which cannot handle nonconsecutive word matches, overcame in our case by the skip-gram measures. Another disadvantage is the hand-made threshold setting which their and many other systems relied on. In our system this process is completely automatic, handled by the machine learning approach.

The other systems listed in Table 1 incorporated resources such as WordNet, lexical chains, logical forms, syntactic parsing etc. The conducted experiment showed that a knowledge poor method like the one we presented, outperformes some systems utilizing external knowledge. However, other participating systems as the one of [22], [21], [17] combined various information sources and covered more entailment relations. Their work directs us in the future toward the incorporation of knowledge rich information sources.

We present some textual entailment sentences that our system was able to identify correctly. Each (T, H) pair belongs to one NLP task.

- CD_task number 1808:
  T: Vanunu converted to Christianity while in prison, and has been living in an anglican cathedral in Jerusalem since his release on April 21.
  H: A convert to Christianity, Vanunu has sequestered himself at a Jerusalem church since he was freed on April 21.
- IE_task number 1871:
  T: The third African Union summit opened in the Ethiopia's capital of Addis Ababa on Tuesday, June 29.
  H: The third African Union summit is held in Addis Ababa.
- MT_task number 1301:
  T: The former wife of the South African president did not ask for amnesty, and her activities were not listed in the political reports submitted by the African National Congress to the Truth and Reconciliation Commission in 1996 and 1997.
  H: Winny Mandela, the President's ex-wife, is requesting amnesty.
- QA_task number 1498:
  T: If Russia is excluded from NATO membership while Poland and Hungary are on the path to becoming NATO allies, how can Moscow avoid the conclusion that a renewed and enlarged NATO retains its traditional objective of confronting Russia?
  H: Moscow is the capital of Russia.
- RC_task number 1112:
  T: Every year, 1.2 million people in America have a new or repeat heart attack.
  H: Every year, 1.2 million Americans have a heart attack.
- MT_task number 1301:
  T: The former wife of the South African president did not ask for amnesty, and her activities were not listed in the political reports submitted by the African National Congress to the Truth and Reconciliation Commission in 1996 and 1997.
  H: Winny Mandela, the President's;s ex-wife, is requesting amnesty.
- IR_task Number 967:
  T: Chadrick Fulks escaped from a Kentucky jail.
  H: Chadrick Fulks gets the death penalty.

The n-gram features we modelled are precise with short sentences. These measures have the tendency to punish large text by considering the final outcome of the ratio of the overlapping words as false e.g. the textual entailment between the sentences does not hold.

Other errors that occurred in the presented approach concern the number and the time mismatching. For sentences like "Bill met Mary in 1998" and "Bill met Mary in 1999", the number of common words is high, however we need a time matching attribute to determine that the entailment relation does not hold because 1998 and 1999 are not the same time period. Our system should be able to reason for the two sentences "I woke up before 10" and "I woke up at 9" that "before 10" indicates "at 9".

We failed in the recognition of other examples where Named Entity Recognition module was needed. We need to identify that "Mexican" and "Mexico" are similar, that "John Parker" and "Parker Ltd" are not the same as one is a name of a person and the other is a name of an organization.

The negation attribute handled surface negations, where the particle "not" was present. However, this attribute lacks in defining that "He is a bad boy" and "He is a good boy" do not infer the same meaning. In order to resolve this problem, antonyms are needed.

Finally, but not on a last place, text similarity module as proposed by [11] and [5] is needed in order to establish the semantic relatedness of the words, e.g. "apple" is a type of "fruit". The presently modelled attributes fail in matching that there is a synonym, hyponym or hypernym relation among the words. The incorporation of semantic information will relate the words and establish the textual entailment relation with better precision.

As can be seen from the conducted experiment and the results of other systems, the resolution of textual entailment is a very difficult, but challenging task. Present systems using sophisticated probabilistic models [7] and various information sources [21],[5] achieve as a maximum 62% accuracy. To our knowledge, we are the first entirely based machine-learning entailment system functioning with word overlaps. Our system can be easily adapted to languages other than English, because counting words between two sentences is not a language dependent task.

5   Conclusions and Work in Progress

In this paper we discussed the impact and the role of textual entailment for various Natural Language Processing applications. In order to handle the language variability matter, we designed and developed a completely automatic and language independent machine learning system. This system was evaluated on several NLP applications such as Information Extraction, Information Retrieval, Question Answering, Comparable Documents, Paraphrase Acquisition, Machine Translation and Reading Comprehension. The overall accuracy achieved by our system is 54.13%. The majority of the correctly resolved entailment relations were found for Comparable Documents and Paraphrase recognition. In a comparative study with other entailment systems evaluated on the same data sets, the results show that our system achieved the highest score for Paraphrase Acquisition and yields comparable results to the other systems.

The attributes we worked with are based on common words and sequences of word overlaps, which makes our system easy to be adapted and incorporated for languages other than English. In our approach we did not need to develop a hand-made threshold through which the system should decide if an entailment relation holds or not. This process was completely automatic, handled by the machine learning algorithm. Besides its facility of language independence, we claim that our system is also resource independent. Tools as WordNet, syntactic, semantic or part-of-speech tagging were neither needed nor utilized. The system we developed is extremely usefull and practical for many NLP tasks and different languages.

In the future, we will tune and specialize the described entailment recognition system, for a crosslingual Question Answering and Information Retrieval needs. We are interested in the exploration and combination of probabilistic models and information from the web as described in [22]. To improve the negation attribute, we will include the antonym relation from WordNet. We will examine the robustness of our entailment system, with the participation in the Second Textual Entailment Challenge[6].

Acknowledgements

This research has been partially funded by the Spanish Government under project CICyT number TIC2003-07158-C04-01 and PROFIT number FIT-340100-2004-14 and by the Valencia Government under project numbers GV04B-276.

References

1. Elena Akhmatova. Textual entailment resolution via atomic propositions. In *Proceedings of the PASCAL Challenges Workshop on Recognising Textual Entailment, 2005.*, pages 61–64.
2. Alina Andreevska, Zhuoyan Li, and Sabine Bergler. Can shallow predicate argument structure determine entailment? In *Proceedings of the PASCAL Challenges Workshop on Recognising Textual Entailment, 2005.*, pages 45–48.
3. Regina Barzilay and Kathleen McKeown. Extracting paraphrases from a parallel corpus. In *ACL, 2001.*, pages 50–57.
4. Regina Barzilay and Kathleen McKeown. Learning to paraphrase: An unsupervised approach using multiple-sequence alignment. In *HTLT-NAACL, 2003.*, pages 16–23.
5. Courtney Corley and Rada Mihalcea. Measures of text semantic similarity. In *Proceedings of the ACL workshop on Empirical Modeling of Semantic Equivalence.*, 2005.
6. Walter Daelemans, Jakub Zavrel, Ko van der Sloot, and Antal van den Bosch. Timbl: Tilburg memory-based learner. Technical Report ILK 03-10, Tilburg University, November 2003.
7. Ido Dagan and Oren Glickman. Probabilistic textual entailment: Generic applied modeling of language variability. In *PASCAL workshop on Text Understanding and Mining, 2004.*
8. Ido Dagan, Oren Glickman, and Bernardo Magnini. The pascal recognising textual entailment challenge. In *Proceedings of the PASCAL Challenges Workshop on Recognising Textual Entailment, 2005.*
9. Thomas G. Dietterich. Approximate statistical test for comparing supervised classification learning algorithms. *Neural Computation*, 10(7):1895–1923, 1998.
10. Oren Glickman. *Applied Textual Entailment*. PhD thesis, Bar Ilan University, 2005.
11. Valentin Jijkoun and Maarten de Rijke. Recognizing textual entailment using lexical similarity. In *Proceedings of the PASCAL Challenges Workshop on Recognising Textual Entailment, 2005.*, pages 73–76.
12. Milen Kouylekov and Bernardo Magnini. Recizing textual entailment with tree edit distance algorithm. In *Proceedings of the PASCAL Challenges Workshop on Recognising Textual Entailment, 2005.*, pages 17–20.

---

[6] www.pascal-network.org/Challenges/RTE2/

13. Chin-Yew Lin and Franz Josef Och. Automatic evaluation of machine translation quality using longest common subsequence and skip-birgam statistics. In *Proceedings of ACL-2004*. Barcelona, Spain, 2004.
14. Dekang Lin and Patrik Pantel. Discovery of inference rules for question answering. *Natural Language Engineering, 4(7)*, pages 343–360.
15. Dan Moldovan and Vasile Rus. Logic form transformation of wordnet and its applicability to question answering. In *ACL*, pages 394–401, 2001.
16. Christof Monz and Maarten de Rijke. Lightweight entailment checking for computational semantics. In *ICoS-3*.
17. Eamonn Newman, Nicola Stokes, John Dunnion, and Joe Carthy. Ucd iirg approach to the textual entailment challenge. In *Proceedings of the PASCAL Challenges Workshop on Recognising Textual Entailment, 2005.*, pages 53–56.
18. Maria Teresa Pazienza, Marco Pannacchiotti, and Fabio Massimo Zanzotto. Textual entailment as syntactic graph distance: a rule based and svm based approach. In *Proceedings of the PASCAL Challenges Workshop on Recognising Textual Entailment, 2005.*, pages 25–28.
19. Diana Pérez and Enrique Alfonseca. Application of the bleu algorithm for recognising textual entailments. In *Proceedings of the PASCAL Challenges Workshop on Recognising Textual Entailment, 2005.*, pages 9–12.
20. Dragomir Radev. A common theory of information fusion from multiple text sources. In *Proceedings of the First SIGdial Workshop on Discourse and Dialogue*, pages 74–83, 2000.
21. Rajat Raina, Aria Haghighi, Christopher Cox, Jenny Finkel, Jeff Michels, Krsitina Toutanova, Bill MacCartney, Marie-Catherine de Marneffe, Christopher D. Manning, and Andrew Y. Ng. Robust textual inference using diverse knowledge sources. In *Proceedings of the PASCAL Challenges Workshop on Recognising Textual Entailment, 2005.*, pages 57–60.
22. Idan Szpektor, Hristo Tanev, Ido Dagan, and Bonaventura Coppola. Scaling web-based acquisition of entailment relations. In *Proceedings of Empirical Methods in Natural Language Processing*, 2004.
23. Dekai Wu. Textual entailment recognition based on inversion transduction grammars. In *Proceedings of the PASCAL Challenges Workshop on Recognising Textual Entailment, 2005.*, pages 37–40.

An Information Retrieval Approach Based on Discourse Type

D.Y. Wang[1], R.W.P. Luk[1], K.F. Wong[2], and K.L. Kwok[3]

[1] Department of Computing, The Hong Kong Polytechnic University
{csdywang, csrluk}@comp.polyu.edu.hk
[2] Department of Systems Engineering and Engineering Management,
The Chinese University of Hong Kong
kfwong@se.cuhk.edu.hk
[3] Information Retrieval Laboratory, Department of Computer Science,
Queens College, City University of New York
kwok@ir.cs.qc.edu

Abstract. In ad hoc information retrieval (IR), some information need (e.g., find the advantages and disadvantages of smoking) requires the explicit identification of information related to the discourse type (e.g., advantages/ disadvantages) as well as to the topic (e.g., smoking). Such information need is not uncommon and may not be satisfied by using conventional retrieval methods. We extend existing retrieval models by adding a re-ranking strategy based on a novel graph-based retrieval model using document contexts that are called information units (IU). For evaluation, we focused on a discourse type that appeared in a subset of TREC topics where the retrieval effectiveness achieved by our conventional retrieval models for those topics was low. We showed that our approach is able to enhance the retrieval effectiveness for the selected TREC topics. This shows that our preliminary investigation is promising and deserves further investigation.

1 Introduction

The effectiveness of information retrieval (IR) systems varies substantially from one topic to another. This may be due to the diversity of the user information need. Common retrieval systems cannot perform well for all the different kinds of topics since they still deploy a relatively simple representation of the user information need. Potentially, the diversity of user information need may be one of the basic problems in IR.

Our approach to solve problems due to the diversity of the user information need ranks documents by matching the desired discourse types and by the topic. In semantics, discourses are linguistic units composed of several sentences. The study of discourse is known as discourse analysis [1], which looks at both language form and function. We define the discourse type as the functions (including properties and relations that cannot exist independently) of the independent entities mentioned in the topics or documents. Table 1 shows some discourse type examples from robust TREC 2004 [2].

C. Kop et al. (Eds.): NLDB 2006, LNCS 3999, pp. 197–202, 2006.

Table 1. Examples of discourse types (Entity: Independent Entity)

Topic	Description field of topic	Entity	Discourse Type
654	What are the advantages and disadvantages of same-sex schools?	same-sex school	advantages and disadvantages
436	What are the causes of railway accidents throughout the world?	railway accident	cause
606	Find documents that discuss banning leg traps used to capture animals.	leg trap	ban

The feasibility of our approach is investigated in this paper by developing a novel retrieval model that considers discourse types. Queries of a particular discourse type do not need any special attention at the moment if they have high MAP values. Therefore, we focus on discourse types that appeared in queries which have low MAP values. More specifically, this paper focuses on the discourse type "advantage and disadvantage" because it:

(a) is relatively abstract and therefore it is unlikely to be investigated before. By comparison, the discourse types about concrete things (e.g. people, country) may be investigated in question answering tasks or in factoid questions [3];

(b) is related to some cue phrases (e.g., "more than") that are composed of stop words. In conventional IR, stop words do not play any significant role in retrieval. By contrast, some stop words may be indicative of the discourse type in a document or passage;

(c) has a reasonable amount (i.e., eight) of TREC topics for investigation ;

(d) is a popular discourse type of information need. As supporting evidence, we found that there are at least 40 questions that are asking about advantages and disadvantages of something at a website providing a community-built collection of frequently asked questions (http://www.answerbag.com).

2   Problem Formulation and the Graph-Based Model

Our approach uses two sets of terms to present the query for a topic. T is the set of query terms that represent the independent entities. We assume that terms in the "title" field of TREC topics compose T. For example, T of topic 308 is { '*implant*', '*dentistry*' }. The other set is D, a set of language units (including terms, inflected forms and structure patterns) that represent the discourse type, which is called discourse terms set. D is fixed for the same discourse type. Section 3 explains how D is obtained.

We believe that the terms appearing near the query terms are more important for retrieval. Hence, we extract text windows around each query term in the documents. We call these text windows *information units* (IU). So the centre term of an IU must belongs to T, see Fig. 1. Our approach is based on the disjunctive relevance decision (DRD) principle [4] which states that any part of a document that is considered relevant implies that the whole document is relevant. The document re-ranking score (DRS) is an aggregated score of the re-ranking scores of all the IUs in the document using a function $Agg_1(.)$ that emulates disjunction in formula (1).

$$S' = S_0 * DRS = S_0 * Agg_i[RS(IU_i(doc), T, D)] \tag{1}$$

where S' denotes the similarity score after re-ranking, S_0 denotes the original similarity score, "*" is the combining function, $IU_i(doc)$ is the i-th IU of the document doc, $RS(.)$ is a function to compute the re-ranking score of an IU with respect to T and D.

Our graph-based model is more general than the vector based models because the graph includes term dependencies. We use a graph $G(V,E)$ to present an IU. Each vertex in V is a term belonging to T or D in a particular location in the IU and each edge in E links two vertices of V. There are five types of edges: Iso-T edge, linking two same terms belonging to T; Allo-T edge, linking two different terms belonging to T; Iso-D edge, linking two same terms belonging to D; Allo-D edge, linking different terms belonging to D and T-D edge linking a term belonging to T and another term belonging to D. We show one example for each of the five edge types for the IU in Fig. 1., although for some edge types more than one edges could be formed.

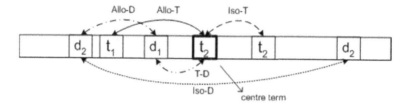

Fig. 1. Example of five edges in a given IU

For each type of edges, we can selectively use all of them or some of them. Six schemes are adopted to select edges. Let us take Allo-T edges for example.

S1: All (atS1): keep all possible Allo-T edges;
S2: Centre (atS2): only Allo-T edges linking the centre term;
S3: Nearest for each pair (atS3): among each pair of two different topic terms, keep the nearest pair;
S4: Nearest for centre (atS4): among each Allo-T edges linking the centre term and another term, choose the nearest one;
S5: Nearest for all (atS5): choose the nearest pair of two different topic terms.
S6: None (atS6): Select no Allo-T edge, i.e., discard this type of edges.

For example, suppose that T consists of three terms t_1, t_2 and t_3. These three terms respectively occur once, twice and once in the IU. The centre term of the IU is t_3. Fig 2 shows the selected edges based on the first five edge selection schemes.

Given a graph $G(V,E)$, let $\sigma(E)$ represent the set of edges selected by applying σ on E. σ is defined by appointing one of the six edge selection schemes for each type of edges. (e.g., σ can be defined as "select Allo-T edges with 'centre' scheme and select T-D edges with 'Nearest for all' scheme, select other edges with 'none' scheme".)

Let $G(V,E)$ be the graph representing $IU_i(doc)$ and the re-ranking score of this IU is aggregated by the relevance evidence score of all edges in the selected edge set $\sigma(E)$:

$$RS(IU_i(doc)) = RS(G(V,E)) = RS(\sigma(E)) = \underset{edge(p,q)\in\sigma(E)}{Agg_2}\{\mathcal{E}[edge(p,q)]\} \qquad (2)$$

where $edge(p, q)$ represents the edge linking term p and term q in E. The relevance evidence score of an edge is specified as:

$$\mathcal{E}(edge(p,q)) = IDF(p,q) \wedge Order(p,q) \wedge Dist(p,q) \qquad (3)$$

where "$\wedge$" denotes a conjunctive function and we specialize it using multiplication in later experiments. This relevance evidence score $\mathcal{E}(.)$ of an edge depends on the specificity and order of the two terms and distance between them in formula (3). For simplicity, $\mathcal{E}(.)$ only depends on the distance in the reported experiments.

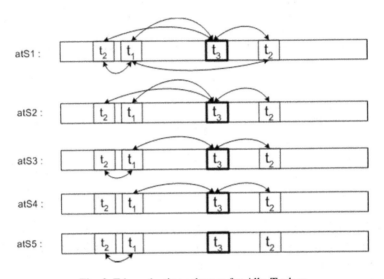

Fig. 2. Edge selection schemes for Allo-T edges

3   Experiment Setup and Results

Our experiments use the topics and documents of TREC Robust Track [2]. We determine the discourse type of a topic by manually reading the "description" field of the topic. The discourse type can be determined by simple pattern matching methods. For simplicity, we determine only one discourse type for each topic. After obtaining the discourse types of all 250 topics, we find that eight of them have discourse type "advantage and disadvantage". The topic IDs are 308, 605, 608, 624, 637, 654, 690 and 699. The following experimental results are based on these eight topics.

Discovery of discourse terms is important for discourse type based IR. For different discourse types, the discourse terms are different in terms of content, representation and occurrence position. Hence, the discovery methods may also be different. We try three methods to find terms for the discourse type "advantage/disadvantage".

(1) Discovery based on statistics: This is a retrospective method since we select single terms that have quite different term distribution in relevant document set and

irrelevant document set. Terms are sorted in descending order by the ratio of the frequency in IUs of relevant documents to irrelevant documents. For each term, we count how many topics have it in the relevant document IUs. After terms with the count number less than four are removed, we select the top 20 terms in the list and compose set d4. Set d5, d6, d7, d8 are built in the same way. We are using these sets of terms in the experiments reported to test the feasibility of our ideas.

(2) Discovery based on linguistic knowledge: We believe that advantages and disadvantages are derived from comparisons. We choose the comparative words (e.g. adjective and adverb) and comparison structures (e.g. more... than) as discourse terms. We find that the higher percentage of comparative words in relevant documents than irrelevant documents for the eight topics that we are investigating.

(3) Discovery based on empirical observations: This is performed by manually extracting the text segments talking about advantages and disadvantages from retrieved results of Internet search engine. By reading these sample text we discover some hints to show the advantage/disadvantage. For example, "success", "fail", "approval" and "oppose" may talk about the positive and negative aspects that relate to advantages and disadvantages. Words ending with "ible" and "able" and their morphological derivations are related with certain capabilities, which often occur in the text segments.

Table 2. Performance of diffent re-ranked methods (Note: Maximum of each topic is marked with bold. We do not compare with PRF since retrieved list for re-ranking is without PRF)

Topic	Original		Graph Model Allo-T Edges				Discourse		Both
	PRF	noprf	atS3	c	c^2	c^2S^2	d4-8	d5-6	c^2S^2d
308	.102	.459	.256	.513	.482	.477	**.693**	.611	.547
605	.339	.067	.053	.053	.057	.063	**.131**	.125	.088
608	.115	.105	.105	.104	**.115**	.113	.081	.082	.080
624	.393	.257	.259	.261	.257	.265	.218	.217	**.277**
637	.347	.435	.508	.505	**.541**	.520	.433	.414	.514
654	.053	.107	.208	.235	.279	.239	.452	**.467**	.391
690	.003	.001	.003	.003	.003	.002	**.005**	**.005**	**.005**
699	.541	.353	.445	.441	**.456**	.434	.381	.369	.433
Mean	.237	.223	.230	.264	.274	.264	**.299**	.286	.292
p<=			.461	.078	.047	**.023**	.250	.460	.055

We re-rank the top 1000 documents retrieved by the 2-Poisson model using the BM11 term weighting scheme [5] without PRF, the performance of which is shown by "noprf" in Table 2. "PRF" is the performance of the same model with PRF as a reference. The RS (IU re-ranking score) of "atS3" is the relevance evidence score of Allo-T edges with atS3 selection. The RS of "c" is obtained by combining the RS of atS3 with dtf (viz. the number of distinct terms of T occurring in IU) by $C=atS3 \times 0.99 + dtf \times 0.01$ in order to assign dtf to the IUs that cannot form any Allo-T edges. The RS of "c^2" and "c^2S^2" is the square of the RS of "c". The RS of "d4-8" is the summation of numbers of terms of d4, d5, ..., d8 occurring in IU. The RS of "d5-6" only counts terms of d5 and d6. The RS of "c^2S^2d" is the multiplication of the RS of "c^2" and the RS of "d4-8". The re-ranked scores(S') of "atS3", "c", "c^2", "d4-8" and "d5-6" are products of the RSD and S_0. The S' of the "c^2" and "c^2S^2d" are products of the RSD with the square of S_0. The aggregating function $Agg_I(.)$ of all the above computations is summation.

4   Related Work and Conclusion

The early work of [6] introduced discourse analysis to IR. Later, researchers in computational linguistics pay more attention to the discourse analysis [7]. Some researchers (e.g. Knott [8], Hutchinson [9]). have studied the discourse terms and discourse types. However, our consideration of discourse type is more implicit and deliberate than the relations used in discourse analysis.

Retrieval effectiveness in terms of MAP after re-ranking is statistically significantly better than our conventional model (baseline) up to 94% confidence level for the reference collection. The confidence level in the significance test has already taken into the account of the sample size (i.e. number of topics). This illustrates that this approach is promising and is worth further investigation.

Acknowledgement

We thank the Center for Intelligent Information Retrieval, University of Massachusetts, for facilitating Robert Luk to develop the basic IR system, when he was on leave there. This work is supported by the CERG Project # PolyU 5226/05E.

References

1. B. Johnstone: Discourse Analysis. Blackwell Publishing Ltd. (2002)
2. E. Voorhees: The TREC robust retrieval track. In ACM SIGIR Forum 39 (1) (2005) 11-20
3. X. Li, D. Roth: Learning question classifiers. In Proceedings of COLING (2002) 556-562
4. Y. Kwong, R. Luk, W. Lam, K. Ho, F.Chung: Passage-based retrieval based on parameterized fuzzy operators, In ACM SIGIR Workshop on Mathematical/Formal Methods for IR (2004)
5. H. C. Wu, R. W. P. Luk, K. F. Wong, K. L. Kwok, W. J. Li: A retrospective study of probabilistic context-based retrieval, In Proceedings of the 28th ACM SIGIR (2005) 663 - 664
6. H. M. Brooks, N. J. Belkin: Using discourse analysis for the design of information retrieval interaction mechanisms. In Proceedings of the 6th ACM SIGIR (1983) 31-47
7. B. Webber, M.Stone, A. Joshi, A. Knott: Anaphora and Discourse Structure. In Computational Linguistics, Vol 29, Issue 4, (2003) 545 – 587
8. A. Knott: A data-driven methodology for motivating a set of coherence relations. PhD thesis, University of Edinburgh. (1996)
9. B. Hutchinson: The Automatic Acquisition of Knowledge about Discourse Connectives. PhD thesis, University of Edinburgh. (2005)

Natural Language Updates to Databases Through Dialogue

Michael Minock

Department of Computing Science
Ume University, Sweden

Abstract. This paper reopens the long dormant topic of natural language updates to databases. A protocol to handle database updates of the IDM (Insert-Delete-Modify) class is proposed and implemented. This protocol exploits modern relational update facilities and constraints and structures update dialogues using DAMSL dialogue acts. The protocol may be used with any natural language parser that maps to relational queries.

1 Introduction

An important issue that received only scant attention in the heyday of research on natural language interfaces to databases, is support for natural language updates [3, 6, 7]. Though there are perhaps better ways to build up the initial state of a large database, we would like users to provide corrections when they notice errors or omissions of content. A simple natural language update seems to be a natural way to accomplish this.

It was recognized early that natural language updates raised several complications beyond natural language querying [3]. One complication is that updates are *referentially opaque*; two phrases with the same extent (i.e. the same tuple or value) can not generally be interchanged and yield the same meaning. For example, "change *the exam grade of Julie Smith* to 96" is not equivalent to "change the exam grade of 92 to 96," where "*the exam grade of Julie Smith*" is currently 92. In contrast a query is *referentially transparent*. In our example "give students with exam grade higher than *the exam grade of Julie Smith*" is equivalent to "Give students with exam grade higher than 92". The consequence of this is that approaches to updates must reason over the access paths to references (i.e. logical queries), not solely over the database objects referred to by such access paths. This implies post parser reasoning must be employed to handle such requests.

Another issue that complicates natural language updates is how to determine the resulting database state of an update. Database updates may in fact be viewed as a form of *counter-factual* reasoning [3]. For example the database update "change the exam grade of Julie Smith from 92 to 96" may be viewed as the counter-factual, "how would the world the database models be different if Julie Smith got a 96 rather than a 92 on her exam?" In ranking the consistent

C. Kop et al. (Eds.): NLDB 2006, LNCS 3999, pp. 203–208, 2006.

databases, preference is given to those that are the nearest to the given database and particularly those that require the fewest changes to the user's view of the database. While in the simple example, it seems sufficient to just change the value of Julie's exam grade and nothing else, harder examples may be concocted. For example consider the request, "change Julie Smith's group leader to Jim Davis". Does this mean (1) to change Smith's group assignment to a group led by Jim Davis or does this mean (2) to assign Jim Davis as the leader of the group that Smith is currently a member of? The informal heuristic in [3] seems to point toward interpretation (2), but this becomes more intricate when one considers the role played by constraints. If a person may lead at most one group and Jim Davis is already assigned to a group, we would be inclined to favor interpretation (1). Again this points toward a significant reasoning component in processing natural language updates. It also points toward the necessity of clarification dialogues with the user to resolve their intended update request.

The early work in natural language updates occurred at a time when basic relational technology was still being developed. While [3] proposes a domain-independent heuristic to rank candidate results of a user's update request, the actual technical specifics are sketchy. The system ASK [7], one of the few early systems to actually implement an update facility, did so over a semantic network, not a relational database. In any case after the initial work of the 1980s, very little work has directly addressed natural language updates to databases. Commercial products have not offered any support for natural language updates and the capability has only been rarely addressed in the academic literature (see for example [9] and [8]).

There are two core problems that must be addressed in processing natural language updates. The first, which is *not* the focus of this paper, is to parse natural language update requests to update specifications in a formal update language. The second problem, which *is* the focus of this paper, is how to resolve ambiguities and handle faults in the formal update request. The approach taken in the work here is to engage users in interactive dialogues to repair faults in their update requests. The types of updates considered are those of the IDM (Insert-Delete-Modify) class [1] and dialogue is modeled using DAMSL (Dialogue Act Markup in Several Layers) [2]. The underlying database formalism is relational and corresponds to what is supported in SQL-92 based databases. A full exposition of this work may be found in the technical report [5] available on the author's web site.

The plan of this paper is as follows: Section 2 gives a brief summary of our approach (see [5] for details). Section 3 discusses current efforts to evaluate the approach. Section 4 discusses this work in the context of prior work and discusses some short comings of the current approach. Finally section 6 gives conclusions.

2   Managing Updates Through Dialogue

Figure 1 shows the basic architecture of a complete natural language interface system which has support for updates. In the ideal case the user's input, a se-

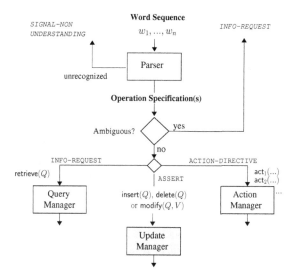

Fig. 1. Architecture of a full NLI to databases

quence of words, is parsed to an operation specification over a logical query expression. Often however the parser does not recognize the sequence of words or the request is ambiguous, leading to several possible interpretations. In the case of non-recognition, a SIGNAL-NON-UNDERSTANDING act results. In the case of ambiguity the system performs an INFO-REQUEST act to resolve the ambiguity. In any case once a unique operation specification is obtained, its type determines which subsystem is invoked. Of interest here are those cases where the operation specification is an *update specification*: insert(Q), delete(Q), or modify(Q, V) where Q is a tuple relational query and V is a vector of values $v_1, ..., v_m$.

2.1   Fault Identification and Repair

If an update specification is meaningful, sufficiently precise, results in a legal state of the database and the user has the permission to perform it, then the update is performed over the database, followed by an ACCEPT act which paraphrases the successful update operation. Often however, there are faults within an update request and such faults will either result in sub-dialogues meant to repair the fault, or result in a REJECT act with an explanation of why an update could not be performed.

We recount the types of faults that must be flagged. *Authorization faults* occur when the user does not have permission to perform an update. *Specification faults* occur when an update operation is ill formed. *Type faults* occur when an attribute value is set to an incompatible type. *Presupposition faults* occur when an update does not actually apply to any tuples in the current database state. *Paucity faults* occur because not enough information is supplied in an update command. *Duplicate primary key faults* occur when an update operation leads to the same primary key value for two distinct tuples. *Non-existent foreign key faults* occur when an update attempts to set the value for a foreign key to reference a non existent tuple. *Dependent foreign key faults* occur when an update operation removes a primary key value upon which another tuple has a foreign key reference. *Null non-null attribute faults* occur when an update operation attempts to set a non null valued attribute's value to NULL. *Ad hoc constraint faults* occur when an update operation leads to a state of the database that violates an ad hoc constraint.

Each of the update specifications: insert(Q), delete(Q) and modify(Q, V) have an associated update protocol. Each call to these protocols results in either a REJECT act in the case of a non repairable fault, an INFO-REQUEST in the case of a repairable fault or an ACCEPT act in case there are no faults. Only in the case of an ACCEPT is the database state altered. See [5] for details.

2.2 Implementation

The update protocol discussed in section 2.1 are implemented within the STEP system [4]. STEP is a natural language interface to databases that uses a highly structured semantic grammar to both parse and paraphrase relational queries. Sentence templates define common sentence patterns in which relational query referring expressions are embedded. While the semantic grammar is build for each new database schema, sentence templates are domain independent. To support the parsing of update requests, STEP was extended with a set of assertion type sentence templates. One for example is the template "There is a NP" which is associated with insert(Q) update specification. Currently there are approximately 20 such patterns, though their number is expected to grow as further experiments are carried out. Surprisingly little work was required to refine the phrasal approach described to handle such assertion statements.

Once STEP parses word sequences to unambiguous insert(Q), delete(Q) or modify(Q, V) specifications, STEP's update manager operates according to the protocols discussed in section 3.1. At a coarse level, ODBC error codes signal which integrity constraints are violated; additional analysis is sometimes required to discern which type of foreign key error occurred. System generated INFO-REQUEST acts are implemented via yes/no questions, menus of possible choices, or single typed value fields to the user. Such a strategy finesses the difficulties of parsing user answers to system generated questions.

Though the protocols discussed in section 3.1 can be used by any natural language interface that maps natural language update requests to insert, delete or modify update specifications, STEP has a full query paraphraser. This paraphraser makes STEP responses much more natural; system utterances are tuned to the query that the user asks. Unfortunately most natural language interfaces to databases are not equipped with paraphrasers, and thus would have to rely on less flexible responses if they were to be extended with an update manager.

3   Evaluation

Limited experiments with STEP's update manager indicates that the system is usable. In fact the author has used the grading example here to record grades for one of his courses, has populated a personal database of his fishing exploits and is using the system to manage paper review assignments and evaluations for the 23rd annual meeting of the Swedish AI Society (SAIS 2006). By using the system in everyday life, bugs are being worked out and an intuition of desirable and undesirable features is being cultivated. A more formal evaluation is planned for the interface which will compare the accuracy of natural language updates over a complex database versus more traditional data entry screens. The hypothesis is that once conceptual complexity of a schema goes beyond a certain bound, there are cases where natural language updates exceed the speed and accuracy of conventional approaches. Naturally the update work will be included in the next system release of STEP, slated for Summer 2006.

A practical requirement, not yet implemented, is a means by which administrators may review user initiated natural language updates before they are permanently committed. Since administrator time and attention is limited, such approvals may take hours (or days) to be performed. However we would like users to immediately see the effects of their updates, particularly in cases in which users will be making multiple updates in a single session. These seemingly contradictory wishes may be accommodated in databases that support *isolated transactions*. At the end of their session, the user's transaction remains pending, awaiting approval by an administrator. Though there are significant system challenges, this approach seems feasible with current generation tools.

4 Discussion

This paper began with the observations, made in [3], that natural language updates are referentially opaque and that there are complex cases in which an update manager must decide how to reflect such updates back into the database. Though these concerns are intellectually appealing, at a practical level, they are not especially significant. For example, all parsed logical query expressions define access paths to referents. Since the update protocols here reason over such query expressions, not just their referents, the approach here manifests a referentially opaque context.

To decide which database state results from an update operation, the approach here is to only accept update operations of the IDM class and to apply such operations only to those objects explicitly mentioned in the update request. Moreover only updates that lead to a state of the database that satisfies the constraints are accepted. When multiple interpretations are still possible, the decision of what update to perform is turned back to the user, not decided through any type of heuristic. Thus in the example from the introduction, the user will receive a paraphrase of both possibilities and then must decide for themselves.

A line of early work questioning the usefulness of domain independent approaches to database updates is [6]. This work argues that a stative relationship between the database and the world is not adequate for database updates. For example in the request "report final grades to the registrar," there is no object in the database that is the rightful referent of 'report'. The action itself will involve checking (or perhaps updating) several tables. The work [6] uses *domain dependent* knowledge encoded in *verb-graphs* to capture the active correspondence between the state of the world and the database. In addition these verb graphs, capture a variety of *domain dependent* dialogue patterns that are involved in performing the action based on available information, etc. The work here side steps these issues by suggesting that the way to model complex actions over the data is as ACTION-DIRECTIVE acts that are processed by a domain dependent *action manager*.

5   Conclusions

The work here, augmented with in [5], lays out a concrete protocol for structuring natural language updates to modern relational databases. The key issue faced is how to interactively resolve faults in the user's update request so that the eventual update respects the constraints of the database. While further development will extend the cases whose repairs may occur, the core of the protocols is expected to provide a durable approach. Prior work on natural language updates to databases has not elaborated such a protocol. In addition, the work here has been implemented and is in the process of being evaluated.

References

1. S. Abiteboul, R. Viannu, and V. Hull. *Foundations of Database Systems*. Addison Wesley, 1995.
2. M. Core and J. Allen. Coding dialogues with the DAMSL annotation scheme. In *AAAI Fall Symposium on Communicative Action in Humans and Machines*, pages 28–35, 1997.
3. S. Kaplan and J. Davidson. Interpreting natural language database updates. In *Proc. of the 19th ACL*, pages 139–141, Stanford, CA, 1981.
4. M. Minock. A phrasal approach to natural language access over relational databases. In *Proc. of Applications of Natural Language to Data Bases (NLDB)*, pages 333–336, Alicante, Spain, 2005.
5. M. Minock. Natural language updates to databases through dialog. Technical Report 06.12, Umeå University, Umeå, Sweden, May 2006.
6. S. Salveter and D. Maier. Natural language updates. In *COLING*, pages 345–350, 1982.
7. B. Thompson and F. Thompson. Ask is transportable in half a dozen ways. *ACM Trans. Inf. Syst.*, 3(2):185–203, 1985.
8. A. Tomasic W. Cohen, E. Minkov. Learning to understand web site update requests. In *Proc. of IJCAI*, pages 1028–1033, 2005.
9. A. Yates, O. Etzioni, and D. Weld. A reliable natural language interface to household appliances. In *Intelligent User Interfaces*, pages 189–196, 2003.

Automatic Construction of a Japanese Onomatopoeic Dictionary Using Text Data on the WWW

Manabu Okumura[1], Atsushi Okumura[2], and Suguru Saito[1]

[1] Tokyo Institute of Technology,
4259 Nagatsuta Midori Yokohama 226-8503 Japan
oku@pi.titech.ac.jp
[2] Sony Corporation

Abstract. As new onomatopoeic words are often created at short notice, existing dictionaries tend to have an insufficient number of their entries. Furthermore, onomatopoeic words seldom appear in collections of newspaper articles, that have been used as corpora in natural language processing. In this work, we present a method of automatically acquiring lexical knowledge for Japanese onomatopoeic words from the WWW. As a result, we could automatically construct a onomatopoeic dictionary that contained 5,130 entries. By manually evaluating 487 newly acquired words that were not in the existing dictionary, we found that we could acquire 266 new onomatopoeic words, and if words in the existing dictionary were regarded as being correct, precision of our automatic acquisition was 83.6%.

1 Introduction

More attention has been paid to automatically acquiring lexical knowledge from a corpus since the middle of the 1980's because knowledge sources such as dictionaries and thesauri are indispensable for the analysis in natural language processing, and it is extremely costly to manually construct a relatively large-scale knowledge source to enable robust analysis. We can now collect a variety of usages for words from a corpus, and can automatically construct a dictionary for them by statistically processing their cooccurrence data. Onomatopoeic words sound like the thing they represent, such as 'hiss' or 'buzz'[1]. Although they are commonly used in everyday speech, no thorough or exhaustive description of them is available in existing lexical knowledge sources. Furthermore, (at least in Japanese) as onomatopoeic words are often newly created, it makes more sense to construct a dictionary of these, automatically rather than manually.

Unfortunately, however, onomatopoeic words seldom appear in collections of newspaper articles, which have been used as corpora in natural language processing. For example, in the 38,383 articles(985,449 morphemes in total) of the Kyoto corpus[2], there have only been 428 occurrences(135 words) of onomatopoeic words that belong to the EDR Japanese Word Dictionary(total of 3,077 entries and 1,618 words)[3], and even the most frequently occurring word uv('kichin-to': accurately) only occurs 45 times in these articles. Therefore, we need to use text data on the Web, which is now available as another useful corpus for linguistic research[4]. We presently have various search

C. Kop et al. (Eds.): NLDB 2006, LNCS 3999, pp. 209–215, 2006.

engines with which we can access text data on the Web, such as Yahoo![1] and Google[2]. Trying to retrieve the word uv, using Google for example, we got about 724,000 hits. Furthermore, as [5, 6] have already pointed out, the advantages of using text data on the Web as a corpus are that the volume of the corpus is huge, and the number of words appearing in the corpus and the variation of their usages are big.

WebCorp[7] is a system that assists linguistic research using text data on the Web as a corpus, and can be used as a search engine where regular expressions can be written, such as "walk*." (With this one expression pages with "walk", "walked", "walking", and "walker" can be retrieved.) Similar systems also can be found elsewhere[3,4,5]. Therefore, it is obvious that retrieving text data from the Web is the most efficient way for automatically acquiring a dictionary of onomatopoeic words. Furthermore, an exhaustive 'living' dictionary of onomatopoeic words that contains newly created entries can automatically be constructed using the huge collection of texts on the Web, including a number of those recently written by individuals, as a corpus and statistically analyzing real usages.

The goal of the work is to 1) try to obtain an exhaustive list of onomatopoeic words, and 2) try to acquire their lexical knowledge. Therefore, to achieve 1), we first have to generate candidate onomatopoeic words automatically, and try to retrieve texts on the Web with a search engine by using the generated candidate words as queries. We can acquire text data that contain the candidate words by retrieval. We then process the text data and determine whether each candidate word is onomatopoeic or not. If the word is judged to be onomatopoeic, its lexical knowledge is acquired from the results of processing the text data. The difficulty in automatically acquiring lexical knowledge for onomatopoeic words is that since we do not have a list of them in processing text data that contain a candidate word, the morphological analyzer that can be easily applied to a newspaper corpus cannot be applied to ours because it does not know the candidate onomatopoeic word and therefore cannot correctly analyze the sentence. Therefore, in processing text data that contain a candidate word, we devised a special method of morphological analysis, which we will explain in Section 3.

Please note that our approach can generally be applied to automatically acquiring lexical knowledge of unknown words, such as the acronyms of proper nouns, if the candidate words can be generated by rule. In Section 2, we briefly outline the characteristics of Japanese onomatopoeia. In Section 3, we explain our approach to automatically construct a Japanese onomatopoeic dictionary. Last, in Section 4, we describe the experimental results with our approach.

2   Characteristics of Japanese Onomatopoeia

2.1   Word Formation in Japanese Onomatopoeia

First let us look at some examples of Japanese onomatopoeic words: u v('mogumogu'; mumble), ułv('gattan';jerk), uv ('chirari-to';glance). While the word forms are various,

---

[1] http://www.yahoo.com/

[2] http://www.google.com/

[3] http://www.kwicfinder.com/KWiCFinder.html

[4] http://prairie.lang.nagoya-u.ac.jp/program/webkwic.html

[5] http://www.edict.com.hk/concordance/

Table 1. Parts-of-Speech in Japanese onomatopoeic words

Adverb	Adjective	Sahen Noun	Others
2492	315	263	7

most of them are formed by the combination of a word base and a pattern. In uv, the base is uv('mogu') and the pattern is uv, where A and B are syllables and a sequence of two syllables 'AB' consists of a base. Similarly, ułv consists of base ułv('gata') and pattern uBv. Therefore, with base uł v and pattern uv, we can create another onomatopoeic word ułłv('gatagata';clatter). According to the Japanese literature on their phonology[8], word formation in Japanese onomatopoeic words can be classified into various classes by pattern. The majority also consist of a base of two syllables, and the most typical form for Japanese onomatopoeic words is repetition of the base(the pattern uv). Therefore, in this work, we have only dealt with those with a base of two syllables and the following 10 patterns: uv, uBv, uBv, uv, uBv, uv, uv, uv, uABv, and uABv, where A and B are syllables, and AB represents a base.

2.2 Parts-of-Speech in Japanese Onomatopoeia

The parts-of-speech for onomatopoeic words in EDR[3] are summarized in Table 1. Therefore, apart from a few exceptions(seven), the parts-of-speech for Japanese onomatopoeic words are: adverbs, adjectives, and sahen nouns, which is a noun followed by verb uv('suru';to do). Furthermore, according to [9], Japanese onomatopoeic adverbs tend to be followed by particle uv('to').

3 Proposed Method

The following illustrates the steps in our proposed method:

1. Generating candidate onomatopoeic words by using the word formation rules for Japanese onomatopoeia,
2. Web retrieval with a search engine,
3. Extracting sentences containing the candidate words from the retrieved web pages,
4. Morphologically and syntactically analysing the extracted sentences,
5. Constructing lexical entries for the candidate words.

3.1 Automatic Generation of Candidate Onomatopoeic Words

Candidate onomatopoeic words are generated in Hiragana(Japanese syllabary characters), as described in Section 2.2, by the following 10 patterns: uv, uBv, uBv, uv, uBv, uv, uv, uv, uABv, and uABv. 'A' in the patterns can be a Hiragana(uv('a'), uv('i'), uv('u'), c) or 2 Hiraganas that form a syllable, such as uv('kya'), uv ('kyu'), or uv('kyo'). 'B' in the patterns can be the same as 'A' or nasal sound change(uv('n')), double consonant(uv), or long vowel(u[v). The words where the second A changes to the dull sound (e.g. uv('shimijimi';feelingly)) are also generated only for the pattern uv.

3.2   Sentence Retrieval from the Web

We then tried to retrieve texts from the Web with a search engine by using the generated candidate words as queries. We first checked the number of hits and obtain URL of the hit page only for the candidate words for which the number of hits exceeded a pre-fixed threshold. Candidate words that could not yield fewer hits than the threshold were discarded, being regarded as 'non-words.' We then extracted sentences in which the candidate word appeared from the pages of the obtained URL. Since sentence boundaries are usually not explicitly indicated in Web texts, we constructed a filter that could extract a sentence correctly from a Web page, and used it to correctly analyze texts on the Web.

3.3   Morphological Analysis

Extracted sentences were then morphologically analyzed with JUMAN[10], which analysed an inputted sentence by looking up words in its word dictionary, trying to segment the sentence into a sequence of words and to identify their parts-of-speech. Unfortunately, as we did not have a list of onomatopoeic words beforehand, JUMAN tended to output erroneous results for sentences that contained an onomatopoeic word that was not in its word dictionary. Therefore, we need to devise a method of performing morphological analysis correctly in sentences containing onomatopoeic words. To segment a sentence correctly into a sequence of words, we applied JUMAN to the sentence by placing a space symbol just before and after a candidate word in the sentence. This was because we could explicitly indicate that the position of the space symbol was a word boundary.

Since the part-of-speech of a candidate word was not identified with the morphological analyzer, we need to develop a method of identifying it separately. Here, we again tried to retrieve texts on the Web with a search engine by using a candidate word followed by suffixes that tended to cooccur with onomatopoeic words of a part-of-speech as queries. We could identify the part-of-speech of a candidate onomatopoeic word to be the one that could obtain the number of hits greater than a prefixed threshold. As we mentioned in Section 2.2, the part-of-speech of onomatopoeic words can be: adverbs, adjectives, and sahen nouns. Therefore, if the part-of-speech of a candidate word was identified to be one other than those listed above, it was judged not to be onomatopoeic, and was discarded.

3.4   Syntactic Analysis

Next, to obtain words that cooccured with the candidate onomatopoeic words, we applied a syntactic analyser to sentences that contained them. We used KNP[11], a Japanese syntactic analyser.

4   Experiments

4.1   Candidate-Words Generation and Web Retrieval

We first generated candidate words with the most typical word formation pattern uv. There were 30,867 words generated. We then tried to retrieve texts on the Web with

Google[6], after obtaining permission, using these generated candidate words as queries. We first checked the number of hits and only obtained URL of the hit pages for candidate words with more than 100 hits. In the candidate words of pattern uv(30,867 words), the number of words for which we could obtain more than 100 hits was 2,812. Next, based on the base ('AB') by which we could generate the candidate words obtaining more than 100 hits with Google, we generated candidate words for the other 9 patterns[7]. We then extracted sentences in which the candidate word appeared. If there were no more than 100 extracted sentences, the candidate word was judged not to be a word and was discarded in the experiments.

4.2 Sentence Analysis

For candidate words that could obtain more than 100 sentences containing them, we did web retrieval with the words followed by some suffixes to identify their part-of-speech. Here, since the patterns uv, uv, and uv included the suffix particle in itself, we did not do the retrieval for the candidate words of the patterns since they were clearly adverbs.

Morphological and syntactic analysis was done for the candidate words that still remained to be considered as onomatopoeic after this step, and the dictionary was constructed with information from the analytical results.

4.3 Evaluation

We evaluated our constructed dictionary by comparing it with existing dictionaries that contained onomatopoeic words. As we previously mentioned, we used the following 3 dictionaries: EDR[3], Gendai[12], and Eijirou[13].

We first investigated the overlap in our constructed dictionary and the existing 3 dictionaries. We can see that our dictionary contained words that were not in the existing dictionaries. However, since the words in the existing dictionaries themselves varied one another, comparing our dictionary with each existing dictionary did not necessarily mean a proper investigation. Therefore, we merged the 3 existing dictionaries into one, and compared our dictionary with this[8].

There were 1,447 stems in the merged dictionary. 487 stems were in ours but not theirs. However, theirs had 583 stems that were not in ours, and the number of stems that were in both dictionaries was 864. If the words in the existing dictionary are considered correct for evaluation, the recall is $864/1,447 = 59.7\%$.

For these 487 stems that were in our dictionary but not in the existing dictionary, we manually evaluated whether they were truly onomatopoeic. The results are listed in Table 2, which shows we could acquire 266 new onomatopoeic stems that were not in the existing dictionary. Some new onomatopoeic words are listed in Table 3. Again, if we consider the words in the existing dictionary were correct for evaluation, our precision is, as Table 4 shows, 83.6%.

---

[6] http://www.google.com/

[7] We can generate candidate words for all the patterns with all possible combinations of 'A','B', similar to pattern uv. However, we adopted the above strategy to do the experiments efficiently.

[8] Here, we take into consideration only the stems that can be generated by the 10 patterns for evaluation.

Table 2. Accuracy of words only in our dictionary

	Correct	Wrong	Total
No. of stems	266	221	487
Percentage(%)	54.6	45.4	100

Table 3. Some newly acquired words

Words	Sample sentences	Synonym in the existing dictionary
('uzouzo')	ł	(in swarms)
('kiran-to')	ł	(with a twincle)
('tekoteko')		(with short steps)

Table 4. Precision of our dictionary

	Correct	Wrong	Total
No. of stems	1,130	221	1,351
Percentage(%)	83.6	16.4	100

5 Conclusions

In this paper, we proposed a method that could automatically construct a 'living' dictionary of onomatopoeic words that were currently being used, utilizing text data on the Web. As a result, we could automatically construct a onomatopoeic dictionary that contained 5,130 entries. Comparing it with an existing dictionary that contained 1,447 stems, which was obtained by merging 3 existing dictionaries, we could obtain 864 stems that were in the existing dictionary with recall of 59.7%. By manually evaluating 487 newly acquired stems that were not in the existing dictionary, the accuracy was 54.6%, and if words in the existing dictionary were regarded as being correct, precision of our automatic acquisition was 83.6%.

As future work, we are planning to do similar experiments to the ones discussed in the last section with patterns that were not used in this work, and on onomatopoeic words in Katakana. We are also planning to automatically construct a thesaurus with the acquired entries, by taking into account their similarity scores. We think we should take at least the following two similarities between entries into account: similarity of word form between entries(ułłv('gatagata'), ułv('gattan'), and ułv ('gatatto') are similar), and similarity of cooccurrence information(uł łkv(trembling), uhv(wavy) are similar).

Acknowledgements

Our thanks go to Google, who kindly gave us the permission to use their search engine for our research.

References

1. Sinclair, J., ed.: Collins Cobuild English Dictionary. HarperCollins Publishers (1995)
2. Kurohashi, S., Nagao, M.: Kyoto university text corpus project. Proceedings of ANLP '97 (1997) 115–118 In Japanese.
3. Japanese Electronic Dictionary Research Institute Ltd.: EDR electronic dictionary technical guide ver.2.0. (1999)
4. Kilgarriff, A., Grefenstette, G.: Introduction to the special issue on the web as corpus. Computational Linguistics **29**(3) (2003) 333–347
5. Dumais, S., Banko, M., Brill, E., Lin, J., Ng, A.: Web question answering: Is more always better? In: Proceedings of SIGIR '02. (2002) 291–298
6. Ravichandran, D., Hovy, E.: Learning surface text patterns for a question answering system. In: Proceedings of ACL '02. (2002)
7. Kehoe, A., Renouf, A.: Webcorp: Applying the web to linguistics and linguistics to the web. In: Proceedings of The Eleventh International World Wide Web Conference. (2002)
8. Tamori, I.: Nihongo onomatope no on'in keitai. In Kakei, H., Tamori, I., eds.: Onomatopia GionEGitaigo no Rakuen. Keisou Shobou (1993) 1–15 In Japanese.
9. Tamori, I.: Nihongo onomatope no tougo hanchuu. In Kakei, H., Tamori, I., eds.: Onomatopia GionEGitaigo no Rakuen. Keisou Shobou (1993) 17–75 In Japanese.
10. Kurohashi, S., Nagao, M.: Japanese Morphological Analysis System JUMAN version 3.61 Manual. (1999) In Japanese.
11. Kurohashi, S., Nagao, M.: Kn parser : Japanese dependency/case structure analyzer. In: Proceedings of the Workshop on Sharable Natural Language Resources. (1994) 48–55
12. Hida, Y., Asada, H.: Gendai Giongo Gitaigo Youhou Jiten. Tokyodo Shuppan (2002) In Japanese.
13. Michibata, H.: Eijirou. 1st edn. Alc, http://www.alc.co.jp/ (2002) In Japanese.

Category-Based Audience Metrics for Web Site Content Improvement Using Ontologies and Page Classification

Jean-Pierre Norguet[1], Benjamin Tshibasu-Kabeya[2],
Gianluca Bontempi[2], and Esteban Zimányi[1]

[1] Department of Computer & Network Engineering
Université Libre de Bruxelles, CP 165/15
50 Avenue F.D. Roosevelt, 1050 Brussels, Belgium
{jnorguet, ezimanyi}@ulb.ac.be
[2] Machine Learning Group, Département d'Informatique
Université Libre de Bruxelles, CP 212
Boulevard du Triomphe, 1050 Brussels, Belgium
{btshibas, gbonte}@ulb.ac.be

Abstract. With the emergence of the World Wide Web, analyzing and improving Web communication has become essential to adapt the Web content to the visitors' expectations. Web communication analysis is traditionally performed by Web analytics software, which produce long lists of page-based audience metrics. These results suffer from page synonymy, page polysemy, page temporality, and page volatility. In addition, the metrics contain little semantics and are too detailed to be exploited by organization managers and chief editors, who need summarized and conceptual information to take high-level decisions. To obtain such metrics, we propose to classify the Web site pages into categories representing the Web site topics and to aggregate the page hits accordingly. In this paper, we show how to compute and visualize these metrics using OLAP tools. To solve the page-temporality issue, we propose to classify the versions of the pages using automatic classifiers.

1 Motivations and Related Work

With the emergence of the Internet, Web sites have become key communication channels in organizations. To satisfy the objectives of the Web site, adapting the Web site content to the users' expectations has become a major concern. In this context, Web usage mining, a relatively new research area, and Web analytics, a part of Web usage mining that has most emerged in the corporate world, offer many Web communication analysis techniques. These techniques include prediction of the user's behaviour within the site, comparison between expected and actual Web site usage, adjustment of the Web site with respect to the users' interests, and mining and analyzing Web usage data to discover interesting metrics and usage patterns [13]. However, Web usage mining and

C. Kop et al. (Eds.): NLDB 2006, LNCS 3999, pp. 216–220, 2006.

Web analytics suffer from significant drawbacks when it comes to support the decision-making process at higher levels in the organization.

Indeed, according to organizations theory [6], higher levels in the organizations need summarized and conceptual information to take fast, high-level, and effective decisions. For Web sites, these levels include the organization managers and the Web site chief editors. At these levels, the results produced by Web analytics tools are mostly useless. Indeed, most of these results target Web designers and Web developers [15]. Summary reports like the number of visitors and the number of page views can be of some interest to the organization manager but these results are poor. Finally, page-group and directory hits give the Web site chief editor conceptual results, but these are limited by several problems like page synonymy (several pages contain the same topic), page polysemy (a page contains several topics), page temporality, and page volatility.

Web usage mining research projects on their part have mostly left aside Web analytics and its limitations and have focused on other research paths. Examples of these paths are usage pattern analysis, personalization, system improvement, site structure modification, marketing business intelligence, and usage characterization [13]. A potential contribution to Web analytics was attempted with reverse clustering analysis [10], a technique based on self-organizing feature maps. This technique integrates Web usage mining and Web content mining in order to rank the Web site pages according to an original popularity score. However, the algorithm is not scalable and does not answer the page-polysemy, page-synonymy, page-temporality, and page-volatility problems. As a consequence, these approaches fail at delivering summarized and conceptual results.

An interesting attempt to obtain such results is proposed in the IUNIS algorithm of the Information Scent model [2]. This algorithm produces a list of term vectors representing the visitors' needs. These vectors provide a semantic representation of the visitors' needs and can be easily interpreted. Unfortunately, the results suffer from term polysemy and term synonymy, are visit-centric rather than site-centric, and are not scalable to produce. Finally, according to a recent survey [3], no Web usage mining research project has proposed a satisfying solution to provide site-wide summarized and conceptual audience metrics.

In this paper, we propose to automatically classify the Web site pages into ontology categories. In Section 2, we introduce the idea of classifying the Web site pages into a taxonomy representing the Web site topics. Then, we explain how to aggregate the page hits along the taxonomy in order to obtain category-based audience metrics. Finally, we formalize these metrics and we explain how to compute them using OLAP tools.

2   Category-Based Audience Metrics

Given a Web site to analyze, we choose a taxonomy or ontology that models the Web site knowledge domain. The taxonomy entries should represent the hierarchy of the Web site topics. For each topic in the taxonomy, we classify the Web site pages that fit into the corresponding category (Figure 1). As in most taxonomies the terms are hierarchically linked by a relationship of type *part of*, *is a kind of*, or *is a* [14], the audience of the lower topics contributes to the communication of the upper topics. As the number of page hits can be retrieved from the Web site logs [8], category-based hits can be obtained by hierarchical aggregation of the page hits from the leaves up to the taxonomy root.

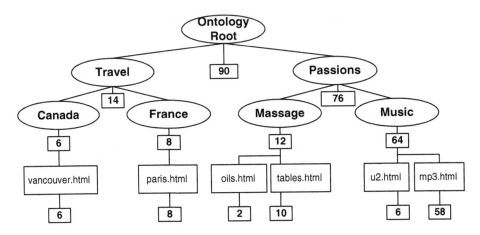

Fig. 1. Classified Web pages in categories and page hits aggregation

Category-based hits can be formalized as follows. For a mining period between days d_1 and d_2 and a given category C_i in the taxonomy, the number of hits for the C_i category is given by the following recursive expression, where C_j are the subcategories of C_i and p_{ij} are the pages classified into C_i:

$$\text{Hits}(C_i, d_1, d_2) := \sum_{C_j} \text{Hits}(C_j, d_1, d_2) + \sum_{d=d_1}^{d_2} \sum_{p_{ij}} \text{Hits}(p_{ij}, d). \qquad (1)$$

Practically, hierarchical aggregation of the page-based metrics into category-based metrics can be computed and visualized using OLAP tools. The computation of Equation 1 with OLAP tools requires a multidimensional model with two dimensions: Time and Taxonomy (Figure 2). The taxonomy dimension should be designed as a *parent-child dimension* to support taxonomies with any number of levels in each branch [5]. The time dimension, hereby schematized, can be designed from an aggregation of days, weeks, months, years, etc. [8]. The cube fact table must contain the daily page hits, which can be computed from the Web logs. The measure to define in the cube is the number of hits. After the cube has been introduced and processed in the OLAP tool, category-based hits can be extracted and visualized with any OLAP client, like Microsoft Excel.

To take the page temporality into account, we use a *content journal* to keep track of the page content evolution [8]. Practically, a content journal records the history of the Web site pages, including the online periods and the publishing URIs. The analyzer can therefore retrieve from the content journal the content

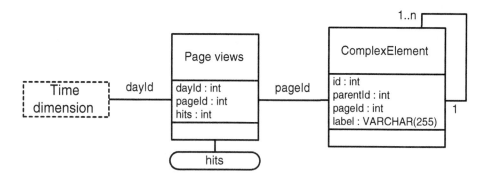

Fig. 2. Multidimensional model for category-based hits

of any Web page sent to the client, based on the request datetime and URI. If the analysis period is long, classifying the content journal pages can be overwhelming. In this case, an automatic classifier can be used. Automatic classifiers require a training phase on an annotated document set. An example of document set can be the latest snapshot of the Web site pages. As the content of Web sites usually expands rather than contracts, this snapshot should ensure a good coverage of the knowledge domain. This should improve the classification of the content journal pages.

3   Conclusions and Future Work

As category-based metrics are summarized and conceptual, they can be exploited at higher levels in the organization. For example, organization managers can redefine the organization strategy according to the visitors' interests. Category-based metrics also give an intuitive view of the messages delivered through the Web site and allow to adapt the Web site communication to the organization objectives. The Web site chief editor on his part can interpret the metrics to redefine the publishing orders and the editors' writing tasks. As decisions at higher levels in the organization are more effective, category-based metrics should significantly contribute to extending Web analytics results.

The main limitation of category-based metrics is their dependency on proper page classification. To improve the classification process, our future work will consider other classification techniques like ontology-based reasoning [4] and decision-tree classifiers [7]. Also, we anticipate that category-based metrics would encounter several limitations before their wide adoption. These limitations include page polysemy, term polysemy, training set availability, and data volume in high-traffic dynamic Web sites. In our future work, we will therefore consider as respective insights: multiple classification [9], word sense disambiguation [12], classifier optimization using external training sets [1], and statistical inference from page samples [11].

References

1. S. Chakrabarti, B. Dom, R. Agrawal, and P. Raghavan. Scalable feature selection, classification and signature generation for organizing large text databases into hierarchical topic taxonomies. *VLDB J.*, 7(3):163–178, 1998.
2. E. H. Chi, P. Pirolli, K. Chen, and J. E. Pitkow. Using information scent to model user information needs and actions and the web. In *Proc. of the SIGCHI on Human Factors in Computing Systems*, pages 490–497, 2001.
3. F. M. Facca and P. L. Lanzi. Mining interesting knowledge from weblogs: a survey. *Data Knowl. Eng.*, 53(3):225–241, 2005.
4. H. Johan, D. Perrotta, R. Steinberger, and A. Varfis. Document classification and visualisation to support the investigation of suspected fraud. In *Proc. of the 4th European Conf. on Principles and Practice of Knowledge Discovery in Databases, PKDD*, 2000.
5. E. Malinowski and E. Zimányi. OLAP hierarchies: A conceptual perspective. In *Proc. of the 16th Int. Conf. on Advanced Information Systems Engineering, CAiSE'04*, LNCS 3084, pages 477–491. Springer-Verlag, 2004.
6. J.G. March, H.A. Simon, and H.S. Guetzkow. *Organizations*. Cambridge Mass. Blackwell, 2nd edition, 1983.
7. T. M. Mitchell. *Machine Learning*. McGraw-Hill Higher Education, 1997.
8. J. P. Norguet, E. Zimányi, and R. Steinberger. Improving web sites with web usage mining, web content mining, and semantic analysis. In *Proc. of the 32nd Int. Conf. on Current Trends in Theory and Practice of Computer Science, SOFSEM*. Springer-Verlag, 2006.
9. A. M. Ráez, L. A. Ureña López, and R. Steinberger. Adaptive selection of base classifiers in one-against-all learning for large multi-labeled collections. In *Proc. of the 4th Int. Conf. on Advances in Natural Language Processing, EsTAL*, pages 1–12, 2004.
10. S. A. Ríos, J. D. Velásquez, E. S. Vera, H. Yasuda, and T. Aoki. Using SOFM to improve web site text content. In *Proc. of the 1st Int. Conf. on Advances in Natural Computation, ICNC, Part II*, pages 622–626, 2005.
11. V.K. Rohatgi. *An Introduction to Probability Theory and Mathematical Statistics*. John Wiley & Sons, 1976.
12. M. Sanderson. Word sense disambiguation and information retrieval. In *Proc. of the 17th Int. Conf. on R&D in IR, SIGIR*, pages 142–150, 1994.
13. J. Srivastava, R. Cooley, M. Deshpande, and T. Pang-Ning. Web usage mining: Discovery and applications of usage patterns from web data. *SIGKDD Explorations*, 1(2), 2000.
14. G. Stumme and A. Maedche. FCA-MERGE: Bottom-up merging of ontologies. In *Proc. of the 17th Int. Joint Conf. on Artificial Intelligence, IJCAI*, pages 225–234, 2001.
15. U. Wahli, J.P. Norguet, J. Andersen, N. Hargrove, and M. Meser. *Websphere Version 5 Application Development Handbook*. IBM Press, 2003.

Automatic Turkish Text Categorization in Terms of Author, Genre and Gender

M. Fatih Amasyalı and Banu Diri

Yıldız Technical University, Computer Engineering Department,
34349 Beşiktaş, İstanbul, Turkey
{mfatih, banu}@ce.yildiz.edu.tr

Abstract. In this study, a first comprehensive text classification using n-gram model has been realized for Turkish. We worked in 3 different areas such as determining the identification of a Turkish document's author, classifying documents according to text's genre and identifying a gender of an author, automatically. Naive Bayes, Support Vector Machine, C 4.5 and Random Forest were used as classification methods and the results were given comparatively. The success in determining the author of the text, genre of the text and gender of the author was obtained as 83%, 93% and 96%, respectively.

1 Introduction

Text categorization (TC) is the process of classifying documents into a certain number of predefined categories. One of the problems in TC is the authorship attribution which is identifying the author of an anonymous text or text whose authorship is in doubt [1]. The other problem is the identification of text genre which is becoming an important application in web information management. The other problem is also a need to classify texts according to author gender.

In the last 35 years there were several studies in the identification of the author of a text. Mosteller and Wallace took the Federalist Papers and determined a very credible attribution of authorship on the basis of a range of discriminates and used Bayesian analysis [2]. Burrows [3] focused on common high-frequency words. Amongst the pioneers of authorship attribution are Brinegar [4], who focused on word lengths, Morton [4], who focused on sentence lengths, and Brainerd [4], who focused on syllables per word. Stamatatos [4] have applied Multiple Regression and Discriminant Analysis using 22 style markers. They have measured these results on ten authors. Fürnkranz [5] described an algorithm for efficient generation and frequency-based pruning of n-gram features. Cavnar et all [6]described a n-gram based approach to text categorization is tolerant of textual errors.

The traditional literature on genre that uses quantitative methods is that of Biber [7], which draws on work on stylistic analysis readability indexing and differences between spoken and written language. Kessler et al [8], who developed a simple and confident method for genre detection.

C. Kop et al. (Eds.): NLDB 2006, LNCS 3999, pp. 221–226, 2006.

Some of the works for determining the gender of a document's author are performed by Mulac et al [9], Herring [10] and Palander-Collin [11]. Koppel et al. [12] employed machine learning algorithms on a genre-controlled corpus of 566 documents taken from the British National Corpus to construct models.

In this work we used character n-grams to achieve the TC. We have figured out the language bi-grams and tri-grams by using a corpus, which is composed of Turkish texts. Using this bi-gram and tri-gram, 6 different datasets were constructed for 3 different classification problems (author, genre and gender) and 2 different n-gram models (bi-gram, tri-gram).

The remainder of the paper is organized as follows: In section 2 a brief description of n-grams and our corpus are introduced. In Section 3 Classification and feature selection algorithms are presented. In Section 4, we have discussed empirical results in our experiments. Finally, we summarize our conclusions in section 5.

2 Testing Ground

2.1 N-Grams

An n-gram is an n-character fragment of a longer string. In literature, the n-gram term is included the notion of any co-occurring set of characters in a string [6].We have handled the text as a whole and we have extracted the bi-grams and the tri-grams.

2.2 Corpus

In the text categorization experiments we chose to deal with texts taken from newspapers, considering the variety of authors publishing their writings in the press. Our corpus consists of texts downloaded from 3 Turkish daily newspapers. This corpus consists of eighteen randomly selected authors writing on different subjects like political, popular interest and sport.

The dataset consists of 630 singly authored documents written by 18 different authors, with 35 different texts written by each author. Also, this dataset has been chosen from 3 different classes such as politic, popular interest and sport in order to be used to determine the genre of the document. Again, the same dataset is composed of 4 female and 14 male authors in order to determine the gender of the author. To determine the author of text, the genre of text and the gender of the author six different data set has been constructed as shown in the Table 1.

While forming the bi-grams and the tri-grams of the corpus the number of occurrences of each feature is counted. At the end of this process we have observed that the number of different bi-grams and tri-grams are too much. In order to avoid the combinatorial explosion in the feature vectors, which consist of bi-grams and tri-grams, we used a threshold value to reduce the number of features. Infrequent features are removed from the feature vectors. The dimensions of the bi-gram and tri-gram feature vectors are 446 and 913 respectively.

Table 1. Datasets

	Bi-grams (446 features)	Tri-grams (913 features)
Author of document (18 classes)	Dataset I	Dataset II
Genre of document (3 classes)	Dataset III	Dataset IV
Gender of author (2 classes)	Dataset V	Dataset VI

3   Classification and Feature Selection Algorithms

In this work, we used 4 different classification methods such as Naive Bayes, Support Vector Machines, C 4.5 and Random Forest that are used in identification of an author, determination of a text genre and gender of an author.

Naive Bayes (NB): Classical Naive Bayes is a probabilistic classifier that uses joint probabilities of words and categories to calculate the category of a given document. In our study, the features are not word frequencies. They have continuous distributions. For this reason, Naive Bayes's WEKA (available at www.cs.waikato.ac.nz/ml/weka) implementation was used for our experiments.

Support Vector Machines (SVM): Support Vector Machines which are based on the structural risk minimization principle and mapping of input vectors in high-dimensional feature space also avoids over fitting and does not need a feature selection. We used WEKA's SVM implementation.

C4.5: The main idea of the classic decision tree algorithm is the division of the feature space into two regions. The division process is repeated until each region contains single-class data or a predefined criterion is achieved. C4.5 is univariate decision tree algorithm. At each node, only one attribute of instances are used for decision making.

Random Forest (RF): The forest consists of several different multivariate decision trees which are trained by different training sets. Different training sets are constructed from original training set by bootstrap and random feature selection. Multivariate decision trees are constructed with CART algorithm. Although, each tree has its own decision, the maximum voted class in the forest is accepted as final decision.

Correlation-based Feature Selection (CFS): CFS is one of the feature selection methods which place in WEKA. Each feature's independent prediction ability is calculated. Subsets of features that are highly correlated with the class while having low inter-correlation are selected.

4   Experimental Results

In our experiments, we showed whether the modeling of Turkish texts with n-grams is successful approach or not for in determining the author of text, genre of the text and gender of the author. For each classification problem, 4 different classifiers were trained on 2 different n-gram models. 5-fold cross validation was used for the evaluation of success ratio. Default performance (dp) is the success ratio when all instances were classified as majority class.

4.1   Author Identification

DataSet-I and DataSet-II were constructed by using bi-gram and tri-gram models for author identification, respectively. Classifiers were trained with all n-gram features and n-gram feature subsets that selected by CFS. Each author has 35 texts of which 28 were used as training set and 7 were used as test set. The success of 4 different classification methods used in determining the author of the text is given Table 2.

Table 2. Author Identification Results

dp : 5.5%	C4.5%	NB%	SVM%	RF%
Dataset-I (446 features)	59.5	76.2	72.2	74.4
Dataset-I CFS: (34 subset feature)	66.2	83.3	79	80.2
Dataset-II (913 feature)	54.4	71.4	69.7	70.1
Dataset-II CFS : (29 subset feature)	61.2	76.2	74.1	74.3

When the feature selective method is not used, Naive Bayes classifier gave the best result in identifying the author of text. Feature selection's improvement on success can be seen for all classifiers and n-gram models. Again, in both two datasets, Naive Bayes gave the best result. Bi-gram model is more successful than tri-gram in determining the author of the text.

4.2   Genre Identification

DataSet-III and DataSet-IV were constructed by using bi-gram and tri-gram models for genre identification, respectively. Classifiers were trained with all n-gram features and n-gram feature subsets that selected by CFS. Each genre has 210 texts of which 168 were used as training set and 42 were used as test set. The success of 4 different classification methods used in determining the genre of the text is given Table 3.

Table 3. Genre Identification Results

dp : 33.3%	C4.5%	NB%	SVM%	RF%
Dataset-III (446 features)	84.9	84.1	90.6	87.9
Dataset-III CFS: (34 subset feature)	88.8	86.2	92.5	92.2
Dataset-IV (913 feature)	79.8	84.3	88.5	88.9
Dataset-IV CFS : (29 subset feature)	84.2	89.8	93.6	92.7

When the feature selective method is not used, while SVM gives good result in DataSet-III, RF gave almost the same result with SVM in DataSet-IV. Feature selection's improvement on success can be seen for all classifiers and n-gram models. SVM gave good result in DataSet-III and DataSet-IV. There is no significant difference between bi-gram and tri-gram models.

4.3 Gender Identification

DataSet-V and DataSet-VI were constructed by using bi-gram and tri-gram models for determining gender of an author, respectively. Classifiers were trained with all n-gram features and n-gram feature subsets that selected by CFS. Female authors have 140 texts of which 112 were used as training set and 28 were used as test set. Male authors have 490 texts of which 392 were used as training set and 98 were used as test set. The success of 4 different classification methods used in determining the gender of the author is given Table 4.

Table 4. Gender Identification Results

dp : 77.7%	C4.5%	NB%	SVM%	RF%
Dataset-V (446 features)	84.9	83.8	88.2	88.3
Dataset-V CFS: (34 subset feature)	90.5	91.6	94.1	92.2
Dataset-VI (913 feature)	86.8	85.1	90.1	87.8
Dataset-VI CFS : (29 subset feature)	88.9	92.2	96.3	92.2

When the feature selective method is not used, while SVM and RF give the best results in DataSet-V, SVM gave better result in DataSet-VI. Feature selection's improvement on success can be seen for all classifiers and n-gram models. There is no significant difference between bi-gram and tri-gram models. SVM again over performed from all other classifiers in both datasets.

5 Conclusion

N-gram models are common and successful approach for text classification. This work is the first comprehensive study on classification of Turkish texts modeled with n-grams. Turkish texts were classified in terms of author, genre and gender. Our study shows that n-grams are suitable models solving different Turkish texts classification problems.

Using the same corpus, 6 different classification problems were constructed by labeling text according to their authors, genres and author genders. 4 different classification algorithms and a feature selection algorithm were used in this work. Default parameters in WEKA were used in all classification problems. It is observed that feature selection increased the classification accuracy on all datasets. Three classification problems are compared in terms of feature selection effect, best classifier and best n-gram model in Table 5.

Table 5. Comparing classification problems

	Author	Genre	Gender
Feature Selection Effect	Success increased	Success increased	Success increased
Best Model	Bi-gram	No difference	No difference
Best Classifier	Naive Bayes	SVM	SVM

As summarized in Table 5, when feature selective model is used we observed that the success of 3 classification problem is increased. Bi-gram model is more successful than tri-gram model in determining the author of the text. Both n-gram models gave the same success in identifying the genre of the text and gender of the author. While the Naive Bayes classifier is successful in determining the author of the text, SVM is more successful in determining the genre of the text and gender of the author.

For future work, combining other text features (lexical, syntactic annotation, stylometry, word n-grams eg.) with character n-grams is planning.

References

1. Love H.: Attributing Authorship: An Introduction, Cambridge Univ. Press (2002)
2. Dale R., Moisl H., Somers H.: Handbook of NLP, Marcel Dekker (2000)
3. Burrows J.F.: Not unless you ask nicely: the interpretative nexus between analysis and information. Literary Linguist Comput (7):pp.91-109 (1992)
4. Stamatatos E., Fakotakis N., Kokkinakis G.: Automatic Text Categorization in Terms of Genre and Author, Computational Linguistics, pp.471-495 (2000)
5. Fürnkranz J.: A Study using n-gram Features for Text Categorization, Austrian Research Institute for Artifical Intelligence (1998)
6. Cavnar W.B.: Using an n-gram-based Document Representation with a Vector Processing Retrieval Model. In Proceedings of the Third Text Retrieval Conference(TREC-3) (1994)
7. Biber D.: Dimensions of Register Variation: A Cross-Linguistic Comparison Cambridge Univ.Press (1995)
8. Kessler B., Nunberg G., Schütze H.: Automatic Detection of Text Genre, Proc. of the 35th Annual Meeting of the Association for Computational Linguistics (ACL/EACL'97), pp.32-38 (1997)
9. Mulac A., Studley L.B, Blau S.: The Gender-linked Language Effect in Primary and Secondary Students' impromptu Essays, Sex Roles, 9/10 (1990)
10. Herring S.: Two Variants of an Electronic Message Schema, in S.Herring ed., Computer-Mediated Communication: Linguistic, Social and Cross-Cultural Perspectives, pp.81-106 (1996)
11. Palander C. M.: Male and Female Styles in 17th Century Correspondence, Language Variation and Change 11, pp. 123-141 (1999)
12. Koppel M., Argamon S., Shimoni A.R.: Automatically Categorizing Written Texts by Author Gender Literary and Linguistic Computing 17(4) pp.401-412 (2002)

Author Index

Lecture Notes in Computer Science

For information about Vols. 1–3906

please contact your bookseller or Springer

Vol. 3959: J.-Y. Cai, S. B. Cooper, A. Li (Eds.), Theory and Applications of Models of Computation. XV, 794 pages. 2006.

Vol. 3958: M. Yung, Y. Dodis, A. Kiayias, T. Malkin (Eds.), Public Key Cryptography - PKC 2006. XIV, 543 pages. 2006.

Vol. 3956: G. Barthe, B. Gregoire, M. Huisman, J.-L. Lanet (Eds.), Construction and Analysis of Safe, Secure, and Interoperable Smart Devices. IX, 175 pages. 2006.

Vol. 3955: G. Antoniou, G. Potamias, C. Spyropoulos, D. Plexousakis (Eds.), Advances in Artificial Intelligence. XVII, 611 pages. 2006. (Sublibrary LNAI).

Vol. 3954: A. Leonardis, H. Bischof, A. Pinz (Eds.), Computer Vision – ECCV 2006, Part IV. XVII, 613 pages. 2006.

Vol. 3953: A. Leonardis, H. Bischof, A. Pinz (Eds.), Computer Vision – ECCV 2006, Part III. XVII, 649 pages. 2006.

Vol. 3952: A. Leonardis, H. Bischof, A. Pinz (Eds.), Computer Vision – ECCV 2006, Part II. XVII, 661 pages. 2006.

Vol. 3951: A. Leonardis, H. Bischof, A. Pinz (Eds.), Computer Vision – ECCV 2006, Part I. XXXV, 639 pages. 2006.

Vol. 3950: J.P. Müller, F. Zambonelli (Eds.), Agent-Oriented Software Engineering VI. XVI, 249 pages. 2006.

Vol. 3947: Y.-C. Chung, J.E. Moreira (Eds.), Advances in Grid and Pervasive Computing. XXI, 667 pages. 2006.

Vol. 3946: T.R. Roth-Berghofer, S. Schulz, D.B. Leake (Eds.), Modeling and Retrieval of Context. XI, 149 pages. 2006. (Sublibrary LNAI).

Vol. 3945: M. Hagiya, P. Wadler (Eds.), Functional and Logic Programming. X, 295 pages. 2006.

Vol. 3944: J. Quiñonero-Candela, I. Dagan, B. Magnini, F. d'Alché-Buc (Eds.), Machine Learning Challenges. XIII, 462 pages. 2006. (Sublibrary LNAI).

Vol. 3943: N. Guelfi, A. Savidis (Eds.), Rapid Integration of Software Engineering Techniques. X, 289 pages. 2006.

Vol. 3942: Z. Pan, R. Aylett, H. Diener, X. Jin, S. Göbel, L. Li (Eds.), Technologies for E-Learning and Digital Entertainment. XXV, 1396 pages. 2006.

Vol. 3941: S.W. Gilroy, M.D. Harrison (Eds.), Interactive Systems. XI, 267 pages. 2006.

Vol. 3940: C. Saunders, M. Grobelnik, S. Gunn, J. Shawe-Taylor (Eds.), Subspace, Latent Structure and Feature Selection. X, 209 pages. 2006.

Vol. 3939: C. Priami, L. Cardelli, S. Emmott (Eds.), Transactions on Computational Systems Biology IV. VII, 141 pages. 2006. (Sublibrary LNBI).

Vol. 3936: M. Lalmas, A. MacFarlane, S. Rüger, A. Tombros, T. Tsikrika, A. Yavlinsky (Eds.), Advances in Information Retrieval. XIX, 584 pages. 2006.

Vol. 3935: D. Won, S. Kim (Eds.), Information Security and Cryptology - ICISC 2005. XIV, 458 pages. 2006.

Vol. 3934: J.A. Clark, R.F. Paige, F.A. C. Polack, P.J. Brooke (Eds.), Security in Pervasive Computing. X, 243 pages. 2006.

Vol. 3933: F. Bonchi, J.-F. Boulicaut (Eds.), Knowledge Discovery in Inductive Databases. VIII, 251 pages. 2006.

Vol. 3931: B. Apolloni, M. Marinaro, G. Nicosia, R. Tagliaferri (Eds.), Neural Nets. XIII, 370 pages. 2006.

Vol. 3930: D.S. Yeung, Z.-Q. Liu, X.-Z. Wang, H. Yan (Eds.), Advances in Machine Learning and Cybernetics. XXI, 1110 pages. 2006. (Sublibrary LNAI).

Vol. 3929: W. MacCaull, M. Winter, I. Düntsch (Eds.), Relational Methods in Computer Science. VIII, 263 pages. 2006.

Vol. 3928: J. Domingo-Ferrer, J. Posegga, D. Schreckling (Eds.), Smart Card Research and Advanced Applications. XI, 359 pages. 2006.

Vol. 3927: J. Hespanha, A. Tiwari (Eds.), Hybrid Systems: Computation and Control. XII, 584 pages. 2006.

Vol. 3925: A. Valmari (Ed.), Model Checking Software. X, 307 pages. 2006.

Vol. 3924: P. Sestoft (Ed.), Programming Languages and Systems. XII, 343 pages. 2006.

Vol. 3923: A. Mycroft, A. Zeller (Eds.), Compiler Construction. XIII, 277 pages. 2006.

Vol. 3922: L. Baresi, R. Heckel (Eds.), Fundamental Approaches to Software Engineering. XIII, 427 pages. 2006.

Vol. 3921: L. Aceto, A. Ingólfsdóttir (Eds.), Foundations of Software Science and Computation Structures. XV, 447 pages. 2006.

Vol. 3920: H. Hermanns, J. Palsberg (Eds.), Tools and Algorithms for the Construction and Analysis of Systems. XIV, 506 pages. 2006.

Vol. 3918: W.K. Ng, M. Kitsuregawa, J. Li, K. Chang (Eds.), Advances in Knowledge Discovery and Data Mining. XXIV, 879 pages. 2006. (Sublibrary LNAI).

Vol. 3917: H. Chen, F.-Y. Wang, C.C. Yang, D. Zeng, M. Chau, K. Chang (Eds.), Intelligence and Security Informatics. XII, 186 pages. 2006.

Vol. 3916: J. Li, Q. Yang, A.-H. Tan (Eds.), Data Mining for Biomedical Applications. VIII, 155 pages. 2006. (Sublibrary LNBI).

Vol. 3915: R. Nayak, M.J. Zaki (Eds.), Knowledge Discovery from XML Documents. VIII, 105 pages. 2006.

Vol. 3914: A. Garcia, R. Choren, C. Lucena, P. Giorgini, T. Holvoet, A. Romanovsky (Eds.), Software Engineering for Multi-Agent Systems IV. XIV, 255 pages. 2006.

Vol. 3911: R. Wyrzykowski, J. Dongarra, N. Meyer, J. Waśniewski (Eds.), Parallel Processing and Applied Mathematics. XXIII, 1126 pages. 2006.

Vol. 3910: S.A. Brueckner, G.D.M. Serugendo, D. Hales, F. Zambonelli (Eds.), Engineering Self-Organising Systems. XII, 245 pages. 2006. (Sublibrary LNAI).

Vol. 3909: A. Apostolico, C. Guerra, S. Istrail, P. Pevzner, M. Waterman (Eds.), Research in Computational Molecular Biology. XVII, 612 pages. 2006. (Sublibrary LNBI).

Vol. 3908: A. Bui, M. Bui, T. Böhme, H. Unger (Eds.), Innovative Internet Community Systems. VIII, 207 pages. 2006.

Vol. 3907: F. Rothlauf, J. Branke, S. Cagnoni, E. Costa, C. Cotta, R. Drechsler, E. Lutton, P. Machado, J.H. Moore, J. Romero, G.D. Smith, G. Squillero, H. Takagi (Eds.), Applications of Evolutionary Computing. XXIV, 813 pages. 2006.